D0866846

SOCIALISM IN INDIA

SOCIALISM
IN
INDIA

Edited by
B. R. NANDA

Issued under the Auspices of the
Nehru Memorial Museum and Library

BARNES & NOBLE, Inc.
NEW YORK
PUBLISHERS & BOOKSELLERS SINCE 1873

First Published in the United States, 1972
by Barnes & Noble, Inc.

ISBN 389 04662 0

© Nehru Memorial Museum and Library, 1972

Printed in India

By Aroon Purie at Thomson Press (India) Limited,
Faridabad, Haryana, and Published by Mrs Sharda Chawla,
Vikas Publications, 5 Daryaganj, Ansari Road, Delhi-6

PREFACE

There is hardly any subject which has aroused keener debate in India during the last twentyfive years than socialism. We may all be socialists now, as we were all nationalists once, but there is a bewildering diversity of views on what constitutes socialism. Socialist ideas are, however, not the outgrowth of the post-independence era; their origins go far back to the days of the struggle for freedom and their impact today can be best understood in the historical perspective.

The Nehru Memorial Museum and Library, which has been developed as a research centre on modern India, with special emphasis on the nationalist movement, selected for its first seminar the theme: "Socialism in India, 1919-39." The choice of the inter-war years was deliberate. Twenty years seemed a long enough period if the papers and discussions were to be in some depth, and original material for the pre-Second World War years seemed more readily available than for the later period. The fact that these two decades were dominated by Gandhi's leadership gave them an underlying unity. It is true that socialist ideas had to compete with the main political issue, the struggle against British imperialism, and the need for a united front against the British often acted as a brake on social and economic radicalism. Nevertheless, the seminal socialist ideas were articulated and found recognition in the writings and utterances of nationalist leaders as well as in the policies of the political parties during this period.

Thirty scholars belonging to fourteen Indian universities and learned institutions participated in the first session of the seminar in November 1968. Dr V.K.R.V. Rao, who inaugurated the session, pointed out that it was the first time that a systematic study of the socialist ideas in India in the 1920s and 1930s was being attempted. A detailed chronology and a select bibliography prepared by the Nehru Memorial Museum and Library had already been circulated to the participants. Twentyfive papers had been contributed, and the discussions, which were spread over five sessions, ranged over the entire political and economic scene in India, external influences from the Soviet Union, Britain and other European countries, the role of the Indian National Congress, the Congress Socialist Party, the Communist Party of India, and the impact of certain dominant personalities such as Gandhi, Nehru and M.N. Roy.

The discussions at the seminar were stimulating and a good deal of ground was covered, but it was felt that another session of the seminar was necessary to explore certain themes which had remained uncovered, such as the effect of socialist ideas on literature, trade unions, and agrarian movements. The second session of the seminar held in October 1969 had thirteen papers before it and was attended by twentyfive scholars.

All the papers were mimeographed and circulated to the participants. The papers contributed to both the sessions of the seminar added up to a thousand pages, and inevitably there was a certain amount of overlapping. It was, therefore, decided to publish a few representative papers to share some of the ideas thrown up at the seminar with a wider audience. The present volume includes in all ten papers. They cover, *inter alia,* the ideology of socialism, the influence of Soviet Russia and the Communist International, the response of the Indian National Congress, the influence of the agrarian movements and the effect of socialist ideas on literature in some of the Indian languages.

I must acknowledge my debt to the distinguished scholars and participants who contributed papers and took part in the discussion. To my colleague Shri V.C. Joshi I am especially grateful for assistance in the detailed planning of the seminar: much of the credit for its success was due to him. In the preparation of the volume for the press both he and Dr K. Raman Pillai have given valuable help. The bibliography—which is an abridged version of the one circulated at the seminar—was prepared by Miss K. Ashta, our Assistant Librarian.

If this volume helps to contribute some new facts and new insights, stimulate discussion and suggest further avenues for research, it would have justified itself.

Nehru Memorial Museum and Library   B. R. NANDA
Teen Murti House
New Delhi-11

CONTRIBUTORS

B. R. NANDA is Director, Nehru Memorial Museum and Library, New Delhi.

DR VIJAY SEN BUDHRAJ is Reader, Department of Political Science, University of Kurukshetra.

DR ZAFAR IMAM is Associate Professor, School of International Studies, Jawaharlal Nehru University.

DR PARTHA SARATHI GUPTA is Reader, Department of History, University of Delhi.

DR P. C. JOSHI is Senior Fellow, Institute of Economic Growth, University of Delhi.

DR BIMAL PRASAD is Professor and Head of the Department of South Asian Studies, School of International Studies, Jawaharlal Nehru University.

DR BIPAN CHANDRA is Professor of Modern Indian History, Jawaharlal Nehru University.

DR BINAY BHUSHAN CHAUDHURI is Reader, Department of History, University of Calcutta.

PRABHAKAR PADHYE is Director, Centre for Indian Writers, Poona.

D. ANJANEYULU is a Telugu writer and journalist.

CONTENTS

SOCIALISM IN INDIA, 1919-1939:
A RETROSPECT

B. R. NANDA

THE GROWTH OF Indian socialism during the two crowded decades which span the first and the second world wars can best be studied in the political and social context of the time. This growth was not, however, in a straight line; it suffered from false starts and set-backs; it was affected by the hostility of the British authorities, recurrent economic crises, the changing international scene, and the rather violent shifts in the attitude of the Communist International towards the nationalist struggle in India. The organization of "Left Politics" took place in the face of official opposition and Congress suspicion. The periods favourable to socialist ideas were those which formed the troughs of the Gandhian waves of Satyagraha struggles.

There is no doubt that socialist ideas and parties gave a certain social content and occasionally a sharper edge to Indian nationalism as represented by the Indian National Congress. That they could not achieve more was due to the internal contradictions of the Left parties, the limitations imposed by their grasp of the political realities, and the charismatic, but dynamic and skilful leadership of the Indian National Congress by Mahatma Gandhi throughout this period.

It is a curious fact that even though Marx was a contemporary of Keshub Chander Sen and Dadabhai Naoroji, and Lenin of Gokhale and Tilak, socialist ideas hardly figured in the Indian imagination in the period before the First World War, when politics constituted probably the only hobby of the educated classes. Some of the Indian leaders had contacts with socialists in Britain: Dadabhai was friendly with Hyndman, Gokhale with the Webbs, Tilak with Lansbury, Lajpat Rai with Colonel Wedgwood. It would seem, however, that British socialists and the Labour Party were viewed by Indian leaders not so much as champions of the British working class, as possible allies in extracting constitutional reforms from Britain.

Indian politicians, extremists as well as moderates, seem to have been too preoccupied with the Herculean task of making a dent in the armour of the British bureaucratic machine, to think of reconstructing the Indian economy. Such a reconstruction was indeed an idle dream so long as all political and economic power rested in an alien agency. There was also a built-in fear of drastic changes. Memories of the civil disorder and instability in the eighteenth century, doubtless exaggerated by British writers, conditioned the first generation of Indian nationalists against root-and-branch reforms. The agrarian disturbances in the Deccan in the 1870's and the 1890's struck the Indian intelligentsia not as the welcome stirrings of an oppressed peasantry, but danger signals of a possible relapse into anarchy. The Congress leaders wanted gradual changes towards a rational, secular, progressive society and an administration at first responsive and ultimately responsible to public opinion.

The Indian educated class constituted a small minority, but it was not merely the mouthpiece of the upper and middle classes. That it did not neglect the interests of the masses is shown by its persistent and persuasive advocacy of increase in the minimum limit for income tax, the abolition of the salt tax, the extension of local self-government, the establishment of the village panchayats, the reduction of land revenue and the institution of free and compulsory elementary education—reforms which would benefit the poorer sections of the community. It is true that leaders of the pre-war Congress did not idealize the masses—nobody did before 1917—but they had a deep concern for the well-being of the peasantry and the weaker sections of the community. They were of course far from being socialists. Indeed the word had a bad odour about it, just as a hundred years earlier the word "Liberal" was looked down upon as a term of abuse by respectable people in Europe.[1]

II

It was the Russian Revolution which was to make socialism a word

[1]Irene Collins, "Liberalism in Nineteenth Century Europe," in W.N. Medilicott, ed., *From Metternich to Hitler: Aspects of British and Foreign History, 1814-1939* (London, 1963), p. 25.

to conjure with. It was only natural that Indian nationalism, engaged in a continual debate with the British Government, should have seen in the fall of Tsarist autocracy the confirmation of its hope that British autocracy in India would also crumble one day. The annulment of the partition of Persia and Turkey by the revolutionary government in Russia was well received in India; it was a practical token of the renunciation of imperialism by a European power. But the other important aspect of the Russian Revolution—the fashioning of a new socio-economic system—seems curiously to have made relatively little immediate impact on the Indian imagination. This may have been due to the fact that Marxist literature had enjoyed little vogue in this country and the news from Russia, filtered through the British press, tended to produce a dark picture of disorder and bloodshed, wholesale executions of political opponents, expropriation of property, censorship and regimentation. "Russia indeed has hinted a moral," Lord Chelmsford told the Imperial Council, "which it would do us all good to take to heart."[2] That the revolution and anarchy were considered synonymous is indicated by Gandhi's comment that India "did not want Bolshevism. The people are too peaceful to stand anarchy."[3]

The Russian Revolution seems to have stimulated the organization of labour and the formation of trade unions in India. In April 1918, Wadia formed a trade union in Madras, and in the same year, Bombay saw the emergence of the Indian Seamen's Union. The G.I.P. Railway Union came into existence in 1919, the Ahmedabad Textile Workers Union and the All India Trade Union Congress in 1920. The success of the proletarian revolution in Russia powerfully affected a few individuals such as the poet Nazrul Islam who wrote his *Byathar Dan* in 1919, and young men like A.K. Fazlul Huq and Muzaffar Ahmed[4] who brought out a new Bengali paper, the *Navayug* in 1920 in Calcutta, and S.A. Dange who published *Gandhi and Lenin* in 1921. The effect on established political parties and its leaders was however hardly perceptible. Raja Mahendra Pratap, Barkatullah and other romantic revolutionaries, who assured Lenin

[2]*Times of India,* 9 September 1918.
[3]*Young India,* 24 November 1921.
[4]Muzaffar Ahmed, *Communist Party of India: Years of Formation, 1921-1933* (Calcutta, 1959), p. 5.

in Moscow that India was ripe for a revolution in 1919,[5] had been so long in the terrorist underground or in exile that they had little knowledge of the real conditions in India. The brilliant M.N. Roy, who had arrived in Moscow via U.S.A. and Mexico, was perhaps in no better position. He impressed Lenin as one of the best representatives of colonial revolutionism and was catapulted into the counsels of the Communist International, but he tended to generalize from his limited experience as a hunted Bengali terrorist. He misjudged the Indian situation, the emergence of Gandhi and the nonviolent non-cooperation movement. Curiously enough, at the meeting of the Second Communist International in 1920, it was not Roy, the expert on Asian colonialism, but Lenin who was nearer the mark in assessing the revolutionary potentialities of the national liberation movements in colonial countries.

Communist ideas, and the news from the Soviet Union, did not immediately influence major political parties and well-known leaders, but it inspired some who were to become the founding fathers of the Communist Party in India. One of them, Muzaffar Ahmed, recalls the enthusiasm of the first converts when they were a mere handful and possessed only a "superficial knowledge of Marxism," but felt an "unquestioned loyalty to the directives of the Communist International."[6] These directives were changed somewhat arbitrarily from time to time according to the reading of the Indian or world situation from Moscow.

The first Communist International in 1919 had expected that the imminent downfall of capitalism in the imperialist countries would ensure the liberation of the colonies. As imperialism did not crumble so easily, the second Communist International in 1920 tackled the problem in dead earnest, and received two theses, one from Lenin himself advocating alliance with "bourgeois democratic liberation movements," and the other from M.N. Roy advocating independent action through the setting up of a proletarian party, untrammelled by restrictions as to means. Roy came to be recognized as the expert on India and largely moulded the thinking of the Soviet leaders in the twenties. The Indian military school which he set up at Tashkent with Russian money and arms to recruit and train an

[5]X.J. Eudin and R.C. North, *Soviet Russia and the East, 1920-1927* (Stanford, 1957), pp. 181-3.
[6]Muzaffar Ahmed, n. 4, p. 8.

army of Indian expatriates for the liberation of India, was still-born. It encountered unexpected difficulties. The Afghan Government was reluctant to allow infiltration through its territory, and the Kremlin itself, anxious to conclude a trade agreement with Britain, could hardly reject British representations for the disbandment of the Tashkent School.[7] The hopes that the road to Bombay and Calcutta would lie via Kabul were thus dashed.[8] Henceforth Roy operated from European capitals with an unending stream of journals, leaflets and letters aimed at potential and actual sympathizers of the revolution in India.

Roy's propaganda and emissaries did not make much headway in India so long as the non-cooperation movement was on the crest of a rising wave. His chance came in the wake of the Chauri Chaura tragedy and the demoralization following the revocation of civil disobedience. Deviating somewhat from his own thesis at the Second Congress, he made a bid to cultivate support within the Indian National Congress and even to wrest the leadership into Communist hands.[9] He tried to win over C.R. Das who was known to be in favour of simultaneously promoting the economic welfare of the masses as well as the struggle for political liberation. Das was too shrewd a politician to play Roy's game and to challenge Gandhi's leadership on non-violence as well as on Council-entry at the Gaya Congress (December 1922). To Roy's discomfiture, he included an anti-Bolshevik broadside in his presidential address. "History has proved over and over again," said Das, "the utter futility of revolutions brought about by force and violence. I am one of those who hold to non-violence on principle."[10]

Roy did not give up all hopes of redeeming the National Congress, but henceforth his efforts were largely directed to the building up of a Communist party in India. These efforts received a check in 1924 when the Government hauled up the more important Communist

[7]L. Shapiro, ed., *Soviet Treaty Series,* Vol. I, 1927-28 (Washington, 1950), p. 102.

[8]Trotsky had suggested that the revolutionary road might lead to Paris and London through Kabul, Calcutta and Bombay. See I. Deutscher, *The Prophet Armed-Trotsky: 1879-1921* (London, 1954), pp. 456-7.

[9]Gene D. Overstreet and Marshall Windmiller, *Communism in India* (Berkeley, 1959), pp. 44-5.

[10]*Congress Presidential Addresses: From the Silver to the Golden Jubilee* (Madras, G.A. Natesan, 1934), p. 572.

workers in the Kanpur Conspiracy Case. Nevertheless he had achieved a measure of success. A number of devoted Communists were enlisted in Bombay, Calcutta, Kanpur, Lahore and other towns, though it was not possible for them to function in the open. In 1927 Jawaharlal Nehru had attended the Congress of Oppressed Nationalities at Brussels, and was elected to the executive committee of the League Against Imperialism, a Comintern sponsored body. There was a great deal of discontent in the countryside and among industrial towns. There was a no-tax campaign in Gujarat in 1928 and strikes in industrial towns. A strong leftist group within the Indian National Congress was also emerging under Jawaharlal Nehru and Subhas Bose. However, just when the climate seemed ideal for the growth of Communist influence in the nationalist movement, the Communist International executed a *volte face*. The Sixth Congress meeting in 1928, on the basis of the recent experience in China, where the Kuomintang had turned upon its Communist allies, came to the conclusion that the national bourgeoisie in all colonial countries had turned counter-revolutionary. The Communists in India were thus enjoined to "unmask" and oppose "all talk of Swarajists, Gandhists, etc., about passive resistance," and to advance "the irreconcilable slogan of armed struggle for the emancipation of the country and expulsion of the imperialists."[11] This was a return to Roy's thesis at the Second Congress, but eight years later, Roy with better knowledge of Indian conditions, thought differently and preferred a united front with the National Congress. He was expelled from the Communist International in 1929.

The result of the new directive was that in the early thirties, as in the early twenties, in the heyday of Gandhi's campaigns against the *Raj*, the Communists were cut off from the mainstream of Indian nationalism. In fact, the official Communist line was that the Indian bourgeoisie, as represented in the Congress, were counter-revolutionary. The eighteen accused in the Meerut Conspiracy Case, who included some of the founding fathers of the Indian Communist Party, in their long statement before the court declared that "to the ordinary Congress leader independence was a phrase with which to keep the rank and file contented and perhaps to threaten the Government," that civil disobedience was a means of "sabotag-

[11]Jane Degras, ed., *The Communist International* Vol. II, 1923-1928 (London, 1965), p. 544.

ing revolutionary movements," that the Congress deliberately eschewed violence, as it did not really want to overthrow British rule, and that Gandhi, Jawaharlal Nehru, and Subhas Chandra Bose were working for a compromise with imperialism in accordance with the interests of the bourgeoisie.[12] With such a reading of Gandhi's movement against the *Raj,* it was obvious that the Communist International and its adherents in India could have no place in it.

III

One reason why the Russian Revolution initially failed to make a great impact on India was that from 1917 onwards the Indian political cauldron itself had begun to boil. The Home Rule Movement, Edwin Montagu's declaration and visit to India in 1917, the publication of the Montagu-Chelmsford Report, the secession of the Moderates from the Indian National Congress, the Rowlatt Act, the Khilafat and the emergence of Gandhi raised the political temperature. Not only the large presidency towns and provincial headquarters, but small towns and villages vibrated to Gandhi's call to non-violent resistance. The Khilafat issue sucked the Muslim middle and lower middle classes into the political arena.

To M.N. Roy and his friends in Moscow, as they looked through the telescope of the Communist International, Gandhi may have seemed a petty bourgeoisie "reactionary,"[13] who was restraining the revolutionary stirrings of the masses. The people and the Government of India had reasons to feel differently. The appeal that Roy sent—with the approval of Lenin and Stalin—to Gandhi at the Ahmedabad Congress in December 1921 to broaden the base of his struggle with the help of peasants and workers went unheeded, almost unnoticed. But Roy had hardly any idea of the burdens and anxieties Gandhi bore in leading a mass movement. In South Africa, his Satyagraha struggles had been waged in a compact area and involved a few thousand Indian immigrants whom he could directly influence. In India the canvas was much larger, almost continental in scale; the people to be controlled were not in thousands but in millions. How to rouse the patriotic fervour of these millions and

[12]Muzaffar Ahmed, (Introduction), *Communists Challenge Imperialism From the Dock* (Calcutta, 1967), pp. 176-7, 236 and 268-9.
[13]*M.N. Roy's Memoirs* (Bombay, 1964), p. 543.

still maintain a semblance of discipline was Gandhi's critical problem. In the very first week of the launching of Satyagraha against the Rowlatt Act in April 1919, riots had broken out in Delhi, Ahmedabad, Nadiad and Bombay. Gandhi discovered with a shock that he had underrated the forces of violence in the country; this was his miscalculation, what he penitentially described as his "Himalayan blunder." Soon afterwards, the Punjab went through the tragedy at the Jallianwala Bagh and the horrors of martial law.

During the next three years, even as Gandhi led the non-cooperation movement, he was reluctant to launch mass civil disobedience without adequate preparation. In February 1922, he succumbed to pressure from within the Congress for launching mass civil disobedience in selected areas, but immediately afterwards, when he heard of the riot at Chauri Chaura, he applied the reverse gear. There is little evidence to show that the reasons which Gandhi gave for cancelling the aggressive phase of his movement were not honest. He knew the outbreak in Chauri Chaura was no revolutionary rising of the peasantry,[14] but another manifestation of the mob violence that had been creeping into his movement. The occasional communal riots culminating in the fanatical Moplah outbreak in Malabar, and the riots at Bombay on the occasion of the visit of the Prince of Wales had disconcerted him. For Gandhi, the Chauri Chaura incident was, as he wrote to Jawaharlal Nehru, "the last straw....I assure you that if the thing [civil disobedience] had not been suspended, we would have been leading not a non-violent struggle, but essentially a violent struggle....The movement had unconsciously drifted from the right path."[15]

IV

As we have already seen, M.N. Roy had failed to win over C.R. Das or any other important nationalist leader. Neither Das nor Lajpat Rai, who had presided over the first All India Trade Union Congress in 1920, was destined to introduce socialist ideas into the Congress. That task was to be performed by one of the younger leaders in the the mid-twenties, Jawaharlal Nehru, the son of the veteran Motilal

[14]This was how it was described by the accused in the Meerut Conspiracy Case. See Muzaffar Ahmed, n. 12, p. 86.

[15]B.R. Nanda, *The Nehrus: Motilal and Jawaharlal* (London, 1962), p. 202.

Nehru and the favourite disciple of the Mahatma. In his student
days in England, Jawaharlal had sampled Fabian literature and heard
George Bernard Shaw in 1907 speak on "Socialism and the University Man."[16] Young Nehru's main driving force at this time was
a passionate nationalism which was fanned on return to India by
the Home Rule Movement and then by the coming of Gandhi. The
contact with the Mahatma rubbed off some of his anglicism and
aloofness, but he owed his first encounter with "the naked hungry
mass" of India to an accidental visit to the Oudh countryside in
June 1920. His interest in economic and social questions developed
in the enforced leisure of the prison in 1922-23 when he delved into
the history of the Russian Revolution. In 1926-7 he visited Europe
for the treatment of his ailing wife and came into closer contact
with the anti-colonial as well as the anti-capitalist crusaders from
Asia, Africa, Europe, and America, particularly at the Brussels
Congress of Oppressed Nationalities. Already a student of Marx
and an admirer of Lenin, he was deeply impressed by his brief visit
to Moscow in November 1927, and returned to his homeland just
in time to attend the Madras Congress where he piloted resolutions
with a radical slant. In the following year he clashed with the Congress Establishment on the issue of Dominion Status versus
Independence. As a gesture of defiance, he joined hands with Subhas
Bose to found the Independence League, vowed to the severance
of all relations with Britain and to "a socialistic revision of the economic structure of society." The Independence League did not last
long, but at least one of its goals, that of complete independence,
was indirectly conceded at the Calcutta Congress, and embodied
in the Congress creed at Lahore the following year when Nehru,
as Congress President, unfurled the banner of "complete independence" on the banks of the Ravi.

Nehru's presidential address at the Lahore Congress was at once
an onslaught on British imperialism, Indian feudalism and capitalism.
He frankly avowed himself as "a socialist and a republican and...
no believer in kings and princes, or in the order which produces the
modern kings of industry...."[17] The philosophy of socialism, he
asserted, had permeated the entire structure of society the world
over, and "the only point in dispute was the pace and methods of

[16]*Ibid.*, p. 96.
[17]*Congress Presidential Addresses*, n. 10, p. 894.

advance to its realization." He questioned the proposition that the Congress should hold the balance fairly between capital and labour, and landlord and tenant. The balance was, said Nehru, "terribly weighted on one side"; to maintain the status quo "was to maintain injustice and exploitation." He called for changes in land laws, a minimum wage for every worker in the field or factory, organization of industry on a cooperative basis and effective liaison between the Congress and the labour movement. That all this was not merely a verbal exercise became evident 15 months later when under his pressure, but with the backing of Gandhi, the Karachi Congress embodied some of his ideas in a catalogue of fundamental rights and economic principles, including a living wage, imposition of death duties, and state ownership or control of basic industries. These may seem "mildly socialist" today; in 1931 they sounded revolutionary.

Nehru's admiration for Marx and Lenin, evident in his books, *Soviet Russia, Glimpses of World History,* and the *Autobiography* was, however, never uncritical or unqualified. Marxism was neither the first nor the most important ingredient in his make-up. In his student days, he had been exposed to Fabian ideas and savoured the Western humanism and liberalism with its rational, aesthetic and human approach to life. From Gandhi, he had imbibed an ethical framework, respect for human dignity, compassion for the underdog, and the importance of truth as a guiding principle in personal as well as in public life. Certain aspects of Gandhi's philosophy jarred him; he did not like the Mahatma's idealization of the simple life, "his glorification of poverty," or antipathy to industrialism. The mysterious, almost mystical, overtones of the Satyagraha movements disconcerted him. Jawaharlal was shocked and bewildered by the Gandhi-Irwin Pact in 1931, and the untouchability fast in 1932. The withdrawal of the civil disobedience in 1934 came when he was in Alipore jail. He felt (he wrote in his *Autobiography*) with "a stab of pain" that "the chords of allegiance that had bound me to him [Gandhi] for many years had snapped."[18]

V

In another jail in Nasik in western India, hundreds of miles away,

[18]Jawaharlal Nehru, *Autobiography* (Bombay, 1962), p. 659.

a group of young Congressmen who were admirers of Nehru, felt
a similar disenchantment with Gandhi's leadership. The members
of this group, Jayaprakash Narayan, Asoka Mehta, Achyut Patwardhan, Yusuf Meherally, N.G. Goray, and S.M. Joshi, were ardent
nationalists as well as ardent socialists. They felt that a new orientation to the Congress was necessary, and drew up the blueprint of
a new political party which was to function within the Congress.
They were later joined by some of the senior Congressmen in the
U.P.—Acharya Narendra Deva, Sampurnanand and Sri Prakasa—
all from the Benares Vidyapeeth. The foundations of the Congress
Socialist Party were laid at Patna in May 1934 when a meeting of
the A.I.C.C. was held there. A few months later, the party had its
first conference at Bombay and adopted a 15–point programme
which included the repudiation of the public debt of India, "transfer
of all power to producing masses," planned development of the
economic life of the country by the State, socialization of key industries, State monopoly of foreign trade, cooperative and collective
farming, organization of cooperatives for production, distribution,
and credit, and the elimination of princes and landlords without compensation. This was a thorough-going socialist programme, which
the Communist Party could well have included in its manifesto.
Indeed the leaders of the new party swore by the Marxian theory,
and believed that planned economic development on the Soviet
model was the answer to the problem of Indian poverty and backwardness. They criticized the Congress leadership, but avowed
loyalty to the organization. Their professed object (in the words
of their senior and most respected leader, Narendra Deva) was "to
resuscitate and reinvigorate the Congress,"[19] to rid it of its "defea-
tist mentality," and to draw into it the mass of workers and peasants,
both to "socialize" the nationalist struggle and to forge a massive
anti-imperialist front. They were critical of Gandhi, of his self-
imposed limitations on the score of non-violence, of his ethical
approach to politics and of his theory of "trusteeship."

The new party with its demands for an alternative programme
and a new leadership for the Congress was bound to clash with the
Old Guard. There was no dearth of issues on which differences
arose: the approach to the Act of 1935, the formation of ministries

[19]Acharya Narendra Deva, *Socialism and the National Revolution* (Bombay,
1946), p. 28.

in 1937, the organization of kisan sabhas and agitation for agrarian reforms, the release of political detenues and agitation in the Indian States. There was the curious spectacle during these years of Congressmen leading agitations against Congress ministries in the provinces. There were prolonged and bitter controversies in which the Congress leadership was continually under fire. "Gandhism has played its part," declared J.P. Narayan. "It cannot carry us further and hence we must march and be guided by the ideology of socialism."[20] The Socialist leaders did not realize the predicament of the Congress executive, harassed as it was by a ceaseless cold war with the Muslim League and never-ending battle of wits with the British Government. Without a minimum discipline in the party and stability in the country, the Congress could hardly speak effectively on behalf of nationalist India.

In the Congress executive, Nehru was ideologically the closest to the Congress Socialist Party; he was in jail when the party was formed, but his encouragement, moral and perhaps financial, was available to its founders in the early years of the party. With some members, such as J.P. Narayan, Narendra Deva and Achyut Patwardhan, whom he included in the Working Committee formed by him as Congress President, he was on particularly cordial terms. Nehru was sympathetic to the C.S.P., but he could not hold a brief for it in the Working Committee for the verbal barrages and acts of defiance on the part of its ebullient members. This may account for Nehru's somewhat querulous equation with them, and the "public rebukes," which, according to Sampurnanand,[21] he was occasionally administering to them.

Gandhi had frankly avowed his differences with the Congress socialists in 1934 and gone so far as to say that if they gained ascendancy in the Congress, he could not remain in it.[22] The talk of class war, expropriation, and violence jarred on the Mahatma. Nevertheless—and this was characteristic of Gandhi—he refused to be a party to the muzzling of the Congress socialists. Indeed he helped them to secure a fairer representation in the All-India Congress

[20]Hari Kishore Singh, *A History of the Praja Socialist Party: 1934-59* (Lucknow, 1959), p. 42.

[21]Sampurnanand, *Memories and Reflections* (Bombay, 1962), p. 81.

[22]D.G. Tendulkar, *Mahatma: Life of Mohandas Karamchand Gandhi* (Delhi, 1952), Vol. 3, p. 363.

Committee by supporting the introduction of the single transferable vote in the election.[23] The gulf between Gandhi and the Congress socialists was not really as wide as it seemed at the time. Though he did not want too many fissures in the national front while the battle with the British remained unresolved, he was no supporter of the status quo or of vested interests. Indeed he was not unwilling to be pushed in the direction socialists desired to go. He had given his powerful backing to the adoption of the resolution on Fundamental Rights and Economic Policy at Karachi in 1931; it was his support which had brought the Congress "crown" to Nehru in 1936 and 1937, and enabled him to spell out his socialist programme from the presidential chair of the Congress.

Gandhi seems to have hoped that in 1936, as in 1929, responsibility of office would have a mellowing effect upon Jawaharlal. "Though Jawaharlal is extreme in presentation," he wrote to Agatha Harrison on 30 April 1936, "he is sober in action....My own feeling is that Jawaharlal will accept the decision of the majority of his colleagues."[24] A little earlier Subhas Chandra Bose had urged Nehru to be firm with the Congress Establishment. "I earnestly hope," he wrote, "that you will utilize the strength of your public position in making decisions....Your position is unique and I think that even Mahatma Gandhi will be more accommodating towards you than towards anyone else."[25] Much as his Left-wing colleagues wanted him to, Nehru could not during these difficult years before the war, defy Gandhi or break away from the Congress. Besides the emotional bond between the two men ("My dear *Bapu,*" is how Jawaharlal started his letters to Gandhi), it is important to remember that Gandhi owed his influence not to any position he held in the Congress, but to his moral authority. Again and again he offered to step off the stage altogether, if his ideas were unacceptable to the Working Committee or the All-India Congress Committee. "I can't tell you," he wrote to Jawaharlal in April 1938, "how positively lonely I feel to know that nowadays I can't carry you with me."[26] "I must not lead," he wrote in October 1939, "if I cannot carry all with me. There should be no divided counsels among the

[23]Sampurnanand, n. 21, p. 77.
[24]Gandhi to Agatha Harrison, 30 April 1936.
[25]Subhas Chandra Bose to Jawaharlal Nehru, 4 March 1936.
[26]M.K. Gandhi to Jawaharlal Nehru, 25 April 1938.

members of the W.C. [Working Committee]. I feel you should take full charge and lead the country, leaving me free to voice my opinion."[27]

Gandhi's departure from the political scene was the last thing Nehru could envisage with equanimity. He was not unaware of his own limitations and those of the left-wing in the Congress organization. He could rouse the masses and inspire the intelligentsia, and slog at the desk, but he was not an expert in party management. "I function," he wrote to Subhas Bose, "individually without any group or second person to support me."[28] This aloofness from party politics may have been commendable in its own way, but it also limited room for Jawaharlal's manoeuvring within the organization. When Bose remonstrated with him for not standing by him, Nehru frankly told him that a head-on collision with the Mahatma was suicidal: "The Left wing was not strong enough to bear the burden by itself. And when a real contest came within the Congress, it would lose and there would be a reaction against it."[29] Even if Bose could win a majority in the Congress, it would not ensure him sufficient backing in the country, and in any case, argued Nehru, a mass struggle against the Government without Gandhi was inconceivable. Finally, Nehru warned Bose that there were many "disruptive tendencies already in the country and instead of controlling them, we would add to them. All this meant weakening our national movement just when strength was necessary."[30]

There is evidence that with closer acquaintance with the balance of forces in the country and in the Congress organization during the years 1937-39, Nehru's own approach to the socialist revolution was changing; it became less doctrinaire and more pragmatic. "I am certainly a socialist," he wrote in 1938, "in the sense that I believe in socialist theory and method of approach. I am not a Communist chiefly because I resist the Communist tendency to treat Communism as holy doctrine, and I do not like being told what to think and what to do....I feel also that there is too much violence associated with the Communist method and this produces untoward results as in Russia in recent years. The ends cannot be separated from the means."[31]

[27]M.K. Gandhi to Jawaharlal Nehru, 26 October 1939.
[28]Jawaharlal Nehru to Subhas Chandra Bose, 4 February 1939.
[29]*Ibid.*, 3 April 1939.
[30]*Ibid.*
[31]Note by Jawaharlal Nehru recorded at Khali. Nehru Papers.

This was the time when Nehru's thinking on socialism, as applied to Indian conditions, was crystallizing, thanks to his association with the National Planning Committee. He began to visualize the actual process of modernizing the Indian economy. Socialism was to be attained not in a single forward leap, but gradually, by measured steps. It was to be a pattern of development which would "inevitably lead us towards establishing some of the fundamentals of the socialist structure." He was already groping towards the concept of, what came to be known later, as a "mixed economy" and democratic socialism through planned economic development, formulated in the Five Year Plans of the post-independence era.

VI

Whatever the differences of the Congress Socialists with the leadership of the National Congress, and however violent the language they used, they had no intention of carrying their opposition to the breaking point. Their socialist blueprint could not be implemented without ousting the British, and they realized that this task, under Indian conditions, could only be performed by the Indian National Congress. The C.S.P. won a great deal of support among the youth, the industrial labour and the peasantry, but it was still a minority, albeit a vocal minority. It was not a homogeneous group, consisting as it did of Marxists like J.P. Narayan and Narendra Deva, Social Democrats like Asoka Mehta and Masani, Gandhians like Patwardhan, and populists like Ram Manohar Lohia. The C.S.P. could not have its own way on several important issues; nevertheless it succeeded in giving to a limited extent, a radical orientation to Congress policies. On the rejection of the federal part of the Act of 1935, the release of the political detenus, the introduction of agrarian reforms, or the resignation of the Congress ministries in 1939, the Socialists' pressure within the Congress organization doubtless made some contribution to the final result. The Second World War and the breach with the Government brought the Congress Socialists nearer to Gandhi and the Congress leadership. The bitter dose of repression in 1942 and the process of political re-education provided by the conduct of other left groups during the war led to a shift in the postures the Congress Socialists had adopted in 1934-38. Gandhism which they had rejected so contemptuously in the thirties was to strike them as more relevant in the forties and the fifties, not only for a political but social revolution.

The Congress Socialists had always been keen to consolidate all Leftist forces in the country. When the Nazi menace led to a change in the stance of the Communist International in favour of "popular fronts," the Congress Socialist Party opened its doors to Communists in 1936. The Communist party was still illegal; its leaders were glad to get a chance of functioning openly, through the C.S.P. and the National Congress. In retrospect, the experiment seemed disastrous to the Congress Socialist Party;[32] at its Lahore Congress in 1938, even its control of the party executive was challenged.[33] In 1940 the Communists were expelled, but they took with them the southern branches of the C.S.P. The "Popular Front" phase brought solid gains to the Communist Party and gave it a foothold in the Congress organization. But before long, Hitler's invasion of Russia caused another reversal of the party line; the Communists now felt bound to support Britain against the Axis Powers. When the Quit India movement brought on the clash between the Congress and the Government, they found themselves on the wrong side of the battleline.

As we see these two decades in the historical perspective the progress of socialist ideas and organization seems to have been affected by a series of events on the national and world stage and a complex interplay of personalities and politics. It is difficult to say what the results would have been if the Second Communist International had endorsed only Lenin's thesis on colonialism; if M.N. Roy had not been the chief guide of the International in the twenties, and Indian Communists had been allowed to function within the national movement during this period; if Nehru and other Left leaders had joined hands in the pre-war years and revolted against the Congress Establishment; if Gandhi, the most charismatic as well as the most tolerant, receptive, and creative leader of nationalism in history had not been at the helm of the National Congress; if Nehru's bonds with the Mahatma had not been as strong as they actually were, and he had chosen to lead the Congress Socialists; and, finally, if the British had not skilfully alternated reform with repression and in 1947 confounded the theoreticians of revolutions by deciding to go while the going was good.

[32]Jayaprakash Narayan, *Socialism to Sarvodaya* (Calcutta, 1958), p. 11.
[33]M.R. Masani, *The Communist Party of India* (London, 1954), p. 71.

THE COMMUNIST INTERNATIONAL AND INDIAN POLITICS

Vijay Sen Budhraj

SINCE THE CHIEF aim of the Communist International was to accelerate the development of events towards world revolution and since, in the Marxian scheme, the spread of capitalism and the intensification of working class misery were the necessary prelude to a socialist revolution, the founders of the Comintern believed that Western Europe and North America, where the proletariat or working class was most numerous and most highly organized, were ripe for the seizure of power. They also believed and hoped that the proletariat of the advanced countries, after their victory in the West, would carry forward the colonies with them into socialism. There was nothing illogical about this once the world was regarded as one unit and the metropolitan working class as a class of selfless crusaders, harnessed for the advancement of communism in the world.

It is true that Lenin gave considerable thought to the struggle of oppressed nations for independence when the war began in Europe in 1914. In order "to sharpen and extend the crisis of capitalism," he was of the view that the socialists should give support to the "more revolutionary element in the bourgeois-democratic movements for national liberation" of the oppressed nations "and assist their rebellion...against the imperialist powers that oppress them."[1] But here he was mainly concerned with the oppressed nations in Europe because he noticed that the colonies in Asia and Africa had no capital of their own and were, therefore, dependent upon European finance capital for their advance towards capitalism, a progressive step according to the Marxist laws of development.

[1] V.I. Lenin, *Selected Works,* Vol. V (London, 1936), pp. 275-6.

With this in mind Lenin asked, "What is the sense of demanding the immediate and unconditional liberation of the colonies?" Secondly, he held that "from a military point of view...the secession of the colonies can, as a general rule, be achieved only with the advent of socialism" in Western Europe.[2] Thirdly, he asserted that the national movements in Europe were "more likely, more possible, more stubborn, more conscious and more difficult to subdue than in the colonies."[3] Finally, he considered any uprising in Europe more important for the advancement of world revolution than an uprising elsewhere.

> The struggle of the oppressed nations *in Europe,* a struggle capable of going to the lengths of insurrection and street fighting, of breaking down the iron disciplines in the army and martial law, will "sharpen the revolutionary crisis in Europe" infinitely more than a much more developed rebellion in a remote colony. A blow delivered against the English imperialist bourgeoisie by a rebellion in Ireland is a hundred times more significant politically than a blow of equal weight delivered in Asia or in Africa.[4]

Thus when Lenin and his associates seized power in Russia and soon thereafter sought to foment revolutionary movements in the world, they had in mind only that part of the world where the great industrial countries were located.

THE FIRST CONGRESS OF THE COMINTERN AND THE COLONIES

All the thirty-nine invitees to the First Congress of the Communist International were, therefore, from the great industrial countries.[5] It was from Europe, not Asia, that delegates came to found the Communist International. Moreover, when the Congress met in Moscow from 2 March to 6 March 1919, attention was focussed mainly on Europe and on the progress of the Western proletariat. The colonial

[2]V.I. Lenin, *The Right of Nations to Self-Determination* (New York, 1951), p. 101.

[3]*Ibid.,* p. 101.

[4]V.I. Lenin, n. 1, p. 304.

[5]For a list of invitees, see Jane Degras, ed., *The Communist International, 1919-22*, Vol. 1 (London, 1956), pp. 3-4.

question was not on the agenda. The manifesto of the Communist International, written by Trotsky and adopted unanimously by the Congress at its last session, mentions the colonial world only casually. About India, it observed that the revolutionary movement "has not been in abeyance for a single day." But this movement was characterized as a movement of purely "social struggle."[6] Again, while exposing the "peace policy" of the big five Allied and Associated Powers, the theses on the international situation, adopted by the Congress, observed that many countries, including India, had been denied the right of national self-determination.[7] How were they to become independent? The manifesto argued that the emancipation of the colonies was possible only in conjunction with the emancipation of the metropolitan working class; that is, when "the workers of England and France have overthrown Lloyd George and Clemenceau and taken the state power into their hands."[8] It emphatically assured the "colonial slaves of Africa and Asia" that "the hour of proletarian dictatorship in Europe" will also be the hour of their liberation.[9]

At this early date, the Comintern delegates believed that the capitalist world was rapidly nearing its end. They were full of excitement and were very hopeful about the revolution in Europe. "Europe," announced Zinoviev in his address to the delegates, "is hurrying towards the proletarian revolution at a break-neck pace."[10] A few weeks later, he wrote that Europe would be communist within a year "and the struggle will have spread to America, perhaps to Asia too."[11] Clearly both Trotsky and Zinoviev were of the view that the liberation of colonies was dependent on communist victory in Europe. The colonial question did not fit into their scheme of world revolution.

This, then, was the atmosphere in which the First Congress met, and where the colonial question was set aside to be considered after the revolution in Europe.

[6]*The Communist International* (Petrograd), No. 1, 1 May 1919, cols. 12 and 13

[7]Jane Degras, n. 5, p. 33.

[8]For text of the manifesto, see *ibid.*, pp. 38-47.

[9]*Ibid.*, p. 43.

[10]*The Communist International*, n. 6, cols. 39-40.

[11]Jane Degras, n. 5, p. 51.

The *Communist International,* official organ of the Comintern, gave only cursory treatment to the events in the colonies. The first issue in its column "Chronicle of Revolutionary Movement" did not mention anything about India, though it took note of the struggle for independence in Ireland.[12] The second issue reported "rioting" in the Punjab and "greater cooperation between the Mohammadans and Buddhists" (*sic*).[13] Evidently, for the official organ of the Comintern, the mighty wave of mass demonstrations, strikes, and unrest witnessed in many parts of India, following the Jallianwala Bagh massacre at Amritsar in April 1919, were of no significance.

THE REVOLUTION THROWN BACK EASTWARD

The expected revolution in Europe did not take place. The destruction of Soviet Bavaria and Soviet Hungary in the summer of 1919 coincided with the height of British and French intervention in Russia. Denikin had seized the Ukraine and was advancing towards Moscow. However, during these same months of 1919 Asia appeared to rise in revolt against the bourgeois West. In India, Gandhi's agitation against the Rowlatt Act and the mass upsurge that followed the Amritsar massacre appeared to have created a "revolutionary situation" which "set in motion Trotsky's political imagination in a curious direction."

In August 1919, Trotsky sent a secret memorandum to the Central Committee, arguing that the revolution had been thrown back eastward and that the gates to Asia were open before the Red Army which might find the road to India much shorter and easier than the road to Soviet Hungary. With the utmost urgency he suggested, among other things, the setting up of "a revolutionary academy in the Urals or in Turkestan" and of "political and military staffs to direct the struggle in Asia." He repeated that the revolution's road to Paris and London might lead through Kabul, Calcutta, and Bombay.[14]

A few weeks earlier, Bukharin had suggested almost the same thing, though somewhat cynically, at the Eighth Congress of the Russian Communist Party. He stated:

12The *Communist International,* n. 6, col. 142.

13*Ibid.,* No. 2 (June 1919), cols. 264-5.

14I. Deutscher, *The Prophet Armed—Trotsky: 1879-1921* (London, 1954), pp. 456-7.

If we propound the solution of the right of self-determination
for the colonies, the Hottentots, the Negroes, the Indians, etc.,
we lose nothing by it. On the contrary, we gain....The most out-
right nationalist movement, for example that of the Hindus, is
only water for our mill, since it contributes to the destruction
of English imperialism.[15]

In this way colonial revolts acquired a new significance for the
Bolshevik leaders when their position was highly precarious; if
Europe did not wake up and strengthen their hands, they could at
least redress their weakness in face of the West by creating trouble
in the rear of Western imperialism, weakening and distracting thereby their enemies.

How was this to be achieved?

In 1919 a few Indians arrived in Russia and they were available
for setting up an organization to direct the struggle in India. They
told greatly exaggerated stories about the political situation in
India,[16] though they had left India immediately before or after the
beginning of World War I. During the war they established the
Indian Independence Committee in Berlin, financed by the German
government, for the purpose of liberating India. The Committee
and the German government sent an Indian Mission headed by
Raja Mahendra Pratap, to Kabul in 1915 where the Raja established
the Provisional Government of Independent India in December
1915, with himself as President and Moulana Barkatullah as Prime
Minister. After the defeat of Germany, the Provisional Government
and the Berlin Committee lost their main source of power—German
gold. They now looked to Soviet Russia for assistance. The President
and the Prime Minister of the Provisional Government visited Moscow as guests of the Soviet government and along with four other
Indians (Maulvi Rab, Acharya, Dalip Singh Gill, and Ibrahim)
met Lenin on 7 May 1919, but their bourgeois nationalism might

[15]Jane Degras, n. 5, p. 138.

[16]For example, an Indian revolutionary, Moulana Barkatullah (who left India
in 1906) said in Moscow: "Conditions for a revolution are ripe in India, condition similar to the one in Russia in October 1917....There are good reasons to
expect that this summer will be a decisive one for the liberation of India." (From
a statement made by the Moulana and published in *Izvestia,* No. 95, 6 May 1919).
For the English translation of its text, see X.J. Eudin and R.C. North, *Soviet
Russia and the East, 1920-27* (Stanford, 1957), pp. 181-3.

not have impressed the Soviet leader. The Raja presented his booklet, *Religion of Love*, with the remark that "unless the Soviet leader guided the new regime in Russia according to the principles formulated therein, the Revolution would fail."[17]
Lenin is reported to have dismissed the delegation with the remark:

> Religion would not save the Indian people. Tolstoy and others like him tried the same thing in Russia but failed. Go back to India and preach class-struggle, and the road to freedom to India will be nearer.[18]

Lenin and Raja Mahendra Pratap belonged to two different worlds. On his way to Afghanistan the Raja came across a British spy at Kagan (also known as New Bokhara) and is said to have told him that he had met Lenin several times and that he disagreed with the revolutionary policy of Lenin because while the latter aimed at the "Dictatorship of the Proletariat" and the extinction of the upper classes, he thought that "you must have an intelligent upper class and this should work for the benefit of the proletariat and not only for itself."[19] Among the Indian nationalists abroad, he was a puzzling figure, who spent more than thirty years in emigration, wandered from country to country, obsessed with the notion that he was destined to spread a new gospel. His attachment to religion and a feudal outlook could not assure him any place in the communist movement.

Moscow did find the Indian it was looking for to preach class-struggle in India: he was M.N. Roy. Roy left India in 1915 to procure German arms and gold for the liberation of India and reached the United States in 1916. But conditions in the United States changed with America's entry in the war in 1917 and he was arrested. He jumped bail and escaped to Mexico. During this period he received large sums of money from the Berlin Committee for meeting his expenses and for helping the Indian revolutionaries in the Americas. In New York and later in Mexico, he made an independent study

[17]*M.N. Roy's Memoirs* (Bombay, 1964), p. 290. Also see I. Andranov, "Awakening East," *New Times,* No. 9, 1 March 1967, p. 11, and *New Times,* No. 10, 8 March 1967, pp. 6-7.

[18]F.M. Bailey, *Mission to Tashkent* (London, 1946), p. 228.

[19]A. Gupta, *ed., India and Lenin* (New Delhi, 1960), p. 33.

of Marxism and founded the Communist Party of Mexico in 1919. Here he met the Comintern emissary, Michael Borodin, and helped him financially when it was learnt that his new friend had landed in Mexico practically penniless in the summer of 1919. Borodin suggested that Roy could fulfil the mission with which he left India in 1915 with the assistance of the Third International and thus lured him to Moscow in 1920,[20] just in time for the Second Congress, as a delegate of the Communist Party of Mexico. Although a few other Indians in Moscow claimed that they were the real representatives of the revolutionary forces in India, the Comintern recognized Roy as the chief architect of Asian Communism. Lenin regarded him as "the best representative of colonial revolutionism,"[21] and Trotsky also acknowledged the breadth of Roy's vision.[22]

THE COLONIAL QUESTION AT THE SECOND CONGRESS: ATTACK ON EUROPE THROUGH ASIA

Whereas the speakers at the First Congress of the Communist International spoke only about the impending revolution in Europe and advised Asia to wait until the establishment of socialism in Europe, at the Second Congress they also talked about the explosive situation in the East. In his speech on the international situation at the opening session of the Second Congress, Lenin observed that the "Soviet movement has begun throughout the entire East, over the whole of Asia, among all colonial peoples"[23] and that the Comintern should determine how to organize the "Soviet movement in the non-capitalist countries."

In order to examine the various aspects of the national and colonial question, the Second Congress set up a Commission which included both Lenin and Roy. But they found that they disagreed on their assessment of the nature of the national liberation movements in Asia, on what should be the attitude of the Communist International towards it, and on communist tactics in Asia. After several discus-

[20]*M.N. Roy's Memoirs*, n. 17, p. 212.
[21]V.I. Lenin, *Selected Works*, Vol. X (London, 1938). Also see F. Borkenau, *The Communist International* (London, 1938), p. 288.
[22]L. Trotsky, *The First Five Years of the Third International*, Vol. 1 (New York, 1945), p. 236.
[23]Jane Degras, n. 5, p. 236.

sions, it was decided that both Lenin's and Roy's theses should be recommended for adoption by the Second Congress.

As Lenin looked at the colonial world, he found it "devoid of the classic prerequisites for revolution in the Marxist sense." The colonies had still to witness the capitalist stage of development, the workers there made up only a negligible portion of their population— far too few to constitute anything like a mass movement, what to say of a communist movement. Though the struggle for national liberation was going on in some of the colonies, the national-liberation movements were controlled and led by the bourgeoisie who demanded political independence. These movements did not envisage the introduction of economic and social reforms when they succeeded in getting political power. As pointed out by G.F. Kennan, the question arose: Should the communists expose and fight them in the name of the struggle against capitalism, or should they support them in the name of the struggle against Western imperialism?[24]

Lenin observed that these movements were "revolutionary" so far as they opposed imperialism and campaigned for a democratic republic—the first of his revolutionary stages. He also saw in them a force determined to wipe out the influence of great Western powers from some of the regions adjacent to the borders of the Soviet state. The forces fighting the same adversary naturally tend to conclude alliances. Accordingly, Lenin talked of "a close alliance of all national and liberation movements with Soviet Russia," called upon all communist parties to "support by action the revolutionary liberation movements" (the name given to bourgeois national-liberation movements) and advised the Communist International to enter into temporary alliances or agreements "with the revolutionary movement of the colonies and backward countries."[25]

M.N. Roy, on the other hand, asserted in his supplementary thesis that the "bourgeois-democratic nationalist movements" were not worthy of Comintern support because they were not "revolutionary" and also because the nationalist bourgeoisie was likely to "compromise with Imperialism in return for some economic and political concessions to their class."[26] As he surveyed the colonial

---

[24]*Russia and the West under Lenin and Stalin* (Boston, 1961),p . 266.

[25]For text of Lenin's Thesis on the National and Colonial Question, see Jane Degras, n. 5, pp. 139-44.

[26]*M.N. Roy's Memoirs,* n. 17, p. 382.

world, he saw two distinct movements in the colonies:

> The bourgeois-democratic nationalist movement, with a pro-
> gramme of political independence under the bourgeois order
> and the mass struggle of the poor and ignorant peasants and
> workers for their liberation from various forms of exploitation.

He saw in the second movement the seeds of progress and urged that
communist parties should be organized in order to revolutionize the
social character of this movement and to "organize the peasants and
workers and lead them to the revolution and to the establishment of
Soviet republics." While Lenin believed that there were no proletarian organizations of any consequence in the colonies, Roy insisted
that "in most of the colonies there already exist organized revolutionary parties which try to keep in close contact with the working
masses" and that the communists should work with them in preference to bourgeois organizations. Though he considered it "profit-
able to make use of the cooperation of the bourgeois national-
revolutionary elements," he held that "the leadership of the
revolution" should be in the hands of a "communist vanguard."[27]
Again, Lenin held that Gandhi was a "revolutionary" because he
inspired and led a mass movement; while Roy maintained that as
"a religious and cultural revivalist" Gandhi was "bound to be a
reactionary socially, however revolutionary he might appear politically."[28]

Finally, M.N. Roy emphatically stated that for the final success
of the world revolution, coordination of the revolutionary forces in
the subjugated countries with the Communist International was
imperative. He based his contention on Lenin's *Imperialism, the
Highest Stage of Capitalism* (written at Zurich in 1916), which asserted that the colonies were the chief resource of European capitalists
and that without their empires, the capitalist states would collapse,
their workers would starve, there would be millions of unemployed,
and that this situation must cause revolution in Europe at an early
date. Correspondingly, Roy pointed out:

> One of the main sources from which European capitalism draws

[27]For text of Roy's thesis, see X.J. Eudin and R.C. North, n. 16, pp. 65-7.
[28]*M.N. Roy's Memoirs,* n. 17, p. 379.

its basic strength is in the colonial possessions and dependencies.... By enslaving the hundreds of millions of inhabitants of Asia and Africa, English imperialism has succeeded in keeping the British proletariat under the domination of the bourgeoisie.

The logical conclusion of this was that "it will not be easy for the European class to overthrow the capitalist system until the latter is deprived of this super-profit."

The differences between Lenin and Roy were very significant and somewhat fundamental and yet both the theses were voted together and passed by the Second Congress. According to Roy, Lenin wanted that they "should suspend final judgment pending practical experience," believing that the two drafts constituted "the greatest possible approximation to a theoretically sound and factually valid approach to the problem."[29]

Evidently, the Communist International was left with the difficult task of putting these vague and contradictory injunctions into practice.

Having said this, one might ask whose assessment was correct and whose approach realistic? Lenin's approach was certainly more realistic, for he did not hesitate to forge a united front with a movement controlled and led by the bourgeoisie. To hit the enemy where it hurts is a well-established principle of *realpolitik*. A policy of collaboration with the national-liberation movement was bound to unnerve or scare the British, and Lenin must have realized that this would at least increase Russia's bargaining power at a time when Moscow was eager to conclude a trade agreement with London. Russia, Soviet or Czarist, has always appeared as a threat to British interests in the Middle East and Asia. The Czars, while posing a threat to the British Empire in India, tried to get concessions from the British government. Similarly, Lenin could also squeeze some advantageous terms from the British by posing or threatening to help the nationalists in India.

It was certainly a good strategy. Did not Karl Marx see in the Taiping rebellion in China (1853), the possibility of a sufficient reduction in the volume of British foreign trade to trigger an economic crisis in Great Britain "which, spreading abroad, will be closely

[29]*Ibid.*, p. 381.

followed by political revolution on the Continent"[30] And it was quite possible that if India could be taken away from the British Empire at that time, the blow to the British nationalist feeling and the economic upheavals resulting from the loss of the Indian market might have led England to revolution. Bertrand Russell feared such a possibility in 1920.[31] Had Lenin not adopted this course, perhaps history would have judged him a poor revolutionary.

M.N. Roy, like a new convert, was nearer to Marx than Lenin and probably thought that the revolutionary and terrorist groups with which he had contacts when he left India in 1915, could form the nucleus of a communist movement. Had he looked carefully at the Indian scene at that moment, he would have noticed that the advent of Gandhi had brought a radical change in the liberation movement in India. Before Gandhi entered the scene, this movement ran into two main channels—the constitutional struggle carried on by the moderate and radical sections of the Indian National Congress, and violent, armed struggle carried on by unorganized, underground revolutionary and terrorist groups in different parts of the country. Gandhi's programme and methods tended to link the two channels. His method was revolutionary and yet it was non-violent. Like revolutionaries, he advocated the break of laws, but this was to be done openly in order to court imprisonment and also to paralyze the government. Like the programmes of revolutionaries, his programme called for many sacrifices (for example, the renunciation of government titles, boycotting of the legislatures, British goods and government educational institutions), but his actions were straight and open. The result was that his programme captured the imagination of the masses, made the Indian National Congress a party of the great masses and the revolutionary and terrorist groups ceased to be a significant force in the national liberation movement. It seems that Roy was unaware of this development. However, in the 1930s, when he returned to India and had a closer look at the situation in India, he came to realize that the Indian proletariat about which he was so hopeful at the Communist International hardly existed.

Apart from this, ever since 1916 the provocative question raised

[30]Qutoted in C.B. McLane, *Soviet Strategies in Southeast Asia* (Princeton, 1966), p. 4.

[31]*The Practice and Theory of Bolshevism* (London, 1949), second edition, p. 73.

by Lala Lajpat Rai in a socialist meeting in New York had been tormenting him: "What difference would it make to the Indian masses if they were exploited by native capitalists instead of foreign imperialists?" This question made him uncomfortable and ultimately led him to the New York Public Library to read the works of Karl Marx and accept Marxism.[32] How could he now think of political independence alone? His commitment to the new social order called for organizing "the poor and ignorant peasants and workers" in the colonial world, specially in India.

STEPS TAKEN TO SPREAD THE REVOLUTION EASTWARDS

Soon after the Second Congress, the Central Asiatic Bureau of the Communist International was set up, "charged with the responsibility, in the first place, of carrying through the revolution in Turkestan and Bokhara, and then of spreading it to the adjacent countries, particularly India." The Bureau consisted of Sokolnikov, Chairman of the Turkestan Commission of the Central Soviet Government; Safarov, a member of the Central Committee of the Bolshevik Party, and M.N. Roy. The first two members of the Bureau rushed to their assignments in Turkestan immediately after the Second Congress, but Roy stayed behind as Moscow was also considering him for filling its diplomatic post at Kabul.[33] In the hope that he could stir up revolutionary forces inside India from Afghanistan, Roy eagerly looked forward to this appointment. But the Afghan government thought that Roy's appointment might estrange Kabul's relations with New Delhi. The plan for sending Roy as Soviet ambassador to Kabul was dropped and soon after the third anniversary of the October Revolution, Roy left for Tashkent with two train-loads of arms (pistols, rifles, machine guns, hand grenades, light artillery, etc.), ammunition, military stores and field equipment, money (gold coins, bullion and pound and rupee notes), dismantled aeroplanes and the complete outfit of an air battalion, the personnel of the latter and the staff of a military training school.

From Tashkent all this material and men were to be transported to Afghanistan where M.N. Roy was to raise, equip and train an army for Indian liberation, to be recruited from amongst those Indian

[32]*M.N. Roy's Memoirs*, n. 17, pp. 28-9.
[33]*Ibid.*, p. 395.

Muslims who, responding to a call by the Khilafat Committee, had left India for Afghanistan in order to proceed to Turkey. This army, with the mercenary support of the tribesmen, was to acquire operational bases in frontier territories, march into India and occupy some territory for the purpose of establishing a revolutionary government in India. Roy was of the view that if the revolutionary government proclaimed and enforced a programme of social reforms, workers and masses would enthusiastically support the new regime with the result that the vested interests and the imperialist power would go down in defeat.[34]

In this way Roy wanted to prepare himself for a direct, armed confrontation with the British rule in India. The plan appears to be romantically adventurous: an army of liberation, composed of religious fanatics and mercenary tribesmen, led by a Marxist and supported by some dismantled aeroplanes (Kabul did not have an airport at that time), marching through the Khyber Pass, believing that the mighty, well-equipped, well-trained and well-organized British army would be demoralized by revolutionary programmes and propaganda leaflets and hoping that the masses in India would rise in revolt as soon as they heard of the establishment of a "revolutionary government." He was unbelievably optimistic and his plan was far removed from realities.

But the establishment of the advance base in Kabul and operational bases on the Indian frontier presupposed the consent and active cooperation of the Afghan government. When contacted, Kabul proposed that arms and money should be deposited with the Afghan diplomatic mission at Tashkent, to be delivered to M.N. Roy in the proper place and at the proper time. This would, it was explained, relieve the "illustrious visitor," M.N. Roy, of the difficulties of travelling with all the requisites of his mission. It was a tricky proposal and a clever move to acquire some Russian arms and gold. Moscow did not fall into the trap; the plan to build a base in Afghanistan for an Indian army of liberation had to be abandoned.[35]

This did not dampen M.N. Roy's enthusiasm and he decided to give political and military training to about 125 *muhajirins* (Indian Muslim emigrants), who had come to Soviet Central Asia in order to cross over to Turkey, in the Indian Military School that

[34]*Ibid.*, pp. 420-2.
[35]*Ibid.*, p. 442.

he had opened at Tashkent. Since most of them were religious fanatics, they refused to be converted to communism and created a number of problems for Roy who characterized them as "indifferent
material."[36] A small number of them eventually became communists,
organized the Indian Communist Party at Tashkent and later, led
by Shaukat Usmani, some of these *muhajirins* returned to India
to work for the communist movement in their country.

In the meantime, negotiations for a trade agreement between
Soviet Russia and Great Britain, which began in May 1920, were
concluded successfully in March 1921. The agreement was subject
to the condition that the Soviet government would refrain from

> any attempt, by military or diplomatic or any other form of action
> or propaganda, to encourage any of the peoples of Asia in any
> form of hostile action especially in India and the Independent
> State of Afghanistan.[37]

Following the agreement, the British government informed Moscow that Roy's presence and activities in Tashkent, the Indian Military School at Tashkent, and the Russian negotiations with Afghanistan for securing facilities for Indian revolutionaries in that country, were an evidence of Soviet aggressive designs against the British
Empire. All this was a clear violation of the Trade Agreement.
Moscow therefore decided to close the school and direct Roy to
move to Moscow or Western Europe, giving the impression that its
opening was a political manoeuvre, designed to squeeze some economic concessions from the British government.

Even otherwise, the Tashkent school had not been a success.
Thus M.N. Roy's hope that Kabul would give him facilities to
launch an attack on India had been belied. King Amanullah even
asked the Indian revolutionaries who had set up the Provisional
Government of Independent India in Kabul in 1915 to leave Afghanistan.[38]

[36]*Ibid.*, p. 469.
[37]L. Shapiro, ed., *Soviet Treaty Series*, Vol. I, 1917-28 (Washington, 1950),
p. 102.
[38]For the activities of Indian revolutionaries in Afghanistan, see this author's
"The Provisional Government of Independent India, 1915-20," *Kurukshetra
Unversity Research Journal*, Vol. I, No. 1 (January, 1967), pp. 212-29.

THE THIRD CONGRESS AND THE COLONIAL WORLD

When the Third Congress of the Communist International met in Moscow in June-July 1921, it had been realized that there was no possibility of an early world revolution in the East or in the West. In his report on the world situation, Trotsky surveyed the various defeats suffered by revolutionary movements since 1919 and concluded that world capitalism had survived the post-war crisis and that the proletariat, therefore, should wait and strengthen its organization for the next opportunity to be afforded by another crisis of world capitalism.[39]

In India, he observed, "the native bourgeoisie," which provided leadership to the masses in their liberation struggle, was neither "consistent nor energetic." It was alleged that the bourgeoisie had tightened its bond with foreign capital, becoming thereby "an agency of foreign capital."[40] He endorsed the main contention of Roy's supplementary thesis when he observed that this created "favourable conditions for the young proletariat of the colonies to develop rapidly and to take its place at the head of the revolutionary peasant movement."[41]

But when Roy repeated that the colonies constituted a potential means for the stabilization of the tottering capitalist system and that, therefore, the most important matter was to deprive capitalism of such reserve, Trotsky explained that the colonies were only one of the three river-beds along which the revolution flowed—the other two being "the rotten Europe and America."[42] From this he concluded that the revolutionary movement in India and in other colonies had become an integral part of the world revolution.[43] The chief task of the Communist International was now considered to be to direct, broaden, and deepen the "defensive struggles of the proletariat."[44] In other words, comrades everywhere were advised to undertake organizational work in their respective countries.

[39]For extracts from the Thesis on the World Situation, see Jane Degras, n. 5, pp. 230-9.

[40]L. Trotsky, n. 22, pp. 222-3 and 236-7.

[41]Jane Degras, n. 5, p. 234.

[42]D. Boersner, *The Bolsheviks and the National and Colonial Question, 1917-28* (Geneve: Libraire E. Droz, 1957), p. 40.

[43]Jane Degras, n. 5, p. 234.

[44]*Ibid.*, p. 239.

Soviet foreign policy too underwent a radical change in 1921. Having failed to spread revolution abroad, the Kremlin sought expediency to effect reconciliation with the West. In pursuance of this policy, Georgi Chicherin, Commissar for Foreign Affairs, wanted that the base of revolutionary propaganda in Tashkent should be shifted to a more convenient place.[45] It was, therefore, decided that

1. The Turkestan Bureau of the Communist International should be abolished.
2. The communist parties in the imperialist countries should be directed through the Comintern to establish contacts with and help the revolutionary movements in their respective colonies.
3. The Communist International should open an Eastern Section in Moscow to supervise and guide the activities of the revolutionary movement in the colonial world through the communist parties in the imperialist countries.
4. A centre for the political training of revolutionaries from Asian countries should be established in Moscow. (This centre came to be known as the Communist University for the Toilers of the East and admitted, among others, twenty-two students of the disbanded Tashkent School. The remaining students of the Tashkent School were given monetary help to proceed to wherever they liked—Persia, Afghanistan, or India.)
5. M.N. Roy should establish contact with India and influence events therein from Western Europe.[46]

Before M.N. Roy left Moscow, the news of the non-cooperation movement in India reached there and the Bolshevik leaders thought for a while that India was in the throes of a revolution and that the non-cooperation movement was "a revolutionary mass upheaval," a vast political wave which they could ride, though the wave had been created by indigenous, non-communist forces. But Roy pointed out that the non-cooperation movement was "politically immature, with little revolutionary potentialities"[47] and held that the situation in India indicated that there was "a spontaneous mass discontent."[48]

[45]*M.N. Roy's Memoirs*, n. 17, p. 526.
[46]*Ibid.*, pp. 525-31.
[47]*Ibid.*, p. 527.
[48]*Ibid.*, p. 543.

He explained that the religious ideology preached by Gandhi "discouraged any revolutionary mass action" and that "a potentially revolutionary movement" was being "restrained by a reactionary ideology."[49]

Could Roy persuade the Indian National Congress to adopt a revolutionary ideology and a concrete programme of economic reforms so that the movement could become "a revolutionary mass upheaval"? With the approval of Lenin and Stalin, Roy decided to appeal to the Indian leaders for this purpose when they were about to meet at Ahmedabad for the 1921 annual session of the Indian National Congress. The appeal to include in the Congress programme such items as would attract the worker and peasant masses was printed in Moscow and Nalini Gupta was specially sent to distribute and broadcast it throughout India and to the delegates at Ahmedabad.[50]

The appeal did not seem to have made any noticeable impact on the Congress.

ROY IN BERLIN

In April 1922 Roy came to Berlin, which in those days, "was a headquarters of a sort for many Indians living in Europe, and a good place to make contacts."[51] It was a good base for directing the forces likely to change the content of the programme of the national liberation movement in India. What tactics were to be followed by Roy? Was he to collaborate with the Indian National Congress for the overthrow of British imperialism as had been stated in Lenin's thesis adopted at the Second Congress, or was he to expose and discredit this body and organize communist groups in India as had been stated in his supplementary thesis? His activities during the next few years reveal that he adopted both the tactics. He was supplied with money (by the Communist International), which enabled him to begin publication of a bi-monthly journal *Vanguard of Indian Independence*. The journal had to change its name to *Advance Guard* and still later to *Masses*. It had also to change its

---

[49]*Ibid.*
[50]*Ibid.*, pp. 545-7.
[51]G.D. Overstreet and M. Windmiller, *Communism in India* (Berkeley, 1959), p. 40.

place of publication to Geneva and later to Paris in the course of the next five years as Roy had to change his headquarters from time to time, owing to steps taken against him by the police. Apart from these journals, Roy published a number of books and wrote innumerable letters, statements and manifestos and despatched them to India together with the official organ of the Communist International, *International Press Correspondence* or *Inprecor*. According to British Intelligence, *Amrita Bazar Patrika* of Calcutta, *Atma Sakti* of Calcutta, *Independent* of Allahabad, and *Nava Yuga* of Guntur were some of the newspapers influenced by Roy's publications.[52]

When his publications and appeals did not seem to have any impact on Gandhi and his close followers, he wrote in desperation:

> The Mahatma proposes 'to touch the masses through their hearts, their better nature.' It is a fascinating proposition, to which Bolshevism would not object, had it been found workable in the practice of liberating the masses....His theory of 'discipline' is also very questionable....It weakens...their will to fight for freedom. All these doctrines about 'heart,' 'better nature,' 'discipline' and the like were the instruments of class domination. Bolshevism challenges the existence of God and denounces all codes of religion and ethics because in the struggle for freedom they are all found arrayed on the side of despotism, tyranny and oppression.[53]

M.N. Roy also sent a number of emissaries to India to distribute propaganda material and form communist groups. Some success was achieved in this matter, for a number of such groups were established in places like Bombay, Calcutta, Kanpur, Lahore, and Madras.[54] The record of the Kanpur and Meerut conspiracy cases, started in 1924 and 1929 respectively, provide testimony to the fact that the Communist International, through M.N. Roy and his emissaries as well as through the Communist Party of Great Britain, was successful in raising "a band of devoted communists

---

[52]Quoted in *ibid.*, pp. 41-2.

[53]In a letter to Gandhi, published in *Young India* of 1 January 1925 and reproduced in *The Collected Works of Mahatma Gandhi*, Vol. XXV (Delhi: Publications Division, Government of India, 1967), pp. 604-8.

[54]*M.N. Roy's Memoirs*, n. 17, p. 572.

in India who had begun to establish their influence over the working class and were giving evidence of their capacity to arouse the militant spirit."[55]

Not only that, the Communist International could also claim to have gained some influence in the Congress when Nehru, as the spokesman of the Indian National Congress, attended the Communist-inspired Congress of Oppressed Nationalities which met in Brussels in February 1927. According to Michael Brecher, it was at Brussels that "the goals of national independence and social reforms became linked inextricably in his (Nehru's) conception of future political strategy."[56] When this Congress founded the League Against Imperialism, Nehru agreed to serve on the nine-man Executive Committee. Upon his suggestion, the Indian National Congress was formally affiliated to the League in 1927 and reaffirmed its support to the League's aims the following year.

Nehru's initial exposure to the Marxist-Leninist ideology at Brussels was widened when he paid a brief visit to Moscow early in November 1927 during the tenth anniversary of the Bolshevik Revolution. "Soviet Russia, despite certain unpleasant aspects," attracted him "greatly, and seemed to hold forth a message of hope to the world."[57] The visit helped to shape his political outlook, for he came to the conclusion that "without social freedom and socialistic structure of society and the State, neither the country nor the individual could develop much."[58]

THE SIXTH CONGRESS AND THE COLONIES

While communist activities and propaganda were making some headway in India, the Communist International decided to change its strategy and tactics at the Sixth Congress, held in Moscow in 1928. The main reason for this was that the policy of collaboration with the bourgeois-national liberation movement in China, led by the Kuomintang, ended in a major set-back to the communist movement in that country in 1927 when, after extending its control over a large part of China in cooperation with the Chinese communists,

[55]*Ibid.*, p. 574.
[56]Michael Brecher, *Nehru: A Political Biography* (London, 1959), p. 109.
[57]*Jawaharlal Nehru: An Autobiography* (Bombay, 1962), p. 166.
[58]J. Nehru, *Towards Freedom* (New York, 1942), p. 128.

the Kuomintang undertook various repressive measures against the Chinese communists, culminating in the liquidation of a large number of communists. The Communist Party of China was outlawed and driven underground.

From this debacle Stalin concluded that the national bourgeoisie had gone over to the counter-revolution in order to suppress the revolutionary movement and thus had become counter-revolutionary.

What was its relevance for India? Was not the Indian National Congress controlled by the same social classes, bourgeoisie and landlords, that controlled the Kuomintang? And if so, would not the communists in India risk the fate that befell their comrades in China, were they to continue their support to the Indian National Congress? The Chinese experience called for a reappraisal of the Comintern's attitude towards the national-liberation movements, controlled and led by the bourgeoisie, in the colonies.

The theses on the colonial and semi-colonial question, adopted by the Sixth Comintern Congress, strongly reflected the Chinese experience, for it was stated that in 1922 the Indian bourgeoisie betrayed the cause of national revolution as it was scared by the "growing wave of peasant risings, and of the strikes against native employers."[59] In other words, the bourgeoisie had ceased to be "revolutionary" as early as 1922.

What should the communists in India do and what should be their attitude towards the bourgeoisie and the Indian National Congress? They were advised to form a union of all communist groups in the country and thus establish "a single, illegal, independent and centralized party." Secondly, they were to

> unmask and, in opposition to all the talk of the Swarajists, Gandhists, etc., about passive resistance, advance the irreconcilable slogan of armed struggle for the emancipation of the country and the expulsion of the imperialists.[60]

The new line was in essence what M.N. Roy had suggested at the Second Congress in 1920. But in 1928 Roy believed that the situation did not warrant the abandonment of the tactics of united

[59]Jane Degras, ed., *The Communist International*, Vol. II, 1923-1928 (London, 1960), p. 531.
[60]*Ibid.*, p. 544.

front. He strongly criticised the ultra-leftist policy. When expelled from the Communist International in 1929, he began strengthening his contacts with the Congress leaders and, along with many other Indians, made an attempt to organize a branch of the Indian National Congress in Germany. He returned to India in 1930, anxious to influence the thinking of the Congress leaders and to strengthen the hands of the radical group inside the Congress.

It can be argued that Roy's assessment and tactics corresponded to the actual situation, for within the Congress a militant left group had grown up which stood for the achievement of complete independence for India and also for the reconstruction of Indian society on the basis of social and economic equality. Nehru's exposure to and attraction towards communism have already been mentioned. Upon his return from Europe in 1928 he became a strong supporter of socialism within the Congress. In his presidential address at the Lahore session of the Indian National Congress (1929), he declared himself "a Socialist and a republican,"[61] condemned both imperialism and capitalism and stated that India would have to adopt a full "Socialistic programme" if she sought "to end her poverty and inequality."[62] Another Left-wing leader in the Congress, S. Srinivasa Iyengar, was in Moscow observing communism in action, while the Sixth Congress of the Comintern was denouncing the Indian National Congress. According to Shaukat Usmani, S. Srinivasa Iyengar met Stalin and sought Soviet assistance for his party.[63] Instead of cooperating with such men in the Congress, and instead of participating in the mass demonstrations organized by the Indian National Congress during the 1930–34 Civil Disobedience Movement, the Communist International advised the Indian communists to attack the Congress, to fight relentlessly against Gandhism, to denounce the Congress as an organ of "counter-revolution," to isolate themselves from the Civil Disobedience Movement," to organize the workers and peasants *independently* ... and *emancipate* them from the influence of the national bourgeoisie, and to wage a bold and persistent struggle against foreign imperialism.[64]

---

[61]J. Nehru, *India's Freedom* (London, 1965), p. 14.

[62]For text of the 1929 presidential address, see *ibid.,* pp. 7-19.

[63]*I Met Stalin Twice* (Bombay, 1953), p. 27.

[64]"Programme of the Communist International," adopted at its Sixth Congress, Jane Degras, n. 59, pp. 519-22. Emphasis added.

The soundness of this advice could be questioned by those who knew the actual strength of the Communist Party of India. How could a handful of Indian communists do all that? The theses of the Twelfth Plenum of the Executive Committee of the Communist International on the international situation, adopted in 1932, admitted that there were only a small number of weak communist groups in India, not united in any way, and "not clearly differentiated in all cases from the national reformists."[65] How could they operate effectively as an independent political force? When they blindly followed the new line, they placed themselves in opposition to the nationalist movement. When they talked and planned of establishing Soviets, the government arrested all senior communist workers.

THE UNITED FRONT AGAIN

Another change occurred in Soviet foreign policy following Hitler's rise to power in 1933. The danger of fascism took the place of the much-publicized danger of an imperialist offensive against Soviet Russia. In view of this the Seventh Comintern Congress, held in Moscow from 25 July to 20 August 1935, rediscovered the revolutionary role of the Indian bourgeoisie, found the Indian communists guilty of sectarian errors and of failing "to participate in all the mass demonstrations organized by the National Congress and its affiliated organizations." It was again realized that "they (the Indian communists) were not strong enough to organize a mass-imperialist movement of their own"[66] and were, therefore, indirectly advised to join actively in the anti-imperialist struggle of the Indian National Congress.

But the role of the Communist Party of India during the 1930-34 Civil Disobedience Campaign and its later decision to support the British government in India (upon the advice of the Communist International) when at the instance of Gandhi the Indian National Congress resolved to launch the "Quit India" movement in 1942, made the Party unpopular and did incalculable harm to the communist movement in India.

It is not implied here that the Communist Party of India would

[65]Jane Degras, ed., *The Communist International*, Vol. III, 1929-43 (London, 1965), p. 220.
[66]*Ibid.*, p. 358.

have gained strength and captured the Indian liberation movement
if it had not isolated itself from the struggles launched by the Indian
National Congress. A violent communist movement controlled
and directed from outside, could not have taken roots in India at
a time when Gandhi held the Indian masses at his beck and call
or when Gandhi had "cast a spell on all classes and groups of people
and drawn them into one motley crowd struggling in one direction."[67] The Indian section of the Communist International,
composed of a handful of young Indians, most of whom had left
India before or during the First World War, was not in a position
to appraise the realities of the Indian situation. Perhaps it could
not have, even if it wanted, after the failure of the revolutionary
attempt in China when Stalin "nationalized" the proletarian
revolution; that is, when the Russian leaders began to think
of themselves and their state more and more as the sole effective
carrier of the revolution. They began to confuse the emancipation
of the working class with the greatness of their state, the propagation of their ideology with the extension of their power. The
programme of the Communist International adopted at the Sixth
Congress, described the Soviet Union as "the true fatherland of
the proletariat" and enjoined the proletariat of the world to forward
the success of socialist construction in the Soviet Union and to
defend the USSR "by every means" as it was considered to be the
bulwark of the world revolution.[68] This was stated more explicitly
in a resolution adopted by the Seventh Comintern Congress in
1935.[69]

It meant that the Communist movement in India, like such other
movements elsewhere, was to be subordinated to this foremost duty.
Perhaps it might be said that the World Congress, defined in Comintern Statutes as the Supreme Organ of the Comintern, which met
periodically could take an objective view of the world situation. But
this important organ of the Comintern receded into the background
after the Fourth World Congress in 1922. The Fifth Congress met
in 1924, the Sixth four years later and the last, Seventh, in 1935;
though the revised statutes of 1924 provided for a Congress at least
once every two years. In addition, the elimination of Trotsky and

[67] J. Nehru, n. 57, p. 25.
[68] Jane Degras, n. 59, p. 513.
[69] *Ibid.*, p. 378.

Roy, plus the successive purges of dissident elements, made these Congresses Stalin's command performances.

CONCLUSION

When the Comintern was dissolved unceremoniously in 1943 by the Presidium of the Executive Committee of the Communist International, M.N. Roy observed that the Comintern was an "unmitigated evil" for India and that its Indian section "has done more harm to the cause of the Indian Revolution than any other factor."[70] It may appear to be a sweeping statement, but there does not seem to be any doubt that the Comintern or its advice made the communist movement in India unpopular and prevented it from acquiring an effective say in the Indian National Congress.

No one would wish to belittle the huge fund of idealism, goodwill, enthusiasm, faith, and courage that was invested in the establishment of the Communist International in those early days. However, when the signals for a proletarian revolution in the West and in the East went unanswered, the Comintern began to concern itself primarily with the interests of the Soviet Union, the leader and the only "socialist fatherland" in the world. It could probably be said that the interests of the Comintern coincided with the national interests of Soviet Russia. For one thing, the world communist movement was likely to rise in stature with the increase in the strength of Russia. Also Soviet experience, like Soviet gold, could be beneficial for the communist parties abroad. Hence, the interests of the communist movements in the colonies had to be subordinated to those of the USSR. But it should not escape our attention that the communist leaders in the colonies, or, for that matter, in the countries considered ripe for revolution in the West, ceased to have any effective say in the formulation of the Comintern policy, strategy and tactic when Stalin and his associates began to dominate and control the Communist International as they did the Soviet state.

This seriously interfered with the ability of the Comintern to get a clear and meaningful view of what was happening in India. The national-liberation movement in India gained momentum from the end of World War I, when Gandhi took over as its leader, until

[70]*The Communist International* (Bombay: Radical Democratic Party, 1943), p. 49.

India became independent. No doubt the struggle was long, still there was no substantive change in the policy of the Congress or in the situation in India during 1919-42 which warranted changes in the attitude of the Comintern towards this movement. To make things inconvenient for the British, the Comintern decided to give unconditional support to the nationalist movement in India in 1920. Lenin's pragmatism convinced him that an investment in the liberation movements in the colonies could benefit the Soviet state. For the same reason Stalin, through the Comintern, called upon the Indian communists to cooperate with the British government in India for the successful prosecution of the war when Hitler's attack on Russia in 1941 made Britain and Soviet Russia allies. Evidently, the "general staff" of the world revolution in later years became an instrument in the hands of the Soviet leaders or "a secondary department of the Soviet Foreign office"[71] and the interests of Russia came to dictate Comintern tactics in the colonial world more than local conditions.

[71]H.J. Laski, *Reflections on the Revolution of Our Time* (London, 1943), p. 63.

THE RISE OF SOVIET RUSSIA AND SOCIALISM IN INDIA, 1917-1929

Z A F A R   I M A M

EFFECTS ON POLITICS AND MOVEMENTS IN INDIA, 1917-20*

Early reaction in India

THE NEWS OF the February Revolution in Russia was enthusiastically received in India. All sections of Indian opinion, both the nationalist and the pro-Government, joined hands in welcoming the beginning of democracy in Russia. But their underlying motives were very different. The nationalist welcomed it for its possible effect—the reform and the liberalization of British Government in India, and, as a first step to avoid a catastrophe, like in Tsarist Russia, the repeal of all coercive and repressive laws was suggested.

The pro-Government section, on the other hand, welcomed it for its repercussions on the conduct of the war. It was believed that the beginning of popular government in Russia would provide a deathblow to the German influence in Tsarist Russia. It would strengthen Russia's military position, enabling her to make an effective contribution to the Allied war efforts.[1]

For a country like the India of 1917, the interval between the February and October Revolutions was too short to allow any idea to form on the real ideological struggle underlying them. In the first few months after the October Revolution, few could have gathered from conflicting and confusing newspaper reports, still further diluted by censors, what that Revolution really stood for.

However, the enthusiasm shown on the previous occasion was

*For a comprehensive account of this period, see the author's article "Effects of the Russian Revolution on India" in S. N. Mukerjee, ed., *St. Antony's Papers*, No. 18 (London, 1966), pp. 74-97.

[1] *Advocate of India* (Bombay), 17 March 1917.

discernible this time as well. The official report on the Indian constitutional reforms, published in 1918, said:

> The Revolution in Russia and its beginning was regarded in India
> as a triumph over despotism notwithstanding the fact that it has
> involved that unhappy country in anarchy and dismemberment;
> it has given an impetus to Indian political aspirations.[2]

But it was the nationalists who showed an interest in the Russian
Revolution. Leading journals both in the English and Indian langu-
ages published articles and commentaries on the happenings in
Russia, emphasizing the force of nationalism working behind them.

Effects on Government Policy during the War

The Revolution in Russia precipitated a sudden change in Government policy, which was expressed in its attitude to the question of
Indian reforms. The policy of the Government on Indian reforms
had always been marked by cautious delay and hesitant action.

But the sudden announcement of the long-deferred reform in
August 1917 was indeed revealing. In August 1917, the internal
situation in India was in complete control of the Government, and
it did not warrant a drastic change of policy. The hasty character
of the announcement was shown by the fact that it caught the Indian
administration unawares and the top civil servants were not sure
how to implement it. Besides, the Montagu-Chelmsford report
on reforms was prepared a year after the announcement; the actual
reforms were not enacted until the end of 1919, and they came into
operation only in 1920.

One of the major considerations in this abrupt change of policy
from a firm and uncompromising stand to a reconciliatory attitude,
was not only internal but also external. The precarious balance
of the war was of course decisive. It was felt that a definite announcement on the future of India, promising more administrative autonomy to the Indians, would increase the tempo of India's war efforts,
and also revitalize her interest in the immediate victory of the Allies.
But the deepening crisis on the Eastern front and the process of the
disintegration of the Russian army made it urgent to keep the Indians

---

[2]*Report on Indian Constitutional Reform* (HMSO, Cmd. 9109, 1918), p. 14.

quiet, divert their attention from external events, and channel it to the need for safety and security of the Indian Empire.

But a sudden announcement of major concessions to the Indian national aspirations precipitated a long acrimonious political controversy in India. Those who had consistently opposed even minor concessions to Indians were perturbed by the sudden change of policy, and found it convenient to attack the proposed reforms by citing the Russian example. It was argued that, like the Russian intelligentsia, the Indian intelligentsia would also fail to carry out their responsibilities of governing the country efficiently if such responsibilities were thrust upon them too soon without adequate experience and training.[3] Lord Sydenham, a former Governor of Bombay and the president of the influential Indo-British Association, declared: "Russia had given us a striking illustration of what happened when authority was destroyed and 80 per cent of the people were illiterate. The result in India would be more disastrous still."[4]

The widespread nature of such propaganda, emanating from influential Anglo-Indian sources, compelled the nationalists to take a defensive position. They argued that Home Rule would not bring about revolutionary chaos, but that in fact a delay in reform could lead to a revolution. Characteristic of the contemporary opinions on this controversy was the following comment from a nationalist daily:

It is not the Home Rule that brought about troubles in Russia. It is the revolution which is the parent of this chaos. Had the erstwhile rulers of Russia had the wisdom to make a timely concession of Home Rule, there would have been no revolution and no outbreak of lawlessness and disorder....Reforms indefinitely postponed are inadequate in their scope and comprehension, and prepare the ground for revolt.[5]

The Impact on the Nationalist Movement

It would be an over-simplification to suggest that this new reali-

[3] Sir Valentine Chirol, "Reform in India: The Russian Example," *The Times,* 10 June 1918.
[4] *The Morning Post* (London), 30 July 1918.
[5] *The Bengalee,* 25 November 1917.

zation in India was brought about only by the Allied war aims and by the speeches of the British and American leaders.[6] The Soviet pronouncement on the right of self-determination of all nations had also played its role, though a minor one, in projecting the concept of self-determination and also its practicability on the Indian scene. Soviet influence proved even more far-reaching and effective than is generally understood because of the sharp contrast in implementing the principle of self-determination in Allied and Soviet Policy. The Indian public realized that self-determination was proclaimed by the Allies but was not applied to India. On the contrary, they noted that the Soviet Government not only promised but also implemented it in the former Tsarist colonies as well.[7]

The President of the Calcutta session of the Indian National Congress, held in December 1917, the first to be held after the Revolution, contrasted the despotic nature of British rule in India with that of its "free and self-ruling neighbours across the northern frontier," and declared that "in future unless India wins self-government, she will enviously look at her self-governing neighbours and the contrast will intensify her interests."[8]

The appeal issued by the Soviet Government on 24 November-7 December 1917 renouncing secret treaties, annulling the partition of Turkey and Persia, and proclaiming the rights of all people and nations to self-determination was heard in India as well.[9] It had its repercussions too. The 1918 annual Congress session was preoccupied with the question of self-determination and its application to India. The discussion that followed the main resolution on the subject showed a remarkable mixture of the traditional hold of British liberalism over the Indian intelligentsia and their faith in the Allied war aims, and of the new finesse introduced by Soviet Russia's declared policy. The Congress session was swayed by Lloyd George's war speeches and President Wilson's Fourteen Points, and they were approvingly quoted. But for all its carefully inculcated British liberalism, when it came to actual implementation of the principle of self-determination, it appeared to have been inspired

[6]The Official Report on the Indian reforms (1918) has very much emphasized this point. See *Report on Indian Constitutional Reform*, n. 2, pp. 21-2.

[7]"Dyerism or Bolshevism," *Bombay Chronicle*, 20 October 1920.

[8]*Indian National Congress Report* (Delhi, 1917), p. 22.

[9]*Bombay Chronicle*, 22 November 1917.

also by the Soviet example. Madan Mohan Malaviya, the president of the session, while defining and explaining how self-determination would apply to India, said in his presidential address that a congress of the people would be called which "will determine and declare what in its opinion should be the measure of reform which should be introduced in the country. Let the British government give effect to the principle of self-determination in India by accepting the proposal so put forward by the representative of the people of India."[10] The question of the "representative of the people" was for the first time brought into the picture in the context of self-determination. Mrs Besant, who moved the main resolution, thus ridiculed the Government's attitude to self-determination:

> We say this in answer to the Government of Great Britain declaring that it cannot govern without these powers (i.e. coercion and despotism).... But the Czar of Russia could only govern with coercion. Are you then no better ruler than the Czar of Russia.[11]

The Congress session carried a unanimous resolution demanding self-determination for India.

By embodying successfully the principle of self-determination both in its internal and external policies, the Soviet Government projected it on to the world scene. It was considered justified on the part of the Soviet Government in demanding that other Governments should do what they had already implemented in their own country. The question was asked, if one country could do this, why not others, and why not Britain herself? Even in India, these doubts manifested themselves and such questions were asked.

Besides, the rise of new forces in the country had slowly begun to transform the Nationalist Movement itself into a mass movement with a definite programme of action and campaign against British rule in India. The main factors contributing to the new awakening were the rapid transformation of the Indian National Congress into a dynamic organization; the renewed activity of a tiny but determined group of men working to win freedom by terrorist and conspiratorial means; and lastly, a sudden shift in Government

[10]*Indian National Congress Report,* 1918 Session (Delhi, 1919), p. 18.
[11]*Ibid.*

policy from reform and concessions to repression after the war ended.

The new force coming up on the Indian political scene was the beginning of an organized working-class movement. There are indeed some records to show that labour organizations in some form were in existence in Bombay in the late 1880's, but they were in no sense properly constituted labour organizations. However, it was in April 1918 that the first organized industrial union was founded in Madras by B.P. Wadia.

The growth of the political role of the working class after 1917-18 was indeed meteoric. The end of the year 1918 was marked by a great strike in the Bombay cotton mills, and by January 1919, 125,-000 workers coming from practically all the Bombay mills were out of work. In April 1919, the response to the strike call against the Rowlatt Bill was amazing. In all, during the first six months of 1920 there were strikes involving 1.5 million workers.[12]

In fact, the beginning of the year 1918 marked the beginning of an organizational period of the working-class movement in India. Obviously, the horrible working conditions in factories, rising prices and falling wages, and the fantastic profits amassed by the employers were the main causes of the beginning of the working-class movement in India. But it is significant, and not a mere coincidence, that the Indian working class movement began immediately after the October Revolution. Also, it is noteworthy that a desire for solidarity with the October Revolution and sympathy for it manifested themselves among the Indian working class right from the very beginning. One of the main purposes of the programme of the All-India Trade Union Congress, adopted in its inaugural session in 1920, was to serve as a "link between Trade Unions in India and the Trade Unions and Labour Movements elsewhere."[13] In spite of the close association of some leaders of the movement with the British labour movement, Singaravelu Chettiar, a noted labour leader of Madras and an old Congressman, moved a resolution in the first AITUC session for sending delegates to the Communist International, but it was rejected.[14] A year later, at its second conference, the AITUC

[12]R.K. Das, *The Labour Movement in India* (New York, 1923), p. 36.

[13]*Report of the First Session of the All-India Trade Union Congress* (AITUC) (Bombay, 1920), p. 33.

[14]M.N. Roy, *Future of Indian Politics* (London 1926), p. 104.

unanimously adopted resolutions which expressed sympathy for the Russian famine and gave a call to the working class all over the world to abolish wars by international actions.[15]

Thus the overall effect of the October Revolution on the Indian labour movement must not be underestimated. Notwithstanding the Fabian orientation of some leading labour leaders like Joseph Baptista, B.P. Wadia, Lajpat Rai and N.M. Joshi, more confused and paradoxical because of their advocacy of the spiritual task of Indian workers,[16] the beginning of consciousness among the Indian workers, of their own importance and of working class solidarity inside and outside the country was all the more quickened under the impact of the October Revolution.

While in the agitational field new forces were coming up, conspiratorial and underground movements in India and abroad had attracted attention from all quarters. Foremost among them were the emigrè movements outside the country.

Among the Indian political movements, the Ghadar and Hijrat movements, though not inspired by the Russian example, were the first to establish contact with the Soviet Government. Many of the emissaries of the Ghadar party from Berlin and of the Hijrat movement from Kabul later made contacts with the Soviet Government. This is a long and interesting story which need not be related here.

Politics in India after the War

Meanwhile, a significant shift in British policy in India had occurred. As soon as the war ended, the Government of India showed less inclination to fulfil all their promises of reforms and concessions, given during the war and confirmed in the Montagu Declaration of August 1917. After the war, the Government caused disappointment by appointing a special commission under Justice Rowlatt. On the other hand, the report on the constitutional reforms published early in 1918 greatly dismayed all sections of Indian opinion, and subsequently most of them refused to cooperate with the reforms. Moreover, in contrast to the delay in enacting the reform bill, the recommendations of the Rowlatt Commission were rushed through the Imperial Legislative Council, which armed the executive with

[15]Evelyn Roy, "The Crisis in Indian Nationalism," *Labour Monthly* (London), Vol. 2, No. 2 (1922), p. 155.
[16]See *AITUC Report*, 1920.

far-reaching powers to arrest and detain persons without trial and formal charges.

As before, the Russian factor in this reversal of policy was important. Once the pressure of the war was removed, the British Government were concerned with consolidating themselves in India against the new challenge of Bolshevism. The increasing momentum of the Nationalist Movement and the rise of a hostile power on India's border made this all the more urgent and important. In September 1918, Lord Chelmsford, the Viceroy, declared in the Imperial Legislative Council:

...The Russian Revolution which took place shortly afterwards was seized upon as a pretext on which to base claims to sweeping changes. I think those who sang a paean of the Russian events have since repented. Russia indeed has hinted a moral which it would do us all good to take to heart.[17]

Later, in 1919, addressing the budget session of the Imperial Legislative Council, Lord Chelmsford again warned the country of the menace of Bolshevism to India. He also informed the Council of the establishment of a special staff to deal with the danger of Bolshevik agents and propaganda.[18] The Government of India issued an ordinance prohibiting the circulation of all rouble notes in the country.[19] The purpose of this ordinance, as officially described, was to suppress the circulation of all the roubles which were believed to be reaching India in connection with Bolshevik propaganda.[20]

It was obvious that in the opinion of the Government the situation had not much altered since the war. In place of the German military danger, the new and more formidable menace of Bolshevism now threatened India. The official report for the year 1919 declared:

With the termination of hostilities, it might naturally be supposed that the menace of India's north-western frontier of which mention was made in last year's report, would disappear....To the German

[17]Lord Chelmsford's Speech reported in *Times of India,* 9 September 1918.
[18]Government of India. *India in the Year 1919* (Delhi, 1920), p. 61.
[19]*Times of India,* 24 November 1917.
[20]*The Times* (London), 20 March 1920.

arms there succeeded the more formidable menace of Bolshevik ideas.[21]

The British Government, no doubt for their own reasons, rightly considered the rise of Bolshevism on India's border a potential threat to their supremacy over the subcontinent. Partly in view of this new threat, their attitude towards Indian national aspirations hardened all the more, and only limited concessions to Indians were granted in the Montagu-Chelmsford reforms of 1919. But in their preoccupation with the danger of Bolshevism, the British Government misunderstood the growing tempo of the Nationalist Movement assuming it to have been mainly engineered by Bolshevik agents.

Gandhi also lashed at the propaganda in his characteristic vein and remarked: "I have never believed in a Bolshevik menace and why should any Indian Government fear Russian, Bolshevik or any menace?"[22]

It was at the height of this controversy that the Third Afghan War broke out in April 1919. The first and immediate reaction in India to the Afghan War vis-a-vis the Revolution in Russia contradicted the officially inspired propaganda of a Bolshevik invasion of India. The Indian nationalists saw for themselves that the trouble came from other than Russian sources and precisely because of those Afghan demands for complete independence and sovereignty to which they themselves aspired for in India. Perhaps this was the reason that a genuine sympathy for the Afghans was widespread in the country.

INDIAN ATTITUDE TO RUSSIAN EVENTS

At this stage, it is worthwhile to recall that by 1920-21, there emerged a new feature in the Indian political scene, what may be called an Indian opinion on international affairs, particularly those with bearings on India. Although the Indian National Congress (INC), in its early days did occasionally express opinions on events outside India, the real interest in international affairs began to manifest itself among the Nationalists as a result of the First World War and its aftermath. In his presidential address to the annual session of the I.N.C. held

---

[21]*India in the Year 1919*, n. 18, p. 168.
[22]M.K. Gandhi, *Young India, 1919-1922* (Madras, 1924), p. 717.

at Amritsar in 1919, Pandit Motilal Nehru made references to Soviet
Russia wanting peace but not being allowed respite by other powers.
In 1921, the Working Committee of the I.N.C., for the first time in
its history, adopted a formal resolution on foreign policy which
attacked the British policy towards India's neighbours, and called
it "as mainly designed to perpetuate the exploitation of India by
Imperial Powers."[23]

This new factor in the politics of the Indian Nationalist Movement
was felt during the growing tempo of the entire movement as a result
of the first wave of non-cooperation which began in 1919. Hence the
Indian attitude to Russian events was both symbolic for further
development of the political consciousness of the I.N.C. and least
surprising as well.

Invariably, Indian opinion was sympathetic to events in Russia.
However, when it was the question of Britain's policy towards Soviet
Russia, the nationalists were more vocal in siding with Soviet Russia,
while the Pro-Government section expressed support to the British
Government. Suffice here to quote some characteristic contemporary
opinions on these events in Soviet Russia.

Allied Intervention and Civil War

Referring to British intervention in Russia, the Hindi nationalist
monthly, *Maryada* (Allahabad) opined:

> It is clear that the former [i.e. the Capital] is wholly opposed to
> the progress and supremacy of the latter [i.e. labour] and is
> trying hard to suppress its efforts. This is why the capital is deter-
> mined to exterminate Bolshevism, the sole strength of labour
> and that is why the British Government, in spite of its repeated
> promises not to interfere any longer in Russian affairs, is continu-
> ing to fight the Bolsheviks.[24]

The Hindi nationalist weekly, *Abhyudaya,* thus opposed the intervention, "Bolshevism should be allowed to run its own course
because the attempts of the Allies to check it is resulting in oppression and repression in Russia."[25] While reviewing Anglo-Soviet

[23]M.N. Mitra, ed., *The Indian Annual Register,* 1921 (Calcutta, 1922), p. 271.
[24]*Maryada, U.P. Native Newspaper Reports,* September 1919, p. 288.
[25]*Abhyudaya, U.P. Native Newspaper Reports,* March 1919, p. 24.

relations during 1917-20, the influential English nationalist daily of Allahabad, *Independent* remarked:

> Both parties are to blame and if the assessment is to be finally made, judgment would go against England.... It has long been evident that Lenin is the only man who can run a government in Russia and now that Warangal has been routed Western Europe has not the barest excuse to think otherwise.[26]

Soviet Russia's relations with Neighbouring States and Anglo-Soviet Relations

The new Soviet Government was hailed for entering into friendly relations with Persia, Afghanistan and Turkey. On the other hand, the normalization of Anglo-Soviet relations, which took place as a result of the signing of a trade agreement between the two countries in March 1921, was received in India with a sigh of relief. It was generally hoped that the agreement would quieten down Soviet Russia and would help in safeguarding British interests in the East. We shall take up only two samples of contemporary opinion on this. One nationalist daily thus commented: "The trade agreement with Russia showed that England wanted to placate Russia to keep her dominions in the East."[27] A pro-government English daily welcomed the treaty as "a wise step taken by the British Government," but it was constrained to warn that "it is premature to say how far it will be able to neutralize Bolshevik designs against the British."[28]

The suspicion among the Nationalists about British intentions towards Soviet Russia was indeed widespread and almost an article of faith for them. A very representative view on this was thus expressed by the influential Hindi Daily of Kanpur, *Partap,* edited by Ganesh Shankar Vidyarthi. In an editorial on 14 January 1921, the paper argued that the Allies did not want Bolshevik Government in Russia and for that very reason they wanted to discredit the present Russian regime; it then asked the Indians to exercise great caution in reading the British Press reports on Russia.[29]

[26]*The Independent, U.P. Native Newspaper Reports,* 21 November 1920, p. 461.
[27]*Partap* (Hindi), *U.P. Native Newspaper Reports,* 24 March 1921, p. 144.
[28]*Advocate* (Lucknow), 31 March 1921.
[29]*Partap* (Kanpur), *U.P. Native Newspaper Reports,* 14 January 1921, p. 27.

No one connected with the Indian Nationalist Movement showed any belief in the officially inspired propaganda, in full swing during 1920-21, on the impending danger of a Bolshevik attack on India with the connivance of the Afghans. The influential English nationalist daily of Allahabad acidly characterized this propaganda as a

> clever lie concocted by our enemies to divert the attention of the nation from the goal on which it has fixed its gaze and to break Hindu-Muslim unity whose strength is staggering to the enemy. ... We are not for change of masters, though we cannot conceive of worse masters than the British bureaucrats.[30]

However, the only exception was the opinion of the Muslim nationalists on events in Soviet Russia. Although the Muslim opinion appreciated and welcomed Soviet Russia's support to Turkey, Afghanistan, and Persia,[31] it was agitated over the reports of "Bolshevik treatment of Islam in Central Asia" which were pouring in India through official and semi-official sources. The Khilafat Urdu weekly *Albareed*, made thoughtful and indeed representative comments:

> Muslims never regard the Bolsheviks as their friends and even if they are constrained to join them it is only because they are the enemies of their enemies....We admit that the Bolsheviks cruelly shed the blood of a few hundred Muslims in the Crimea and at the Persian Consulate at Armvir, but have not the Armenian beasts of prey devoured one million Muslims....The number of Muslims killed by the Bolsheviks is a mere bagatelle when compared with these figures....We declare that Muslims in India or elsewhere are not supporters of Bolsheviks, but their helpless condition forces them into the arms of the Bolsheviks.[32]

Later, during the following years, the Muslim opinion on Soviet Russia continued to get more and more critical mainly because of

[30]*The Independent* (Allahabad), 12 May 1921.
[31]See, for example, *Oudh Ahkbar* (Lucknow), *U.P. Native Newspaper Reports,* 10 January 1920, p. 10.
[32]*Albareed* (Kanpur), *U.P. Native Newspaper Reports,* 11 February 1920, p. 34.

the anti-religious orientation of the Bolshevik Party. Less and less attention was given to the subsequent developments in Soviet Russia, and the Muslims, in general, became completely cut off from any ideological impact of the Soviet system of Government. This was indeed regrettable, in view of the fact that a fairly large number of Indian Muslims had seen and experienced life in Soviet Russia during 1918-21, to which references have been made earlier.

EFFECT ON INDIAN POLITICS, 1920-1922

Having thus spotlighted the sympathetic attitude of the Indian Nationalists, it would be wrong to conclude that they had begun to evince interest in the ideological aspect of the Soviet system of Government. Indeed, they were hostile to the ideology of the Soviet Government. This was made abundantly clear by the contemporary opinion on the interesting episode of the Reuter News Agency giving publicity to M.N. Roy's blueprint for the Indian Revolution just on the eve of the 1922 Gaya session of the I.N.C. Suffice here to quote from two representative opinions. Even a usually pro-Government daily, *Advocate* thus commented:

> To say that the Indian leaders are inspired by Bolshevik ideals because there is some resemblance between certain items of programme drawn up by Mr Roy is a gross perversion of truth.... There is not the ghost of a chance of India substituting the leadership of Lenin for that of Mahatma Gandhi.[33]

The nationalist daily, *Independent,* expressed this view:

> The object of giving publicity to Mr Roy's programme is to damn the Indian National Congress as a body depending for its inspiration on the Bolsheviks and alienate from it the sympathies of the landlords, employers and the professional classes....Our faith is non-violent, non-cooperation based on love-force. Mr. Roy's plan has no room whatever for love-force.[34]

[33] *The Advocate* (Lucknow), *U.P. Native Newspaper Reports,* No. 1 of 1923, p. 67.
[34] *The Independent,* 12 May 1921, p. 7.

To put the record straight, it must be pointed out that after the end of the Civil War and foreign intervention, the Soviet leaders had begun to show interest in India. The second Comintern Congress, held in the summer of 1920, marked the real beginning of the activization of a policy which might be called a Soviet policy towards India. A discussion of the ideological and geo-political importance of Soviet policy towards India is beyond the scope of this paper. But reference can be made to some practical steps the Soviets took in an effort to implement this policy. In the formative period of Soviet state, the main *modus operandi* of the policy towards the colonial world was still considered to be propaganda and appeals rather than concrete actions. This was true of Soviet policy towards India as well. In September 1922, an emissary from the Comintern (Charles Ashleigh by name and a member of the British Communist Party) arrived in Bombay to contact the Indian Communist leaders for the forthcoming Fourth World Congress of the Comintern.[35] However, he had to leave India within a few days because the police got wind of him. The Fourth Comintern Congress itself made a direct bid to interfere in Indian politics. It sent a message to the All-India Trade Union Congress expressing solidarity with the Indian workers' movement, and assured them of the sympathy and support of the Soviet workers. On the other hand, it also warned the Indian Labour Unions of "the false friendship and misleading advice of labour leaders that are subservient to imperialism."[36]

Indirect tactics were employed in utilizing the services of M.N. Roy in order to gain access to the Indian nationalist movement and influence it from within.

However, as pointed out earlier, all these attempts proved futile as far as the Indian nationalist movement was concerned. But the Government of India was fully aware of these efforts because of the police vigilance in India and the mass of intelligence reports pouring into the British Foreign Office and War Office. Hence the Government of India, on their part, never failed to emphasize the menace of Bolshevism to India. The official report of the Government of India pointed out:

[35]"Early History of the Party," *New Age* (New Delhi), 6 February 1966, p. 14.
[36]CPGB, *Resolution and Thesis of the Fourth Congress of the Communist International,* 1923, p. 15.

The defiant utterances of Lenin and Kamenof [sic] during 1922 show that England is still regarded as the greatest enemy in the world of the Red International. And it is in India that the Bolsheviks believe that they see the Achilles' heel of the British Commonwealth....It would be idle to deny that the Bolsheviks, aided by the present political uncertainty, have been to some degree successful in deferring the consummation of peace in the Near East.[37]

At the other extreme, the press in Britain was almost unanimous in saying that the Bolsheviks and the Indian nationalists were in league with one another. *The Times* accused the Indian nationalist press of receiving subsidies from Moscow in return for their sympathies for Soviet Russia. It even went on to explain that the favourable disposition of the nationalists towards Soviet Russia was "largely the outcome of the influence of Gandhi whose teachings correspond in many ways closely to the doctrines of Lenin."[38] *The Morning Post* reported that *Zinoviev* had spent seven million gold roubles in supporting and maintaining "the revolutionary spirit amongst Gandhi's adherents in India."[39] Likewise, in India, the Anglo-Indian and semi-official press repeated such accusations with greater equanimity.

But the Government of India viewed the developments in the Gaya Session of the I.N.C. (1922) with considerable apprehension. The official report of the Government of India commented:

Dr Das [the leader of the Swaraj party] has adopted an attitude far more socialistic than that generally found in the addresses of the Indian political leaders....Sentiments such as these have excited considerable discussion among the educated classes and there was a tendency in some quarters of a leaning towards Bolshevism.[40]

The semi-official and Anglo-Indian press took the cue from the Government, levelled more wild charges and called the programme of

[37]The Government of India, *India in 1922-23* (Simla, 1924), p. 24.
[38]*The Times,* 19 August 1922.
[39]*The Morning Post* (London), 13 June 1922.
[40]Government of India, *India in 1922-23* (Simla, 1924), p. 291.

the INC "a fruitful soil for the machination of Bolsheviks."[41] Besides, C.R. Das, the leader of the Swaraj party, was under strong suspicion of maintaining close contacts with the terrorists and Bolsheviks.[42]

It was obvious that the British were inclined to identify the normal political activities of the Indian nationalists with the machination of the Bolsheviks. Expression of sympathy for Soviet Russia by the nationalist press added to the Government's suspicion of the nationalist movement. In suspecting the nationalist movement of collusion with the Bolsheviks, the British Government not only tended to ignore the social, political, and economic background of the movement, but also rejected its persistent denials of having anything to do with the Bolsheviks. The result was that while direct appeal and propaganda carried out by the Soviets showed no influence on the programme and policies of the Indian nationalist movement, it seriously affected the British Government in their attitude towards the movement, and also in their dealings with Soviet Russia.

The establishment of an openly hostile power like Soviet Russia on British India's border, revived in the British Government the old and traditional fear of Russia's drive towards India with greater potential danger than ever before.

The British Government, for their own reasons, rightly saw in the Soviet interest in India a potential threat to their supremacy over the subcontinent. They were indeed wise in doing everything possible to thwart all forms of Soviet activities directed towards their rule in India. But they grossly overrated the effects of Soviet policy on the Indian Nationalist Movement and wrongly suspected it to be inspired by the Soviet leaders. They failed to distinguish between the Soviet efforts to challenge their supremacy in India and the actual success they achieved in their objectives. Moreover, British rule was so firmly entrenched in India during the period under review, that it would have required something more than mere propaganda and hostile activities conducted by a foreign power inside and outside the country, to oust it. Besides, it could have been fairly obvious to a careful observer of that time, not to speak of the Government in power, that the Indian Nationalist Movement could hardly have been regarded as a suitable ground for applying and implementing the strategy and tactics devised by the Soviet leaders.

[41] *Pioneer* (Lucknow), 2 January 1923.
[42] The Earl of Lytton, *Pundits and Elephants* (London, 1922), p. 65.

Yet the British Government tended to ignore these factors and throughout the period under review, showed an imbalanced concern for Soviet propaganda in India. This not only brought the external factor of Soviet propaganda and hostile activities in the internal politics of India, but also exposed the British Government to the nationalists' accusation of deliberately fostering the fear of a harmful effect of Soviet policy to silence and discredit the entire nationalist movement. These developments further alienated the nationalists from the Government and created additional difficulties for Britain in India. The cumulative effect of all these factors was that the British Government throughout entertained an exaggerated fear of Soviet propaganda and hostile activities against the British Empire.

EFFECT ON INDIAN POLITICS, 1923-1928

During the period 1923-28, although radicalization of the Indian Nationalist Movement continued at a steady pace, the emphasis in its politics shifted from agitation and non-cooperation to Parliamentary opposition and cautious cooperation. It was also the period when the communist movement in India began to take an organizational form. The Peshawar Conspiracy trial of 1923 and the Kanpur trial, and later in 1929, the Meerut Conspiracy Case presented the incipient communist movement as something distinctive in character and somewhat alienated from the main goals and objectives then before the Indian Nationalist Movement.

On the other hand, as the commitments of the Indian Nationalist Movement to its own national goals and objectives became more and more firm, Soviet policy towards India began to shift from an all-out support for the bourgeois-nationalists to growing impatience towards them. The high-water-mark of Soviet disillusionment with the bourgeois-nationalists was reached in the Sixth Comintern Congress, held in the summer of 1928. The Sixth Comintern Congress unequivocally gave a call against any form of cooperation with the Indian National Congress and asked the Indian Communists to work both for national freedom and social revolution. It was indeed symbolic that this *volte-face* in Soviet policy towards India occurred precisely at a time when the Indian Nationalist Movement was about to enter into its decisive phase with the proclamation of India's independence in the Lahore Session of the I.N.C. in 1929.

Moreover, Anglo-Soviet relations during this period were strained further and the rupture of diplomatic relations between Britain and Soviet Russia occurred in 1927. The Conservative Government obviously decided to ignore Soviet Russia, which eventually contributed to the undermining of the traditional British fear of Bolshevik threat to the British Empire.

Sympathy and support for the Soviet Union, particularly in her relationship with Britain, nevertheless increased among the Indian nationalists. In 1927, the Nehru family, and later in 1928, a former Congress President and a few other persons connected with the labour movement, visited the Soviet Union, and came back very much impressed with what they saw.[43] Their impression, particularly that of young Nehru, which he made public in a series of articles published in a nationalist newspaper, created a very favourable image of the Soviet Union in the country. They also encouraged opposition among the nationalists to Britain's policy towards the Soviet Union. Besides, attracted by the idea of developing international contacts, the I.N.C. sent Jawaharlal Nehru as a delegate to attend the Brussels Conference of the League Against Imperialism, and later formally associated itself with it. In November 1927, the All-India Trade Union Congress (AITUC), in its annual session, passed a resolution congratulating the Soviet Union on the tenth anniversary of the Bolshevik revolution and also expressed solidarity with her in the event of British intervention against her.[44] As a result of the devotion and organizing ability of the Comintern emissaries, Philip Spratt and Ben Bradley, the Workers' and Peasants' Party became active in Bombay and in the United Provinces and in 1927 the Workers' and Peasants' Party of Bengal claimed a membership of 10,000.[45] Moreover, in 1927, Sapurji Saklatvala, the Communist M.P., successfully toured India. Although he refrained from direct propaganda in favour of Communism, he fully exploited his privileged position as a M.P. and his tour was a great personal success. The Central Committee of the Communist Party of India met for

[43]See Jawaharlal Nehru, *Soviet Russia: Some Random Sketches and Impressions* (Bombay, 1929). See also Krishna Hutheesingh, *With No Regrets* (Bombay, 1943).

[44]*The Indian Annual Register,* 1927, Vol. II (Calcutta, 1928), pp. 111-7.

[45]See *Meerut Communist Conspiracy Case Committal* (Meerut, 1929), p. 128 and *Simla, 1932-33,* Vol. *I,* p. 155.

the first time in Bombay in May 1927, and the leading Communists, though still few in number, attended. The question of affiliation with the Comintern was considered but no decision was taken except one for solidarity with that body.

These developments seriously disturbed the Government of India. The official report for the year 1926-27 noted the growth of the Workers' and Peasants' Party in Bengal and the increasing activity of the CPGB in India and concluded: "During 1926-27, Communism in India has been both more active and more vocal than in the preceding years."[46] But the Government of India were still not disposed to distinguish between the growth of the nationalist movement and the new connections between the Communist movement and the Soviet Union. Both these developments were generally regarded as part of one big move against British rule in India. Again the old fear revived of a combination of disorder at home and the hostile actions of an unfriendly neighbouring power. Every year, the Government of India had been steadily increasing defence expenditure. In March 1927, when a Swarajist member of the Assembly raised the whole question of increased military expenditure, Sir William Birdwood, the C-in-C of India, defended it on the grounds of potential danger behind the Bolshevik menace.[47] He dryly told his critics in the Assembly: "Those who have seen the correspondence that has taken place between the Home Government and Russia, I think, will realize that we are not in a state of being to sit down and disband our army."[48]

On the other hand, Britain's action in breaking relations with the USSR evoked extremely hostile comments from the nationalist leaders and the press. On British policy, the INC at its annual session in Madras in December 1927, passed a resolution expressing grave concern over the possibility of war against the Soviet Union after the break in diplomatic relations, and refused to support any such British Plan.[49] The nationalists became all the more reluctant to understand the extreme concern of the British Government at Soviet

[46]Government of India, *India in 1926-1927* (Simla, 1927), p. 288.

[47]*Council of States Debates,* Vol. IX. No. 14, 1927, p. 440. (See also Lord Birkenhead's speech in the House of Lords on 30 March 1927, *Parliamentary Debates, House of Lords,* 5 Series Vol. 66 Cols. 869-70.)

[48]*Ibid.*

[49]*Report of the Forty-Second Session of the Indian National Congress,* p. 61.

activities in India and elsewhere, and considered this to be a part
of the campaign to discredit and frighten them with a threat, which,
in their opinion never existed. The Indian Government on their
part always emphasized the Bolshevik danger, but did not pay much
attention to explaining British policy to the Indians. On the contrary,
they still suspected the nationalist movement of having a liaison
with the Soviet Union. It was, therefore, not surprising that the
suspicion of British policy towards the USSR entertained by the
nationalists continued to grow and deepened their resentment against
the Government.

In the meantime, during 1928, there were new developments on
the Indian political scene. On the one hand, the Workers' and Peasants' Party became very active in Bombay and Calcutta. In Bombay,
the Party was instrumental in organizing a successful strike by
textile workers which lasted for seven months,[50] and caused shut-
down in fifty mills. On the other hand, various units of the WPP
merged themselves into an all India Workers' and Peasants' Party
in a Conference held in Calcutta in December 1928. Besides, a
phenomenal rise of the labour strikes took place all over India during
the year 1928-29.

Moreover the INC showed more interest in outside events affecting India, at its annual session in 1928. On Jawaharlal Nehru's
insistence, the Congress declared that "the struggle of the Indian
people for freedom is a part of the general world struggle against
Imperialism and its manifestations."[51] Similar resolutions were
passed supporting the League Against Imperialism, and others
on the dangers of war which implied that Britain was making preparation for waging a war against the Soviet Union.[52] Dr Ansari,
a former Congress President, who moved the resolution on the danger
of war declared:

We Indians have no quarrels with Russia. We do not know really

[50]During the Bombay strike, the committee sent a few thousand rupees to the
strikers presumably through London. This was openly admitted by the Bombay
Labour leader, N.M. Joshi, on the floor of the House. (*Legislative Assembly
Debates,* Vol. III, 1928, p. 473.)

[51]*Report of the Forty-third Session of the Indian National Congress* (Calcutta,
1928), p. 97.

[52]*Ibid.,* p. 95.

whether the quarrel that England has with Russia is not really another pretext to perpetuate our own slavery. Therefore, it is proper and right that we should not allow ourselves to be made tools in the hands of imperialistic England to conquer other nations.[53]

Besides the gradual transformation of the INC into a mass party with a well-defined political programme and the phenomenal rise of the labour strikes, new organizations like the All-India Socialist Youth Congress and the Independence of India League, etc. had sprung up. These organizations were not only paper organizations but came into being with definite political and social programmes which appealed to the young and radical intelligentsia.

As a matter of fact, the year 1928 was a milestone in the history of the Indian freedom movement. It was the moment in the history of the Indian freedom movement when indecision and confusion gave way to decision and advance.

EFFECT ON INDIAN POLITICS, 1928-29

After 1928, the events in Soviet Russia were understood by the nationalists not only in the context of Anglo-Soviet relations but also within the framework of Soviet national and global objectives. Thus began the full ideological impact of the rise of Soviet Russia on the nationalists. Yet it was significant that the majority of the nationalist leaders continued to show strong disbelief in the Communist threat and in the theory of extension of a Bolshevik power to India. In 1928-29, they opposed tooth and nail the passage of the Public Safety Bill through the Central Legislative Assembly.

Srinivasa Iyengar, a former Congress President, spoke for all when he thus opposed the Bill in the Assembly: "The object of this Bill, I say most advisedly, is not really to deport Bolsheviks, or Communists or anything of that kind. The object of this Bill is really to put down all kinds of movements in this country, agrarian or industrial."[54]

The growing tempo and the radicalization of the Indian nationalist movement had made it increasingly difficult for the British

[53]*Ibid.*
[54]*Legislative Assembly Debates,* Vol. IV, 1928, p. 1365.

Government to explain the unrest and nationalist urge in terms of foreign conspiracy and Bolshevik machinations. Thus forced by the march of events beyond their control some sanity was restored to the policy of the British Government and a more realistic approach to the Indian problem was discernible from 1928 onwards.

But this shift in the Indian Government's policy—from suspecting the nationalists of cooperating with the Bolshevik agents to curbing the spread of Communism in India—also changed the Government's attitude towards the nationalist movement. They now recognized that unrest in India was a result of internal conditions and not because of Soviet conspiracy.

On the other hand, the changes in Soviet policy had made abundantly clear that the Indian nationalist movement led by the INC had neither the support nor the sympathy of the Soviet Union. There was no longer any danger for Britain that a foreign Power would back the nationalist demands and thus turn them into an embarassing issue with world support and sympathy.

Secure in this knowledge, the British Government could henceforward deal with the Indian nationalists as they thought desirable and expedient. Such a correct appreciation of the situation no doubt strengthened the hands of the British Government in exercising control over India.

The nationalists were no longer seriously suspected of extraterritorial connections and sympathies. But Communism in India and Soviet machinations still posed a grave potential threat to British imperial interests. Hence it was considered a desirable policy not only to check the spread of Communism in India but also to ensure that the nationalists did not patronize the Communists. While commenting on the strong nationalist opposition to the Public Safety Bill, the *Times* warned the nationalists against the growing Communist influences in India and accused them of "feeding the brute."[55] The paper even warned them against a possible Soviet armed invasion of India.[56] A bomb throwing incident in the Central Hall of the Indian Legislative Assembly was cited by the responsible Anglo-Indian and British Press as a clear proof of a Communist conspiracy of taking over India.[57] On the other hand, following

[55]*The Times*, 7 February 1929.
[56]*The Times*, 15 February 1929
[57]*Ibid.*, 9 April 1920; *Pioneer*, 10 April 1929.

the arrests of the Communist leaders, stringent measures like the limitation of the right to strike, and a special enquiry into Communist activities in Bombay, were adopted.

The Ideological Impact on the Nationalists

Reference to contemporary writings and speeches of the nationalists shows that some attemps were made to understand the nature of the Bolshevik Revolution. We have noted the far-reaching influence that the Bolshevik Revolution and Russian events exercised on the course of Indian politics. But taking the Bolshevik revolution as a whole and the underlying Bolshevik ideology, one is struck by the marked ignorance about it among Indians, even if this ignorance was mingled with sympathy.

The bloodshed and turmoil in Russia during the Revolution were very unwelcome to Indian minds. They were thought to be a necessary corollary of a revolution, no matter where it occurred. At a public meeting, Srinivasa Sastri, a leading Congress member of Madras, declared that he was "one of those who had acclaimed that the Russian Revolution was a symbol of deliverance and regeneration"; but later he came to look upon it as a historical calamity, because "the prophets who had foretold ruin and disaster had also proved only too late."[58]

Bal Gangadhar Tilak, the noted radical nationalist leader, was reported to have explained that Bolshevism could not spread in India not only because it was an external cult but also due to the fact that all its principles were already enshrined in the Gita.[59] Likewise, Young India, Gandhiji's weekly, foresaw the failure of Bolshevism in India because "temperamentally nothing is so opposed to the Indian mind as the pulling down of all authority, the destruction of all social and judicial sanction and in particular the weakening or wiping out of the institution of private property and marriage."[60]

In 1919-1921, Gandhiji, at the threshold of his career, with his pronounced views on violence, had repeatedly declared his dislike for revolutionary methods and the ensuing chaos. Writing in his weekly, Young India, he remarked:

[58]Madras Mail, 18 May 1919.
[59]Government of Bombay, Bombay Native Newspaper Reports 1920, No. 15, p. 2.
[60]Young India, (Ahmedabad), 2 April 1919.

India does not want Bolshevism. The people are too peaceful
to stand anarchy. They will bow to the knees of anyone who
restores order. Indeed we have made religion subservient to
peace.[61]

Here it is necessary to keep in mind that the Indian intelligentsia
understood the Revolution in Russia only in the context of a general
historical phenomenon closely linked with the history of Europe.
But when it affected relations between the master and subject nations,
it became more an Asian event, hence an object of special interest.
In September 1919, Lala Lajpat Rai, the Congress leader, wrote:

They (the people of Asia and Africa) at any rate have nothing to
lose by the triumph of Bolshevism. They may be intellectually
unfit to grasp it. They may be politically helpless to benefit by
it, but they have no reason to rail at it.[62]

A century of careful inculcation of liberalism through education
and other social reforms of a limited nature had not created an atmosphere conducive to revolution and its ideals. Hence
the Indian intelligentsia vaguely admired the Bolshevik Revolution,
and looked at it with a well marked critical appreciation, while
the restrictions imposed by the censorship made it more confusing
and baffling. The prevalent ignorance about the Bolshevik Revolution was therefore understandable and the confusion of the intellectuals was explicable. It was believed, for example, that revolution
could come only through revolutionary propaganda of a destructive
nature and that the actual conditions in a given country played little
or no part in its failure or success. Characteristic of such opinions
were the remarks of a leading Congress leader from Madras who
said that, "the revolution in Russia was brought about only by the
great spread of ideas through decades of literature of a very revolutionary character."[63]

It is, however, paradoxical that while the Bolshevik Revolution
was so well received in India and affected the political life of the
country, yet the revolution and scientific socialism appeared to the

[61]M.K. Gandhi, n. 22, p. 279.
[62]*The Independent,* 2 September 1919.
[63]*Madras Mail,* 18 May 1919.

Indian leaders as something foreign to their country. In the midst of the growing upsurge of nationalism of that period, all things foreign were fast becoming things least wanted and desired. The Bolshevik Revolution, however much appreciated, could not therefore have easily and instantly moved the Indians to follow its example. Moreover, in spite of the rising new forces of the working class movement and the radical intelligentsia, the basic character of the Indian nationalist movement during 1917-29 and the nature of its leadership, was marked by a natural reluctance to go further than was necessary and expedient. It was therefore not surprising that some of its leaders had to be extremely cautious, to save the movement from the charge of collusion with Soviet Russia—a charge which was then being levelled by the Government supporters and over-zealous empire loyalists.

CONCLUSIONS

The Bolshevik Revolution and the rise of Soviet Russia introduced an explosive new factor in Indian politics to all intents and purposes. This affected the policies of the British Government both internally and externally. Internally, it created a deep-rooted suspicion of the *bonafides* of the nationalist movement partly because of the apparent community of interest between the Indian nationalists and Soviet Russia—a concurrence which was largely accidental rather than designed, as far as the Indian Nationalists were concerned. The British Government looked with alarm and suspicion at every demand the nationalists advanced and every agitation they undertook. In them, the British detected a mysterious Bolshevik connection and failed to evaluate the nature of the growing upsurge of nationalism objectively. In the external field, as a result of the Bolshevik Revolution, a new Power had arisen on the borders of British India with the declared purpose of liquidating imperialist interests all over the world. This suddenly posed the serious problem of defending the British Raj against any possible Soviet military aggression, and also of safeguarding it against a hostile propaganda campaign. The British Government became increasingly concerned with the safety and security of India, and their external policy had to be reoriented to meet this new challenge to their supremacy in India. Viewed from London, Britain's nightmarish dream of a hostile neighbour facing British India and rebellious subjects in her rear appeared to have come true. In point of fact, as a result of the Bolshevik Revolution, British Rule in India suddenly became an international issue: it was one of the main causes of friction between Soviet Russia and Britain.

In the ultimate analysis, the Bolshevik Revolution, later events in Soviet Russia, and Soviet interest in colonial affairs, did exercise a remarkable influence in the whole process of the beginning of the liquidation of British rule over India and in the growth of socialism in India. Firstly, as has been shown in this paper, the Bolshevik Revolution, and later, the various phases of Soviet policy towards India, acted as a catalyst in raising the tempo of the Indian Nationalist Movement; they also posed a new problem for the Government which widened the gulf between the nationalists and the British Government in India and stimulated the interest of the Nationalists in the Soviet Union. Although there was neither evidence of a Bolshevik or Soviet conspiracy in India, nor was there any direct influence of Soviet propaganda and Soviet policy towards India on the work of the Indian Nationalist Movement, the Indian nationalists looked to the Soviet Union with sympathy, admiration and good-will. This widened their perspective, which had always been traditionally confined to Britain, and encouraged them to take a radically new approach to the socio-economic problems then confronting the country; and thus to gain more and more support from the various strata of the Indian masses, particularly the workers, peasantry and lower middle classes. Secondly, Soviet Russia was the only country in the world, which, at least in theory, openly proclaimed itself in favour of the end of the imperialist system. Because of this Soviet stand, the colonial question thus became an international issue which the Communist parties in various countries, particularly in the imperialist countries, promoted and encouraged in order to project it on to the world scene. This effect of Soviet interest in the colonial countries was particularly marked in Anglo-Soviet relations vis-a-vis India. In spite of the fact that under Stalin, Soviet policy towards India was entirely motivated by the interests of the Soviet state, India and the Indian nationalist movement became an irritant in international relations during the inter-war years. Undoubtedly, Britain's fear of Soviet propaganda and hostile activities and the wide publicity given to this by the Bri-

tish and Anglo-Indian press did help in promoting the image o
the Soviet Union as the only foreign Power interested in bringin
about the end of British rule in India. All this helped in fostering
world interest in the independence of India.

From the viewpoint of the Indian nationalists, Soviet interes
in their affairs, however limited by its special circumstances an
difficulties, was indeed welcome and useful mainly because o
its long-term effect on world opinion. A new realization began an
grew among the Indian nationalists that their cause had acquire
an international character of anti-imperialism shared and supporte
by Soviet Russia. Thus, by 1929, anti-imperialism became the mai
hallmark of the Indian Nationalist Movement which paved the way
for the development and propagation of the socialist movemen
and socialist ideas later in the thirties.

BRITISH LABOUR AND THE INDIAN LEFT, 1919-1939

PARTHA SARATHI GUPTA

THE PURPOSE OF this paper is to analyze the mutual interaction of the British Labour movement and the Indian Labour and Socialist movements in the twenty years between 1919 and 1939. How did different leaders and institutions of the two movements regard one another? What did they expect of one another, and how far were these expectations fulfilled? A full length study of the attitudes of the British Labour Party to the question of Indian independence has already been done by Dr Fischer, a French scholar.[1] He has touched on the party's attitude to Indian labour,[2] but has not attem-

(I am grateful to Shrimati Indira Gandhi and the Nehru Memorial Museum and Library for permission to consult and quote from the correspondence of Jawaharlal Nehru. Thanks are due to the Nehru Memorial Museum and Library also for permission to use the files of the All-India Congress Committee, the papers of N.M. Joshi, and the newspaper files at their library. Thanks are due to the National Archives of India and the West Bengal Government Archives for permission to consult their records.

The following abbreviations have been used in the notes: N.A.I.—National Archives of India; W.B.G.A.—West Bengal Government Archives; I.L.P.—Independent Labour Party; N.M.J.P.—N.M. Joshi papers kept in the Nehru Memorial Library; J.L.N.P.—Jawaharlal Nehru Papers kept in the Nehru Memorial Library; A.I.C.C.—Files of the All-India Congress Committee kept in Nehru Memorial Library).

[1]G. Fischer, *Le parti travailliste et la decolonisation de l'inde* (Paris, 1966). Dr Fischer has not used the archival sources available in India, and, even with regard to British sources, has more or less concentrated on published sources. Besides, his approach is that of an analytical political scientist and not that of a historian. Consequently, having taken the twenty-five years 1914-1949 as one unit, and analyzed ideas in terms only of their subject matter and divorced from their time-context, he has failed to bring out the ebb and flow of mutual understanding, which I have attempted in these pages.

[2]*Ibid.*, pp. 268-80.

pted to analyze the ebb and flow of mutual understanding and co-operation in course of these twenty years. Besides, his concern is mainly with the Labour Party, whereas the present study aims to cover the British Trades Union Congress as well as the Independent Labour Party (I.L.P.), both of which were important elements in the British Labour movement. The Communist parties of Britain and India fall outside the scope of this enquiry, but due weight has been given to the effects of their policies.

The First World War had created divisions inside the British Labour movement, divisions between the anti-war Independent Labour Party and the pro-war majority, including all the trade unions and many Fabians. War-time economic problems had created a militant left-wing trade union movement in Glasgow and other places on the Clyde. In politics many of these trade unionists were attracted to Marxism, and joined either the I.L.P. or the British Socialist Party, a left-wing party unaffiliated to the Labour Party. Many non-socialist Liberals with a genuinely internationalist outlook (like E.D. Morel, Charles Trevelyan) had joined the I.L.P. after the war, as a result of which, at the beginning of our period, the I.L.P. was a coalition of radical socialists as well as democratic pacifists, their unity welded together by the shared experience of persecution for their beliefs during the war.[3]

A bird's-eye view of the traditional attitudes of these groups to the British Empire and the ideal of international co-operation would help understand their approach to the social and political problems of India. The I.L.P. had always been strongly anti-imperialist politi-cally, and its view of internationl aeconomic relations was based on Cobden-ite principles of free trade. Over the question of tariff reform and an Imperial Customs Union suggested by the Conservative

[3]There is a huge literature on the subject matter of this paragraph. The books most useful for the conclusions of this paragraph are as follows: B.C. Roberts, *The Trade Union Congress, 1868-1922* (London, 1958); A.M. Mcbriar, *Fabian Socialism and English Politics 1884-1918* (Cambridge, 1962); H. Pelling, *The British Communist Party* (London, 1958); L.J. Macfarlane, *The British Commu-nist Party, its Origin and Development until 1922* (London, 1966); R.E. Dowse, *Left in the Centre: the Independent Labour Party, 1893-1940* (London, 1966); C. Tsuzuki, *H.M. Hyndman and British Socialism* (Oxford, 1961); F. Brockway, *Inside the Left* (London, 1942); A.J.P. Marwick, "The Independent Labour Party, 1918-32" (Unpublished B. Litt. thesis, Oxford 1960, microfilm copy avail-able in Delhi University Library).

supporters of Joseph Chamberlain, the I.L.P. and the rest of the Labour Party had followed the Liberals in opposing it.[4] Yet the anti-imperialist I.L.P.-er did not visualize a dissolution of the political links of the empire, but rather its transformation into a commonwealth of equal sovereign states. This stemmed partly from the idea of socialist international cooperation, and partly from a belief in socialist trusteeship of underdeveloped colonial lands—a belief to be found even in the writings of the noted anti-imperialist J.A. Hobson.[5] Some Fabians, with their neo-Benthamite preference for efficient administration and their belief in the efficacy of permeating the existing political parties and the existing civil service with their ideas, took socialist trusteeship one stage further, and contemplated as their goal a prolonged period of modernization under enlightened colonial administration.[6] On India, all the British socialists in the pre-War era took a stand in favour, not so much of granting self-government, as of improvement in administrative standards in the interests of the people, and of gradual progress towards self-government.[7] Greater emphasis on administrative improvement as opposed to the grant of self-government was characteristic, naturally, of the Fabians. In the pre-War days some cooperation had developed between Indian leaders and British Labourites, between H.M. Hyndman and Dadabhai Naoroji, and Keir Hardie and Gokhale and Bipin Chandra Pal.[8]

[4]R.E. Dowse, *Left in the Centre* (London, 1966), p. 11; the Fabians were split on the tariff question and took a pragmatic viewpoint (A.M. Mcbriar, *Fabian Socialism and English Politics, 1884-1918* (Cambridge, 1962), pp. 131-34. Ramsay Macdonald had criticized the Australian Labour party for supporting the idea of an imperial tariff (G. Fischer, n. 1, p. 80, n. 45).

[5]In fairness to J.A. Hobson, although arguments to justify trusteeship could be found in Part II, Ch. iv of his famous classic, the general trend of the argument of his book was a refutation of the claims of trusteeship made by contemporary imperialists (J. A. Hobson, *Imperialism–a Study*, London, 1938 ed., pp. 230-84).

[6]Mcbriar, n. 4, pp. 125-30.

[7]After a visit to India in the first decade of this century Ramsay Macdonald wrote, "Thus for many a long year British sovereignty will be necessary for India... Britain is the nurse of India." (R. Macdonald, *The Awakening of India*, London, 1910, p. 301). Also see Fischer, n. 1, pp. 38-42.

[8]On Hyndman and Naoroji see C. Tsuzuki, *H.M. Hyndman and British Socialism* (London, 1961), pp. 23, 48, 76, 127, and R.P. Masani, *Dadabhai Naoroji* (New Delhi, Publications Division, 1960), pp. 82-5, 110 f. On Tilak see S. Wolpert, *Tilak and Gokhale* (Berkeley, California, 1962), p. 227. On Bipin Chandra

The Bolshevik revolution in Russia in 1917, the conclusion of a separate peace by Russia with Germany in 1918, and the founding of the Third International (Comintern) in March 1919 evoked somewhat different responses from different sections of the British Labour movement. The entire movement was united in opposing allied intervention in Russia (their most dramatic gesture being the dock and shipping strike of August 1920 to stop arms going to the Poles), and also for recognizing the Soviet Union, but sharp differences arose over the policy of the Comintern and the emergence of a Communist Party in Britian.[9] When the Comintern eventually developed its own strategy of political action in India and the rest of the colonial world, the policies of different socialist groups in Britain to Indian problems was bound to be affected by the way they looked at Communist tactics and policy.

II

Among the different organizations in Britain in 1919, working for political change in India, only two had obvious connexions with the Labour movement—the London section of the Indian Home Rule League founded by Mrs. Besant in 1916 to lobby the government for constitutional reforms,[10] and the Workers' Welfare League of India founded in 1916 for work among Indian seamen in London.[11] Thanks to Mrs. Besant's personal contacts through Theosophism, the former organization had enlisted the active cooperation of three theosophist Labour-ites—David Graham Pole, George Lans-

---

Pal, I.L.P., *Annual Report* 1910, p. 83, for the speech by Pal at the I.L.P. annual conference.

[9]The best volume on this is Stephen R. Graubard, *British Labour and Russian Revolution* (Harvard, 1956). See in particular, pp. 104-16, 291 ff.

[10]Arthur H. Nethercot, *The Last Four Lives of Annie Besant* (London, 1963), p. 220.

[11]The actual date of the foundation of the Workers Welfare League is 1916, but the efforts had started since 1911. (S. Saklatvala, "India in the Labour World," *Labour Monthly,* November 1921). Other organizations on India were the British Committee of the Indian National Congress (rather too moderate), "Britain and India," and students' associations. Some idea of all these organizations and their political roles will be found in the perceptive contemporary despatches sent by Sant Nihal Singh for Mrs Besant's paper, the *Commonweal.* See in particular, Sant Nihal Singh, "When the Deputation arrives in London," *Commonweal,* 25 April 1919 and 2 May 1919, pp. 258 f, 278-80.

bury, and John Scurr. The last two were also anti-war I.L.P.-ers, and in course of 1917-18, their speeches aroused a fair measure of interest in Indian self-government in I.L.P. branches and local trades councils all over South Wales and Yorkshire, and also in some big industrial towns elsewhere.[12] A prominent Indian expatriate leader of the Workers' Welfare League, Shapurji Saklatvala, was also a member of the Home Rule League;[13] since the Bolshevik revolution he had been fired with a zeal to convert the I.L.P.—of which he had been a member since 1909—actively to support Bolshevism, and he devoted all his spare time to lecturing to I.L.P. branches on Bolshevism and allied topics.[14] In the beginning of 1919 his policy was to urge the pro-Indian I.L.P.-ers to persuade moderate Indian nationalists to be more socialistic in their political and economic programmes. To the resolution of John Scurr at the annual conference of the I.L.P. in April 1918 asking for a "measure granting self-government to the Indian people," Saklatvala moved a supplementary pleading for "immediate legislation to improve the hours, wages, and general conditions of workers, and an open advocacy of the nationalization of lands, railways, mines, and other large and important industries." Both resolutions were carried.[15]

It is quite possible that the resolution on India which the Labour and Socialist International (2nd International) adopted at its first post-war meeting in Berne in February 1919, was influenced by the policy adopted by the I.L.P. the previous April at Saklatvala's suggestion, because it was sponsored by the Labour Party delegation,

[12]Note by P. Quinn, Superintendent of Police of the search on the offices of the Home Rule for India League on 7 November 1917. (NAI, Home-Pol. May 1918, A36-54, proc. No. 50, enclosure); also see NAI, Home-Pol. May 1918, A158-161.

[13]The minute book of the Home Rule League, discovered and noted by the British police during their search in November 1917, mentions among names of leading members "Mr. Saklatarals." This most probably is a misprint for Saklatvala. His relations with the Home Rule Leaguers at this time were good for they were all members of the I.L.P. His references to the League in his *Labour Monthly* article of November 1921 are complimentary. (n. 11, p. 449.).

[14]Intelligence report in the U.K. on search of Saklatvala's house, 18 October 1920 (NAI Home-Pol., January 1921, Part B 306-7), gives full details of these activities). Also see A.J.B. Marwick, "The Independent Labour Party, 1918-32" (Unpublished B. Litt. thesis, Oxford, 1960), pp. 97-100 and 113-16.

[15]I.L.P., *Report of the Annual Conference held at Leicester, April* 1918 (London, 1918), pp. 80-1.

which included a strong I.L.P. contingent. This resolution, in addition to criticizing the "capitalistic and imperialistic policy in India" and the Rowlatt Act, and supporting the efforts of "the Indian population to claim...the establishment of democratic governments," demanded "direct representation" of Indian working classes in the Legislative councils. It added, "As the extreme poverty and misery of the Indian working class is the consequence of the exploitation of Indian labour by the great Indian and English landowners and capitalists, which yearly exposes millions to death by famine and disease, the conference is of the opinion that the land and soil, railways and mines of India should be socialized."[16]

In linking up the question of political change in India with the plea for social and economic reconstruction of a radical nature, Saklatvala was trying to link up the leftwing of the British Labour movement with that of the Indian nationalist movement. To paraphrase his own words in April 1918, "His imagination carried him to the time when the Independent Labour Party might have ten million members" in India.[17] In keeping with the same policy, five left wing British trade unionists had petitioned the Secretary of State, in January 1919 on behalf of the Workers' Welfare League of India, protesting against inadequate safeguards for the labouring classes in the reform bill and attributing it to the "non-inclusion of the representatives of organized British labour in committees which have been appointed and are now working in India." They opposed transferring to the provinces questions affecting industrial labour, especially as the provincial assemblies were to be on a narrow franchise, pleaded for keeping the questions with the central government, and ended with a plea that "British labour representatives...should continue to exercise the privilege of recommending to those responsible for Indian affairs in parliament the needs and rights of their Indian fellow-workers."[18]

While the signatories to this memorial were all near-Marxists, such an approach could equally be consistent with a Fabian policy of prolonged tutelage under progressive governments in Britain. Philip Snowden and Ramsay Macdonald, although members both of the I.L.P. and the Home Rule League, did regard themselves

[16]Labour Party, *Annual Report* 1919, p. 229.
[17]I.L.P., n. 15, p. 81.
[18]NAI, Home-Pol., April 1919, Part B 92.

as trustees for the Indian masses. When Austen Chamberlain had raised Indian cotton duties against Britain early in 1917, the opposition of Liberals and the Lancashire trade union M.P., Tom Shaw was to be expected, but Philip Snowden puzzled his Indian admirers by his opposition, until he explained his position: as long as India did not become a dominion with fiscal autonomy, the British Labour representatives have to protect the unrepresented Indian masses "against the rise in price of a necessity of life."[19]

Notwithstanding these differences in approach, the British Labour Party was united in 1919 in supporting the Constitutional Reform Bill (which included fiscal autonomy). As Colonel Josiah Wedgwood, a new recruit to the I.L.P. and a friend of Indian nationalists said, "India is as much entitled to make her own tariffs as Canada, or any other community within the Empire."[20] What all of them were concerned about was simultaneously to secure clauses in favour of the wage-earning and agricultural classes' franchise, especially as British and Indian Capitalist interests had got special privileges in the new constitution.[21] Their plea for a direct working class franchise was so strongly stressed when the bill returned from committee,[22] that Montagu, the Secretary of State, felt obliged to urge the Viceroy, in the despatch enclosing the Act, to see "what can be done to allay the apprehensions" of Labour members on this matter.[23] The provin-

[19]*Commonweal,* 20 April 1917, p. 297.

[20]Sant. Nihal Singh, "An interview with Col. Josiah Wedgwood, M.P.," *Commonweal,* 2 May 1919, p. 275. Wedgwood had joined the Home Rule League and written a preface to the English edition of Lajpat Rai's book, *Young India,* which was published by the London Home Rule League in 1917. (NAI, Home-Pol., May 1918, A36-54, proc. No. 54).

[21]Wedgwood said, "India wants no Manchester slums, and exploitation. Indian capitalists are as dangerous as British." *(Commonweal,* 2 May 1919, p. 275). During the Cotton duties controversy of 1917, H.N. Brailsford, the distinguished labour journalist, urged Indian nationalists not to regard a concession given to Bombay capitalists by the Conservative supporter of Imperial preference, Austen Chamberlain, as a measure in the long-term interests of the Indian masses. In his opinion there was a danger of a docile Indian capitalist class being created by modest tariff concessions within imperial preference, and this class would be an obstacle to national independence. (H.N. Brailsford, "The Affairs of the West: Lancashire v. Bombay," *Commonweal,* 4 May 1917).

[22]U.K. *Parliamentary Debates (Commons),* 5th Series, Vol. 122, Col. 474.

[23]Despatch from the Secretary of State to the Government of India, 25 December 1919, para 7. (NAI, Reforms Office-General, April 1920, A133-37, proc. No. 133.).

cial bureaucracies were unenthusiastic about the extension of the working class vote in places like Calcutta and Bombay, one official commenting, "This is a wild-cat franchise which, at the instance, I understand, of the labour party at home we are asked to provide."[24] The matter was shelved.

The effective liasion between Indian nationalists and British Labour in 1919 was Mrs Besant's Home Rule League, which occupied at this time a centrist position between the Indian Liberals under Srinivasa Sastri and those Congressmen under Gandhiji who later launched the non-cooperation movement.[25] Whatever the future might hold, at this time the Home Rule League and its trade union connexions appeared dangerously radical to the Government of India, as was evident from the furore over nominating the first Indian trade union representative to the International Labour conference at Washington.[26] B.P. Wadia, a follower of Besant who since 1918 had organized Madras textile workers in the Madras Labour Union, spent the summer of 1919 in Britain giving evidence on behalf of the Home Rule League before the parliamentary committee on the Montford reform bill, and spoke at the annual conference of the British Trade Union Congress. The British T.U.C. undertook to help financially and with expert advice the growing trade union movement in India and presented Wadia with its gold badge.[27] Faced with the suggestion from certain Indian unions in favour of Wadia's representing Indian labour at the Washington conference, the Government of India hesitated, as one official considered him "an extremist in politics"[28] and another "an advertising politician."[29] Montagu preferred Wadia, in view of his standing with

[24]Note by H. Wheeler, 12 January 1920 in the keep-withs of the following file: WBGA, Appointments dept. April 1920, A3-10 (File 6R-2).

[25]Nethercot, n. 10, pp. 290-8; S.R. Mehrotra, *India and the Commonwealth* (London, 1965), pp. 110-12. Srinivasa Sastri, who had founded the Liberal federation when Mrs Besant elected to remain in the Congress, commented on her change of front on Montagu's reforms proposals by saying, "That woman is mad, I tell you." (Srinivasa Sastri to Tej Bahadur Sapru, 5 March 1919 (NAI, Srinivasa Sastri Papers, Correspondence (1) No. 306).

[26]All the documents on this are in the following file: NAI, Commerce & Industry-Factories, February 1920, A1-75.

[27]Telegram from Montagu to Chelmsford (private), 15 September 1919, (NAI, Commerce & Industry-Factories, February 1920, A1-75, keep-withs, p. 29.).

[28]Note by C.G. Freke, 11 September 1919, in *ibid.*, p. 23.

[29]Note by G.S. Barnes, 15 September 1919, in *ibid.*, p. 29.

the British T.U.C., and warned the Indian Government that any spurious government-nominated labour leader ran the risk of having his credentials challenged in Washington.[30] The government ultimately nominated N.M. Joshi (a fellow worker of Srinivasa Sastri and the late G.K. Gokhale in the Servants of India Society), but Montagu insisted, against the Viceroy's wish, on Wadia being also sent in an advisory capacity, doubtless in deference to the British Labour movement.[31]

The wider significance of the episode was threefold. It helped to bring the All-India Trade Union Congress into being next year, so that future delegates to the I.L.O. could be authorized by some co-ordinating body of trade unions in India. It illustrated the growing interest in the political and economic destinies of Indian labour on the part of the British T.U.C. It also showed, however, that whatever the political sympathies of Indian trade union leaders, any international association was liable to be interpreted as a political act. The last phenomenon was to affect Indo-British labour relations throughout the period under review.

In the immediate aftermath of the foundation of the A.I.T.U.C., it was kept somewhat insulated from the controversies of nationalist politics, partly because by the end of 1920, Mrs. Besant and the Indian Liberals held practically identical views in favour of a critical acceptance of the Montford reforms.[32] So non-political trade unionists like N.M. Joshi, and R.R. Bakhale could cooperate with Wadia, J. Baptista, B. Shiva Rao and others in building up a trade union movement and using the machinery of the new constitution to further its prospects. In this task, until the middle of 1922, a fairly united support was given by different wings of the British Labour movement. The London Home Rule League dissolved itself in October 1920, saying, "We feel it will be best in future to work through the Labour Party, especially as our chairman, Mr George Lansbury, is on its executive committee."[33] The Workers' Welfare League became

[30]Secretary of State to Viceroy, 13 September 1919. (NAI, Commerce & Industry-Factories, February 1920, A1-75, proc. No. 61).

[31]NAI, Commerce & Industry-Factories, February 1920, A1-75, proc. Nos. 68-71, and keep-with, p. 31.

[32]Nethercot, n. 10, p. 303.

[33]George Lansbury to Mrs. Besant, 27 October 1920, quoted in K. Dwarkadas, *India's Fight for Freedom, 1913-1937: An Eye-Witness Story* (Bombay, 1966), p. 135. (Dwarkadas was able to draw on Graham Pole's papers as well as his

the British representative of the A.I.T.U.C.,[34] thus maintaining a link between the Indian Labour leaders and left wing British trade unionists, some of whom soon joined the Communist Party.[35]

Near-communist, I.L.P.-er, or moderate Fabian, all Labourites deplored the non-cooperation movement and the boycott of British goods, though for slightly different reasons. To Josiah Wedgwood, who was not a Socialist, opposition to the idea of self-government within the Empire might make the Congress-Labour Party co-operation "more difficult, if not impossible."[36] Members of the Workers Welfare League, "at considerable cost to their popularity (sc. in Britain) steadfastly differentiated between the international solidarity of Labour and the non-cooperation movement as a temporary political weapon in India against the imperialist exploiter."[37] One of their members, J. Potter-Wilson, justified the case for trade union legislation in India on the ground that the rise in Indian workers' standards of living would expand markets for British goods and reduce competition between Indian and British industries.[38] Left wing trade union leaders could indeed be won for radical change in India only by underplaying non-cooperation and emphasizing the areas of co-operation between progressive forces in Britain and India. Not surprisingly, in February 1922, the National Joint Council of Labour (a representative cross-section of the trade union and Labour party leadership which at this time included left wingers like Robert Smillie, A. Pugh, and C.T. Cramp) passed a resolution criticizing both the government of India and the non-cooperators. The latter were mistaken in not using the parliamentary institutions granted

---

personal contacts with many of the leading personalities. Therefore, if one discounts an anti-Gandhi bias in the book, his book can yield a lot of useful and correct information).

[34]D. Petrie, *Communism in India, 1924-1927* (Simla, Home Dept. Confidential Report, 1927), p. 278.

[35]J. Potter Wilson, Secretary of the Workers' Welfare League, was one of the I.L.P. dissidents who joined the Communist party.

[36]Mehrotra, n. 25, p. 117.

[37]Saklatvala, "India in the Labour World," *Labour Monthly,* November 1921, p. 450.

[38]See Potter-Wilson's remarks at the T.U.C. deputation to Montagu on 22 March 1921, in Minutes of Proceedings at a deputation from the Trade Union Congress Parliamentary Committee to the Secretary of State for India....22 March 1921. (NAI, Industries & Labour, October 1921, A1-7, proc. No. 3 (enclosure),

so far, and the former were criticized for political repression and urged to grant an amnesty, have talks with Indian leaders, and set a dateline for Dominion Status.[39] While this resolution was ignored by the people to whom it was addressed, the Labour movement had meanwhile set in motion one line of development, legal security of trade unions in India.

When at the end of 1920 the judgment of the Madras High Court in *Buckingham Mills Co. vs. B.R. Wadia* raised legal obstacles in the way of trade union work, the efforts of N.M. Joshi in the Legislative Council was supplemented by lobbying in Britain.[40] The Parliamentary Committee of the Trade Union Congress, accompanied by Potter-Wilson of the Workers' Welfare League, urged the Secretary of State on 22 March 1921 to grant trade unions in India the same immunity from prosecution as the British trade unions enjoyed apropos of the tortious acts of its agents.[41] As they were insistent on ensuring that any future legislation should provide genuine legal safeguards, Montagu urged the government of India to think seriously on such legislation and also to let him have the draft bill.[42] The government of India took time over it; two years passed eliciting opinion of local governments, and then anxiety about preventing strikes in public utility services delayed further action.[43] Only when, early in March 1924, within six weeks of assuming office, Lord Olivier, the Secretary of State in the first Labour government, telegraphed the Indian government to hurry up with the proposal, did the machine start moving again.[44] One civil servant commented wryly. "I rather anticipated this enquiry when the Labour government came into power at home."[45]

[39]Labour Party, *Annual Report* 1922, p. 37.

[40]N.M. Joshi raised the matter in the Legislative Assembly on 1 March 1921.

[41]NAI, Industries & Labour, October 1921, A1-7, proc. No. 3 (enclosure).

[42]Telegram from Secretary of State to the Viceroy, No. 2010, 14 April 1921. (NAI, Industries & Labour October 1921, A1-7, proc. No. 1).

[43]See note by A.H. Ley, 5 November 1923, in keep-withs of NAI, Industries & Labour-Labour, 1924, File L-925 (coll. 21); also note by A.C. Chatterjee, 13 March 1924, in the keep-withs of the same file.

[44]Telegram from the Secretary of State to the Government of India; No. 754, 6 March 1924 was terse and to the point: "Your secretary's letter L. 925 of 28 Sep 1921. Trade Union legislation. May I expect to receive proposal shortly?" (NAI, Industry & Labour-Labour, 1924, File 925 (coll. 21) Series No. 101).

[45]Note by A.H. Ley, 10 March 1924, in the keep-withs of the file mentioned in the previous note, p. 29.

The T.U.C. delegation to Montagu had a pro-communist spokesman on behalf of India, but they did not all think alike on Indian
problems. Where trade union questions were not involved, J.H.
Thomas, of the railwaymen's union, was inclined to believe in government propaganda.[46] Early in 1920 he had discussed with Rushbrook
Williams, the government's publicity officer, how to ensure "that the
Labour Party should derive its information concerning India from
authentic rather than from tainted sources." The publicity officer
had failed to get official sanction to get a labour delegation "of the
right type," "neither cranks nor notoriety hunters," brought out to
India at government expense.[47] He had, however, been unofficially
permitted to try out "if something (sc. could) not be done with the
Members of Parliament who (sc. were) coming out to attend the
Congress (sc. of 1920)."[48] This process of gradual persuasion of
very moderate labour leaders into an acceptance of the government's
case started sharpening the divisions inside the British labour movement on the policy best suited for India. Communist-labour tensions
also contributed to this. By 1928 fairly clear-cut alignments had
developed between British and Indian leaders, disturbing the pattern
of co-operation that had worked so far.

III

In April 1921, Saklatvala left the I.L.P. to join the Communist
Party along with Potter-Wilson, Ellen Wilkinson and others.[49] The
majority of the I.L.P., being unable for justifiable reasons to accept
the twenty-one conditions of the second Comintern Congress but

[46]Thomas had reacted sharply to a suggestion from Montagu on 22 March
1921, that the British T.U.C. should help the Indian government "in getting the
Trade Unions on to the right lines." (NAI, Industries-Labour, October 1921,
A1-7, proc. No. 3 (enclosure).)

[47]L.F. Rushbrook Williams, "Memorandum on the education of public opinion in Britain in matters relating to India, 29 July 1920." (NAI, Home-Pol.,
November 1920, A212 (enclosure).

[48]Note by Rushbrook Williams, 9 October 1920 in the keep-withs (p. 6) of the
file mentioned in the previous note; also see note of E.H.F., 3 November 1920
in the keep-withs (p. 4) of NAI, Home-Pol., February 1921, A360-64. The Labour
M.P.s at the Congres Session of 1920 were Ben Spoor, Holford Knight, and Col.
Josiah Wedgwood.

[49]Marwick, "Independent Labour Party" (B. Litt. thesis 1960, Oxford), p.
108 ff. Ellen Wilkinson came back to the I.L.P. soon after.

also being reluctant to accept Ramsay Macdonald's recommendation to join the Second International, had joined the Vienna Union. The latter tried in vain during 1922 to see if co-operation between the three internationals could be brought about on a permanent basis. When these failed the I.L.P., along with the Vienna Union, rejoined the Second International in 1923, but from the end of 1925 the I.L.P. tried, once again in vain, to renew negotiations between the two internationals.[50]

The position of British Communists (including Saklatvala) became ambivalent vis-a-vis the other groups in the British Labour movement after 1921. The directives of the Comintern to Communists in Western Europe and Britain, it has been rightly remarked, contained within them a "latent incompatibility... between a policy of peaceful infiltration on the national plane and a policy of frontal attack on the international plane."[51] By indiscriminatingly blaming non-communist trade union leaders whenever a strike failed, the British Communists lost ground in the Labour party, and the charge of subservience to Moscow killed their plea for affiliation to the Labour Party.[52] Saklatvala, who was returned to parliament as a Labour M.P. in 1922 lost his Labour Whip after this. While he continued to be in parliament till 1929, except for the year 1924, he carried weight only with the extreme left wing of the parliamentary Labour party, and occasionally on Indian questions got support from people like Wedgwood or T. Wheatley. While he himself was very critical of Indian Liberals,[53] Srinivasa Sastri's first impressions of him was that of "an able, sincere, and patriotic man."[54]

Communist-Labour rivalry in helping Indian labour was somewhat

[50]Dowse, n. 3, pp. 51-9; Marwick, n. 49, pp. 112, 219-21.

[51]E.H. Carr, *The Bolshevik Revolution*, 1917-23 (London, 1953), Vol. III, p. 207.

[52]Graubard, n. 9, Ch. vii & viii, *passim*, and pp. 146-8, 152, and 164-82 in particular.

[53]"Jamnadas, Dwarkadas, Sir Ali Imam, Sir Sankaran Nair, Right Honourable Srinivasa Sastri, S.R. Bomanji...none of them has ever given any assistance, either organizing or financial, to the workers' and peasants' movement in India, and... they are all of them determined opponents of any real move towards working-class freedom." (Saklatvala to N.M. Joshi, 10 March 1926 (N.M.J.P. File No. 8, p. 277).

[54]Srinivasa Sastri to Vaman Rao, 16 July 1924 (NAI, Srinivasa Sastri Papers-Correspondence (1) Series No. 405).

masked in 1924-26 because of the increasingly left-wing trend inside
the General Council of the Trades Union till the General Strike of
1926.[55] Leaders of the type of Earnest Bevin, Walter Citrine, and A.
Pugh (who was also a member of the Workers' Welfare League)[56]
were at this time class-conscious trade unionists in favour of a militant policy, and further to their left stood George Hicks, Alonzo
Swales, and A.A. Purcell. Purcell had visited Russia in May 1920,
had supported Lenin's idea of a new trade union international and
joined the Communist Party at its foundation.[57] He probably left
the Communist Party in the early twenties, to save his links with the
Labour Party, and to keep his parliamentary seat.[58] Nevertheless
he worked for unity between the two internationals, inviting Tomsky
to the Hull Trade-Union Congress over which he presided, setting
up the Anglo-Russian trade union committee, and trying to persuade
the International Federation of Trade Unions (I.F.T.U.) and the Red
International of Labour Unions (R.I.L.U.) to come together.[59]

The first Labour government widened the gulf between moderate
Labour-ites and Indian nationalists. Even a moderate like Annie
Besant was disappointed at Oliver, instead of Wedgwood, being the
Secretary of State.[60] In spite of the pressure of the I.L.P., the Cabinet
ignored the Swarajists' request for an immediate conference between
the government and representative Indian opinion for further consti-

[55]For a general account, see J. Lovell and B.C. Roberts, *A Short History*
of the T.U.C. (London, 1968), pp. 72-86; Lord Citrine, *Men and Work: an
Autobiography* (London, 1964), pp. 73-215; and A. Bullock, *Life and Times of
Ernest Bevin,* Vol. I; *Trade Union Leader* (London, 1960), pp. 260-84.

[56]He was one of the signatories to the memorial sent by the Workers' Welfare
League to Montagu in January 1919 (*vide* note 18 above); his name recurs as
a member of its council for 1924 in the printed circular of the League (Circular
of the League, June 1924, N.M.J.P., File No. 5, p. 33).

[57]Carr, n. 51, p. 206; H. Pelling, The *British Communist Party* (London, 1958),
p. 9; James Klugmann, *History of the Communist Party of Great Britain,* Vol.
I, 1919-1924 (London, 1968), p. 79.

[58]Dr Henry Pelling, in a letter to me (17 May 1969) has suggested the early
twenties as the date when Purcell might have left the Communist Party for the
sake of his parliamentary career.

[59]Citrine, n. 55 pp. 89-93; for a general account of these efforts at Anglo-
Russian Trade Union co-operation, see Lewis L. Lorwin, *The International Labour Movement* (New York, 1953), pp. 97-109. Purcell was also active in other
attempts at Communist-Labour co-operation for a left-wing policy in Britain,
vide L.J. Macfarlane, *The British Communist Party* (London, 1966), pp. 142-4.

[60]Nethercot, n. 10, p. 340.

tutional change.[61] The appointment of the Reforms Inquiry Committee satisfied few people. The moderate Liberal, Srinivasa Sastri, while lobbying in Britain, was disappointed to note that the Cabinet "had no big plan for India" and only wished "to tide over the difficulty somehow." He found Oliver weak, and Chelmsford "dead against advance."[62]

If a Liberal felt disappointed, it is not surprising that Swarajist leaders readily believed the Labour government to be as imperialist as its predecessor. Motilal Nehru refused to serve on the Reforms Enquiry Committee,[63] and in Bengal C.R. Das successfully wrecked the system of diarchy, embittering the Liberal governor Lord Lytton.[64] Wedded as they were to the idea of gradual constitutional evolution, the Labour Cabinet sympathized with Lytton's condemnation of the Swaraj Party's tactics, and supported the official request for promulgating the Bengal Ordinance. Sydney Webb, who was a party to it, thought that they had taken care not to penalize expressions of opinion and only to punish violence,[65] but nevertheless the Ordinances tarnished the image of the government in the eyes of most nationalists.[66] They were too much even for Srinivasa Sastri, who refused support to the renewed efforts at lobbying the Labour Party by the ever hopeful Mrs. Besant.[67]

Left-wing critics of the government's policy, headed by Lansbury,

[61]I.L.P., *Annual Report 1924*, p. 68 f; I.L.P., *Annual Report 1925*, pp. 15, 68; Mehrotra, n. 25, p. 128 f; B.R. Nanda, *The Nehru's, Motilal and Jawaharlal* (London, 1962), pp. 227-32.

[62]Sastri to Patwardhan, 22 May 1924, quoted in T.N. Jagadisan, ed., *Letters of Srinivasa Sastri* (Bombay, 1965), p. 134 f.

[63]Srinivasa Sastri to Vaman Rao, 5 June 1924 (NAI, Srinivasa Sastri papers–Correspondence (i) Ser. No. 401).

[64]J.H. Broomfield, *Elite Conflict in a Plural Society: Twentieth Century Bengal* (Berkeley & Los Angeles, 1968), pp. 187-91, 244-57.

[65]Sidney Webb, "The First Labour Government," *Political Quarterly*, Vol. XXXII (January-March 1961), pp. 23-4. (This note on the Labour Cabinet was written by Webb shortly after the fall of the government, while the issues were fresh in his mind. It was published, years after his death, in 1961).

[66]Subhas Bose, *The Indian Struggle, 1920-42* (Bombay, 1964 ed.), p. 107 ff. Lest Bose's verdict be considered biased, attention is also drawn to the remarks of a member of the British I.L.P., who toured India on the eve of the second Labour government and came to the same conclusion. (V.H. Rutherford, *Modern India: its problems and their solution*, London, 1928, p. 260 f).

[67]Srinivasa Sastri to Annie Besant, 4 November 1924, quoted in T.N. Jagadisan, ed., *Letters of Srinivasa Sastri* (Bombay, 1963), p. 140 f.

had also tried to stop the persecution of Communists in India, just as they had tried to smooth the difficulties in the Anglo-Soviet negotiations which had followed the recognition of the U.S.S.R. in February 1924.[68] They were successful in the latter, but not in the former, because the government was sensitive to charges from Conservative benches of permitting revolutionary violence in India. Apropos of the Kanpur Conspiracy Case against Communists, which tried M.N. Roy *in absentia,* Lansbury and James Maxton tried to get a British lawyer to argue that "apart (sc. from) actual breaches of law Indians have same legal right (sc. of) forming working Communist parties as British subjects have in all dominions."[69] These were as unsuccessful as M.N. Roy's application to Ramsay Macdonald for an amnesty so that he could return to India.[70]

Roy tried from abroad to persuade his Indian contacts to prevent N.M. Joshi from affiliating the A.I.T.U.C. to the I.F.T.U. at its conference in April 1924.[71] He cleverly emphasized the chinks in the armour of British trade union leaders——Tom Shaw's support of the excise duty on Indian cotton, the discriminatory attitude of Havelock Wilson and Harry Gosling to Indian seamen, and so on. His criticism of the British T.U.C. was unfair, for not only was it not subservient to the Labour government, but it was a useful lobby for the A.I.T.U.C., supplementing the efforts of the Workers' Welfare League.[72] On 25 July 1924, a delegation of leading trade unionists consisting of Purcell, Swales, Hicks, Cramp, Lansbury, Robert Smillie and four others met Lord Oliver. The delegation (the left-wing character of which was obvious) discussed a whole range of labour

[68]Marwick, n. 3, p. 172. (The mediatory role was played by E.D. Morel, G. Lansbury, A.A. Purcell).

[69]Telegram from Lansbury, Maxton and Macmanus to the government of the U.P., enclosed in a letter from the U.P. government to the Indian government, 28 March 1924. (NAI, Home-Pol. 1924, File 261, Ser. No. 78.

[70]M.N. Roy to J.R. Macdonald, 21 February 1924 (copy in NAI, Home-Pol. 1924, File 111); in this effort Rajani Palme Dutt was helping him (cf. R. Palme Dutt to M.N. Roy, 6 March 1924, intercepted by the government, in NAI, Home-Pol. 1924, File 176).

[71]M.N. Roy to the Editor, *Bombay Chronicle,* date indecipherable from the postmark on the envelope, but from internal evidence and provenance most probably February or March 1924. Intercepted copy, kept in NAI, Home-Pol. *Secret,* 1924, Part B, File No. 72).

[72]Circular of the Workers' Welfare League, June 1924. (Kept in N.M.J.P. File No. 5, p. 33).

questions, ranging from miners' hours and plantation labour to trade union legislation, and asked the government to conduct an enquiry into the economic conditions of labour in India.[73]

The next four years saw attempts at trade union co-operation between the two countries, which were partially successful, but were also bedevilled by continuing differences between the Labour Party leadership and radical Indian nationalists on the one hand, and on the other by Communist-Labour relations.

In February 1925 the Dundee jute-workers sent money to Joshi to help organize jute-workers in India,[74] and in the following June their secretary, with Saklatvala's assistance, got in touch with Joshi in London, because he was "arranging to go out to India to help the jute-workers there, and to find out ways and means of continued cooperation."[75] H.W. Lee, the lifelong associate of H.M. Hyndman in all his agitations, including those on behalf of India,[76] was then working at the T.U.C. headquarters, and "wanted to maintain as much interest as possible in Indian labour affairs."[77] His suggestions for sending a top-level delegation of the General Council of the T.U.C. proved futile because time and money could not be spared. To his alternative suggestion "that two or three trade union organisers should come over and spend, say, six months among the Indian workers,"[78] Joshi was agreeable. "It is a very good idea," he wrote, and added: "As they will not know any of our languages they will not be able to do much work themselves. But they will be able to teach methods of organization to those who are already

[73]Labour Party, *Annual Report* 1924, p. 58 f.

[74]Sime to N.M. Joshi, 5 February 1925. (N.M.J.P. File 8, p. 315).

[75]Saklatvala to N.M. Joshi, undated but internal evidence points to its being written not more than a week before the 19 June 1925. (N.M.J.P. File No. 7, p. 223).

[76]H.W. Lee, who was in his late fifties at this time, had acted, since the nineties as secretary to the Social Democratic Federation, its successor Social Democratic Party, and its successor the British Socialist Party. In the split in the British Socialist Party over the war of 1914-18, he had sided with Hyndman and left the organization. (On this and other information on him, see Tsuzuki, n. 3).

[77]H.W. Lee to N.M. Joshi, 29 January 1926. (N.M.J.P. File No. 8, p. 319); see also an earlier letter referring to his work with Hyndman for India, Lee to Joshi, 29 July 1925 (N.M.J.P. File 7, p. 81).

[78]Lee to Joshi, 22 March 1926 (N.M.J.P. File No. 8, p. 293); also see Lee to Joshi, 29 January 1926 (N.M.J.P. File No. 8, p. 319).

doing some work here. You can therefore take up the suggestion and see if it could be carried out."[79]

Similar suggestions were made by the I.L.P. in its special report on India published in March 1926 by a committee under the chairmanship of Fenner Brockway, and the research assistance of the Indian I.L.P.-er, T.P. Sinha.[80] Foundation of a trade union college "in the East with its centre in India" was suggested as a task for the International Federation of Trade Unions and the Labour and Socialist International, pending which "it might be possible to make special arrangements for Indians to attend our Labour colleges, and for a British trade unionist of judgment and experience to go to India, for a time, in an advisory capacity."[81] These suggestions never materialized, for the British Trade Union Congress was caught up in the crisis of the General Strike, soon after. Nevertheless, Joshi used his personal contacts to get copies of rules and regulations of various British Unions (in the textile and railway industry for example), their journals, and details of labour legislation—all of which he hoped to use as possible models for work in India.[82]

During the first year of the Anglo-Russian co-ordination committee, the British Communists, much against the wish of M.N. Roy, had tried to concentrate the direction of colonial work in their hands.[83] Receiving reports from Percy Gladding (a Communist member of the Amalgamated Engineering Union who had visited

[79]Joshi to Lee, 9 April 1926 (N.M.J.P. File No. 8, p. 301).

[80]"India today and the duty of British Socialists towards it," in I.L.P., *Report of the Annual Conference, April* 1926 (London, 1926), pp. 9, 53-5. Tarini Prasad Sinha was at this time working in the I.L.P. office and was closely associated with Fenner Brockway. He assisted Jawaharlal Nehru when the latter went to Brussels for the Oppressed Peoples' Conference, and later helped Brockway in his campaign on behalf of the Meerut prisoners. His subsequent history is not known. (Information derived partly from A.I.C.C. Foreign department files, N.M. Joshi papers, File No. 8, and a letter from Lord Brockway to myself, dated 1 February 1969).

[81]*Ibid.,* p. 55.

[82]N.M. Joshi to H.W. Lee, 24 September 1926 (N.M.J.P. file 8); N.M. Joshi to M. Brothers, 22 May 1927 (N.M.J.P. file 9, p. 49); N.M. Joshi to H.S.L. Polak, 15 April 1927 (N.M.J.P. file No. 9, p. 95).

[83]Report by R.W. Robson on a Colonial Conference held at Amsterdam, 11-12 July 1925, pp. 80-83. (This was document No. 42 among the Communist papers seized by the British government by a raid on the offices of the C.P.G.B.), reproduced in *Parliamentary Papers* 1926, (Cmd. 2682), XXIII, p. 686 ff.

India and spoken at the A.I.T.U.C. congress early in 1925) that the number of Communists in India were negligible, they decided, against Roy's wish, to influence the A.I.T.U.C., first through contacts with N.M. Joshi, Chaman Lall and T.C. Goswami during their visit to Britain in June and July 1925.[84] They had already made the Workers' Welfare League a Communist-controlled unit.[85] The Indian leaders were thus able to include among their contacts not only the British T.U.C. and the Indian committee of the parliamentary Labour party, but also Communist Front organizations like the Workers' International Relief, the National Minority Movement and communist leaders like C.P. Dutt.[86] Except for a very short-lived stance taken in favour of these organizations by Chaman Lall in the winter of 1925–26,[87] hardly any conversion to the Communist theory of trade union work took place—the Indian leaders remained, in Leninist terms, attached to "economism."

Non-communist British friends of Joshi were, however, worried about Communist infiltration. H.W. Lee wrote repeatedly to Joshi about this, inquiring first about the effects of Gladding's speech to the T.U.C.,[88] later about reports of efforts to "Bolshevize" the Indian trade union movement, and of the possible affiliation of the A.I.T. U.C. to the R.I.L.U. Pointing out that talks between the I.F.T.U. and R.I.L.U. were still going on, he added that the talks will succeed only if the Russian trade union movement became "more independent of the Communist Party than it (sc. had) been hitherto."[89] "When the trade unions are more powerful," he wrote, "it will be for them to consider the political action they shall take, but at present, I should imagine, strong political policies would be rather disruptive than anything else. Certainly anything in the way of affiliation with the Red Trade Union International would be a false move from

[84]*Ibid.,* pp. 84-6.

[85]C.P.G.B., Report of Colonial Activities, p. 99. (Document No. 46 in *Parliamentary Papers* 1926, Cmd. 2682, XXIII, p. 701 ff).

[86]Helen Crawford to N.M. Joshi, 19 June 1925 (N.M.J.P., file 7, p. 217); C.P. Dutt to N.M. Joshi, 21 July 1925 (N.M.J.P. file 7, p. 75); Harry Pollitt to N.M. Joshi, 5 October 1925 (N.M.J.P. file 7, p. 47).

[87]D. Petrie, *Communism in India, 1924-1927* (Simla, Home Department confidential report 1927), p. 167.

[88]Lee to Joshi, 15 July 1925 (N.M.J.P. file 7, p. 171).

[89]Lee to Joshi, 7 January 1926 (N.M.J.P. file 8, p. 367).

the point of view of the progress of the Indian Trade Unions."[90]
Joshi did not take seriously Lee's fears about Communist infiltration: "I do not see here any effort on the part of the Communists
to Bolshevise the Indian Trade Union Movement. As a matter of
fact there are very few communists in India. Even these very few
people who call themselves communists are, in my judgement,
not real communists. They are nationalists before everything else."[91]
As regards international affiliation, he had, in the previous year,
had talks with the left-wing British leaders most active in the efforts
to achieve international trade union unity,[92] but he did not encourage
any suggestion of unilateral affiliation to the R.I.L.U.[93] Joshi privately was inclined in favour of the I.F.T.U., but asked Lee's opinion
on the wisdom of affiliation.[94] Lee, while preferring the I.F.T.U.,
wondered "whether the issue might not raise divisions in your ranks
just when every effort and attention (sc. was needed) to consolidate
and extend."[95]

The general secretary of the British T.U.C., Walter Citrine, in
reply to an official query from Joshi regarding affiliation, consulted
Purcell and others informally and suggested, in March 1926, that
"it will be well for the All Indian Trade Union Congress to affiliate
at once to the International Federation of Trade Unions at Amsterdam."[96] Possibly they felt that this would strengthen their hands
in their negotiations with the Soviet Trade Union. It also fitted in
with the suggestions of the I.L.P. that the I.F.T.U. should help the
Indian labour movement. Joshi, however, had realized that the Indian
"trade union movement (sc. was) likely to be divided over this question."[97] He knew that Saklatvala's preference for the R.I.L.U. was
likely to influence some of his colleagues, and Saklatvala's Workers'
Welfare League had recently been reappointed as the official agent
of the A.I.T.U.C. in Britain.[98] "If I find that our movement is likely

[90]Lee to Joshi, 29 January 1926 (N.M.J.P. file 8, p. 319).

[91]Joshi to Lee, 25 February 1926 (N.M.J.P. file 8, p. 323).

[92]R. Page Arnot to N.M. Joshi, 19 June 1925 (N.M.J.P. file 7, p. 215).

[93]"There is absolutely no talk of affiliation with the Red International," wrote
Joshi to Lee, 25 February 1926 (N.M.J.P. file 8, p. 323).

[94]*Ibid.*

[95]Lee to Joshi, 2 March 1926 (N.M.J.P. file 8, p. 29).

[96]Walter M. Citrine to N.M. Joshi, 11 March 1926 (N.M.J.P. file 8, p. 267).

[97]Joshi to Lee, 9 April 1926 (N.M.J.P. file 8, p. 301).

[98]*Ibid.;* also see Saklatvala to Joshi, 4 February 1926 (N.M.J.P. file 8, p. 317).

to be divided I shall avoid decision. Of course, we cannot consider this question till next December or January," wrote Joshi privately to Lee,[99] and officially he simply told Citrine to wait until the next January.[100]

Politically, Joshi at this time had become a member of the I.L.P.[101] The A.I.T.U.C. office thus was made familiar with the creative socialist thought which the I.L.P. through its journals and pamphlets was putting about.[102] Nevertheless, he did not wish to break with Saklatvala, partly in order not to divide the A.I.T.U.C., and partly out of genuine regard for him. H.S.L. Polak, at the behest of Gillies of the international department of the British T.U.C., had written that to retain the Workers' Welfare League as the official agent of the A.I.T.U.C. in Britain was "a very grave practical mistake as that body (sc. had) not any influence with the Labour Party, and (sc. was) usually associated with 'Leftwing' activities of an objectionable kind."[103] Joshi had replied, "I am avoiding raising this question for the fear that it will unnecessarily create complications here. As I am in direct contact with the Secretary of the General Council of the British Trade Union Congress there is no practical harm done by the Workers' Welfare League continuing as our agent in name."[104]

The position in the Indian trade union movement, Joshi knew, was different from that in Britain. In Britain, the aftermath of the General Strike had been characterized by vituperation against all leaders of the T.U.C. on the part of the Soviet and British Communist Parties, so much so that it convinced people like Bevin and

[99]Joshi to Lee, 9 April 1926 (N.M.J.P. file 8, p. 301).

[100]Joshi to Citrine, 9 April 1926 (N.M.J.P. file 8, p. 269).

[101]N.M. Joshi to Fenner Brockway, 15 April 1926 (N.M.J.P. file 8, p. 263); Tarini P. Sinha to N.M. Joshi, 17 July 1926 (N.M.J.P. file 8, p. 157); John Paton to N.M. Joshi, 21 July 1926 (N.M.J.P. file 8, p. 153); N.M. Joshi to Tarini P. Sinha, 22 October 1926 (N.M.J.P. file 8).

[102]Dowse, n. 3, pp. 122 f, 130-6.

[103]H.S.L. Polak to N.M. Joshi, 1 July 1926 (N.M.J.P. file 8, p. 105). Polak, who was a friend of Mahatma Gandhi from his South African days, was at this time closely associated with the moderate Labour Party members who supported Mrs. Besant's Commonwealth of India League. He was also on the advisory committee of the Labour Party on colonial affairs, of which Leonard Woolf was secretary. Leonard Woolf, *Downhill All the Way* (third volume of the autobiography), London, 1967, p. 223).

[104]Joshi to Polak, 16 July 1926 (N.M.J.P. file 8).

Citrine that it was futile to continue the work of Anglo-Soviet trade union co-operation.[105] In India Saklatvala, during his visit in the first half of 1927, played a generally constructive role at the A.I. T.U.C. session in April,[106] although he naturally took every opportunity to push the communist ideology. When Joshi sounded Lee privately whether Saklatvala would be acceptable as a fraternal delegate to the Edinburgh T.U.C., he pointed out, "He being a member of Parliament Indians are naturally proud of him."[107] When Lee vehemently protested, because it would create a wrong impression,[108] Joshi dropped the idea, commenting, "I fully appreciate the attitude of the British Trade Union movement towards the Communists. As the Communists here in India have not started the trouble which they have created in Europe our people here do not fully appreciate your position."[109]

A year after the General Strike, the Edinburgh T.U.C. in September 1927 authorized A.A. Purcell and J. Hallsworth to visit India on their behalf and present a report. They attended the Kanpur Trades Union Congress in November 1927, toured India and produced a valuable report.[110] Neither in his speech to the conference nor in his report did Purcell speak the language of Fabian trusteeship, but attempted a Marxian socialist analysis of the need for co-operation. Criticizing the distorted imperial history on which working-class children were brought up in British schools, he made out a case that Indian and British workers' interests were identical, because to a large extent their enemies were the same—British capitalist and financial interests in both countries.[111] In his joint report with Hallsworth he urged British trade unionists to accept the inevitability of Indian industrialization, approved the rapid growth of the Indian trade unions, and stressed the need of the British Trade Union movement to assist it, both on the grounds of altruism and self-interest.[112]

[105]Bullock, n. 55, p. 384 f; Citrine, n. 55, p. 92 f.

[106]*Indian Quarterly Register,* January-June 1927, Vol. I p. 436 f.

[107]Joshi to Lee, 29 April 1927 (N.M.J.P. file 9, p. 81).

[108]Lee to Joshi, 18 May 1927 (N.M.J.P. file 9, p. 55).

[109]Joshi to Lee, 3 June 1927 (N.M.J.P. file 9, p. 31).

[110]A.A. Purcell and J. Hallsworth, *Report on Labour Conditions in India* (London, T.U.C. General Council, 1928).

[111]*Indian Quarterly Register,* July-December 1927, Vol. II, p. 112 f.

[112]Purcell and Hallsworth, n. 110, p. 42 f.

By April 1928, when this report came out, there was less and less
prospect of a united British labour movement assisting the Indian
labour movement. At the T.U.C. of September 1928 Citrine obtained
a clear mandate to conduct a full inquiry into the disruptive role of
Communists in the British trade union movement.[113] By that time in
India Communist trade union workers, with the help of a few British communist trade unionists like Ben Bradley, had built up a
powerful group in the A.I.T.U.C., and on international questions
they followed R.I.L.U. In these circumstances no one heeded the
plea of Purcell, who had been disappointed in his efforts at international trade union unity, that the task of helping trade unionism in
India was so urgent that it could not "wait upon the caprice of various
International units each wondering what its advantage (sc. was)
likely to be and then moving swiftly or slowly as (sc. suited) the individual case."[114]

IV

On the political plane, too, by 1928, the distance between radical
nationalists and many British Labour-ites had grown wider than it
had been even five years before. The Indian labour delegation to the
Commonwealth Labour Conference in July 1926 included the Swarajist leader T.C. Goswami, Diwan Chaman Lall, and N.M. Joshi.
Probably because Purcell presided over one session, the Indian leaders
were able to get adopted an unscheduled resolution approving the
grant of "immediate self-government" to India in that session.[115]
This was followed by the British T.U. Congress of September 1925,
passing a resolution recommending the freedom of India and criticizing British imperialism in Marxist terms.[116] Both these resolutions
were anathema to Fabian gradualists like Lord Oliver, who thought
that only "immediate anarchy" would follow if "the cement of
British control" was replaced by "immediate self-government."[117]

[113]Lovell and Roberts, n. 55, p. 106.
[114]Purcell and Hallsworth, n. 110, p. 43.
[115]Labour Party, *Annual Report* 1925, p. 59; *Indian Quarterly Register,* July-
December 1925, Vol. II.
[116]Quoted in the appendix of B. Shiva Rao and D. Graham Pole, *Problem
of India* (London, 1926), p. 95.
[117]Lord Olivier in his preface to Shiva Rao and Graham Pole, n. 116, p. 3 f.

In Britain in June and July 1925, Goswami and Chaman Lall had tried to "repudiate the idea which had obtained some credence in England that (sc. the Swarajists) were afraid of democracy and... favoured the establishment of an Indian oligarchy."[118] This belief, however, died hard. Graham Pole, after a visit to India in the winter of 1925-26, gave some evidence to sustain this belief in an article he wrote for *Lansbury's Labour Weekly*.[119] The charge was to some extent justified, because the Swarajists really had very little base among the working-class or the peasantry, and their efforts at organizing labour agitations had been almost at the level of political stunts.[120] From this analysis, however, people like Oswald Mosley and Graham Pole mistakenly drew the conclusion that Indian nationalist sentiments could be ignored and that efforts should be made to develop political movements like an Indian Fabian society or an Indian Labour Party.[121] Fenner Brockway's approach was different. Speaking on the main resolution on India in April 1925 he had rejoiced in the steps being taken to form an Indian Labour Party under the leadership of Mr. Lajpat Rai, who was himself a member of the I.L.P.,"[122] but he had not visualized the new party as an alternative to nationalism but a supplement. His resolution had fully endorsed C.R. Das's last political initiative and had urged the immediate appointment of a commission to revise the constitution.[123]

Hardly any progress was made with the Indian Labour Party. Lajpat Rai and N.M. Joshi knew that a party formed purely on the platform of labour interests would invite the charge that it was dividing the national movement in the interests of foreign capitalists.[124] Although the A.I.T.U.C. in January 1926 decided to elicit

[118]Speech by T.C. Goswami at a meeting in Essex Hall, London, 22 July 1925. *(Indian Quarterly Register,* July-December 1925, Vol. II, p. 152 (c).)

[119]D. Graham Pole, "Mr Gandhi's Fall," *Lansbury's Labour Weekly,* 6 March 1926, p. 12. (Cutting kept in N.M.J.P. file 8).

[120]Broomfield, n. 64, pp. 214-19, on the Chandpur strike; N.M. Joshi to F.J. Ginwalla, 22 July 1924 (N.M.J.P. file 2, p. 71); Joshi to Saklatvala, 9 April 1926 (N.M.J.P. file 8, p. 279).

[121]*Indian Quarterly Register,* January-June 1925, Vol. I, p. 19; *ibid.,* January-June 1926, Vol. I, p. 9; L.P. Sinha, *The Left Wing in India, 1919-1947* (Muzaffarpur 1965), pp. 198-9.

[122]I.L.P., *Report of the Annual Conference 1925* (London, 1925), p. 161. These remarks were greeted with applause from the delegates.

[123]*Ibid.,* p. 159.

[124]Fischer, *Le parti travailliste* (Paris, 1966), p. 283.

opinions on the advisability of forming a Labour Party, the real difficulties were pointed out by N.M. Joshi to Brockway: "Very few workers have votes."[125] Saklatvala had urged Joshi not to let the labour movement be split from the national movement, in particular, from the Swaraj Party, and also asked him publicly to repudiate Graham Pole's charges against it.[126] Joshi refused to dispute in public with Graham Pole, especially as he "did not believe that either the Swaraj party or any other political party in India (sc. cared) very much for Indian Labour."[127] Privately, later in the year, he reminded Graham Pole that, however laudable, efforts to start a Labour Party or a Fabian Society in India were "extremely small, spasmodic, and the result (sc. was) transient." In order that British Labour should not have any illusions on this he added, "What makes me apprehensive is the desire of these people to send calls to England about matters which are scarcely heard of in India. These methods of disproportionate advertisement give a false idea to people in England of the movements (sc. in) India which I am anxious to avoid."[128]

The efforts of Graham Pole and his colleagues of the Commonwealth of India group in 1925-26 had been unrewarding both in England and in India—in England because they failed to get the sponsorship of the Labour front bench for their constitution,[129] and in India because their efforts to create parties in their own image was regarded with either hostility or scepticism by Indian leaders. Only the I.L.P., which had by the end of 1925 come under the left wing leadership of men of the stamp of Brockway and Maxton,[130] understood that the only way the British Left could have a progres-

[125]Joshi to Brockway, 15 April 1926 (N.M.J.P. file 8, p. 263).

[126]Saklatvala to Joshi, 10 March 1926 (N.M.J.P. file 8, p. 277).

[127]Joshi to Saklatvala, 9 April 1926 (N.M.J.P. file 8, p. 279).

[128]Joshi to Graham Pole, 22 October 1926 (N.M.J.P. file 8, p. 1).

[129]The list of sponsors of the Commonwealth of the India Bill of 11 December 1925 does not include any Labour front benchers. They include, among people who became important much later, George Lansbury, Hugh Dalton, and H. Lees-Smith. Others were active members of the I.L.P. empire committee, viz., H. Snell, Haden Guest, John Scurr, and, of course, Col. Wedgwood. Parliamentary Papers (Commons), 1924-1925, I, pp. 499-556. Also see Nethercot, n. 10, p. 360. When a similar bill was reintroduced on 11 February 1927, there was hardly any change in the absence of front bench support. Parliamentary Papers (Commons), 1927, I, pp. 249-306.

[130]Dowse, n. 3, p. 124 ff; Marwick, n. 3, pp. 237-64.

sive influence on Indian affairs was by supporting both the cause of national independence and the emancipation of the toiling masses. The Empire Policy Committee of the I.L.P. had not visualized the break-up of the Commonwealth,[131] but on India, on the advice of the special committee under Brockway, the I.L.P. passed a resolution implicitly endorsing the demand for Purna Swaraj: "The I.L.P. recognizes the full right of the Indian people to self-government and self-determination. Should they elect to belong to the British group of Nations, it must be on the basis of equality and freedom."[132]

The report of the I.L.P.'s Special Committee on India was in many ways a masterly analysis of the Indian political and economic situation. By emphasizing in detail that the Montford Constitution denied India "rudiments of self-government," and was based on a franchise of privilege, and by asking the government to "respond to the proposal of the Legislative assembly" for a "Convention to submit a scheme of Indian self-government for immediate adoption," it firmly placed itself in opposition to the gradualists of the Labour Party leadership.[133] The report also made proposals for working-class and peasant enfranchisement, for giving "immediate effect...to the Universal and compulsory educational Acts passed by Provincial Councils," for getting the Royal Commission on agriculture widen its terms of reference "to include the root question of land tenure"[134] —all with the hope that the labouring classes would be able to keep their end up in a free India.

Paralleling Purcell's efforts at international trade union unity, the I.L.P., against the wishes of the Labour Party, authorized towards the end of 1925, Fenner Brockway, its representative on the Second International executive, to persuade the Second International to negotiate with the Comintern.[135] Brockway failed in this,[136] but succeeded in getting the Zurich congress of the Second International accept the policy of the I.L.P. of helping colonial workers with the assistance of the I.F.T.U. To quote Brockway's own words, "The reception of these proposals by the Executive was encouraging, but

[131]Marwick, n. 3, p. 208.
[132]I.L.P., *Report of the Annual Conference* 1926, p. 53 f.
[133]*Ibid.*
[134]*Ibid.*, pp. 54-5.
[135]Marwick, n. 3, pp. 219-21.
[136]Labour Party, *Annual Report* 1926, p. 28 f.

months passed and little was done."[137] Meanwhile the Communists seized the initiative by organizing the League against Imperialism in February 1927.

The League against Imperialism was started under Comintern auspices with Communists like Willy Munzenberg in key position in the secretariat at a time when Comintern policy was to direct Communist movements in colonial lands to support the nationalist movement.[138] Jawaharlal Nehru attended its first meeting in Brussels in February 1927, was tremendously impressed by it, and got the Indian National Congress to become affiliated to it.[139] While he was aware that the League had many Communist members, he doubted the possibility of Communist domination because the delegates were "by no means purely Communist."[140] In the case he made out to the Congress for affiliating to it, he rebutted two possible arguments that could be used against it. The socialist character of the League ought not to be a handicap; while nationalism took precedence in colonial countries "of all other sentiments," he agreed with western socialists that "such...nationalism...might derive its strength from and work specially for the masses, the peasants and the other workers." Secondly, the danger of Russian foreign policy utilizing "the League to further their own ends" was not very great. "The presence of Lansbury as chairman and some others in the executive committee shows that it is not an one-sided affair."[141] Nehru was impressed by Lansbury's speech urging nationalists to become socialists and asked the A.I.C.C. to circulate it.[142] He was equally

[137]F. Brockway, *Inside the Left* (London, 1942), p. 167.

[138]R.N. Carew Hunt, "Willi Munzenberg," in D. Footman, ed., *International Communism: St Antony's Papers,* No. IX (London, 1960), p. 76 f; J. Degras, ed., *The Communist International: Documents* (London, 1960), Vol. II, pp. 354, 529; A.I.C.C., Foreign Department (Correspondence, 1926-1927), File G 21 (T.L. No. 79).

[139]Report on the International Congress Against Imperialism held at Brussels... Submitted by Jawaharlal Nehru to the Working Committee of the Indian National Congress, 20 February 1927 (A.I.C.C., File No. G 29, 1927 Part II, T.L. No. 82-A, pp. 80-114). Later references are to the pages of this manuscript.

[140]*Ibid.,* p. 9 f.

[141]*Ibid.,* pp. 16, 18 f.

[142]J. Nehru to Rangaswamy, 16 March 1927 (A.I.C.C. File G 29, Part II (T.L. 82-A, 1927, p. 68). The speeches of Lansbury and Harry Pollitt which Nehru commended, are in A.I.C.C. File G 29, Part I (T.L. No. 82-A), 1927, pp. 27 ff, 38 ff.

appreciative of the stand taken against British imperialism in China
by the British delegation which included I.L.P.-ers like Fenner
Brockway, Ellen Wilkinson and Lansbury himself.[143]

Nehru could not, however, appreciate the hesitation felt by these
I.L.P.-ers on the possibility of getting the I.L.P. or the Labour Party
to directly affiliate to the League against Imperialism, although
he heard that the I.L.P. leaders had braved the displeasure of the
Second International in coming to the congress.[144] Not being familiar with the rather bitter history of Communist-Labour cooperation till 1927, nor understanding how the Communist "fraction"
in a "front organization" was always able to manipulate it to their
own ends, he wrote, "The executive committee of the League has,
I believe, a majority of non-Communists and there is no reason
why they should be led by the nose by the minority."[145] He understood by February 1930[146] that the League was basically subservient
to the Comintern but in the intervening three years he used the League (including its British branch under Reginald Bridgman) as a
main channel of communication to the British Left. This created
awkward problems for people like Lansbury, Brockway, and James
Maxton—all of whom, while supporting the anti-colonial aims of
the League, gradually had to withdraw from active participation in
it because of pressures from the Second International or the Labour
Party. (Lansbury left late in 1927, Brockway retired from the
executive of the League in 1928, and Maxton, who succeeded
Brockway as the I.L.P. representative, was forced out by the
Communists in the late summer of 1929, in pursuance of the
sectarian policy enunciated at the sixth Comintern congress.)[147]

Eight months after the first congress of the League against Imperialism, the Labour Party conference unanimously carried a resolution moved by Lansbury recommending Dominion Home Rule

[143]J. Nehru to Rangaswamy, 16 March 1927 (A.I.C.C., File G 29, Part I, p.
116 ff).

[144]"Report on the International Congress Against Imperialism held at Brussels...submitted by Jawaharlal Nehru to the Working Committee of the Indian
National Congress, 20 February 1927," p. 9 (A.I.C.C., File G 29, Part I.).

[145]J. Nehru to Rangaswamy, 7 March 1927, enclosing a "Note for the Working
Committee" (A.I.C.C. File G 29 (T.L. No. 82-A), 1927, Part II), p. 6.

[146]A.I.C.C. File No. F.D.-1 (T.L. No. 175-D), 1929-1930, Document No. 17.

[147]F. Brockway, n. 137, p. 168; for Maxton's exit see Marwick's thesis, which
has used Maxton-Chattopadhyaya-Bridgman correspondence, n. 3, p. 277,

in India.[148] Yet within a month the rapport between Indian nationalism and the Labour Party was broken. Against the wishes of Lansbury, Ellen Wilkinson, T. Wheatley, Wedgwood and other I.L.P.-ers,
Ramsay Macdonald agreed to let two Labour members (Clement
Attlee and Vernon Hartshorn) participate in the Simon Commission.[149] Fenner Brockway, who visited India in the winter of 1927-
28, was not only impressed by Jawaharlal's socialist leanings but
also by the social revolutionary justification given by Jawaharlal
for the demand for "Purna Swaraj."[150] On his return he tried to get
the parliamentary Labour Party to withdraw the Labour members
from the Simon Commission, without much success.[151] In sharp
contrast to July 1925, the Commonwealth Labour conference of
July 1928 saw a walk-out by the Indian trade union delegation when
they were not allowed to table a resolution criticizing the Simon
Commission. Most Labour Party leaders felt that the interests of
Indian workers were not being served by bringing a prestige question
of nationalist politics in this forum—a view which all Indian labour
leaders (including moderates like R.R. Bakhale) resented.[152] After
this episode, at a meeting organized by the British branch of the
League Against Imperialism, Srinivasa Iyengar of the Indian
National Congress was very caustic about Labour party politicians,
who could be at the same time "a member of the I.L.P., also a
member of the Labour Party, Liberal in certain tendencies and cooperating with the Tories." "Great causes," he added, "could

[148]Labour Party, *Annual Report* 1927, pp. 255-9.

[149]*Indian Quarterly Register,* July-December 1927, pp. 92-8.

[150]F. Brockway, *The Indian Crisis* (London, 1930), p. 114 describes his discussion with Nehru on "Purna Swaraj" early in 1927 before Nehru left Europe;
also see Brockway, n. 37, ch. 18 *passim.*

[151]F. Brockway to J. Nehru, 11 May 1928 (A.I.C.C. File 28 (T.L. No. 88-M),
1928).

[152]Labour Party, *Annual Report* 1928, pp. 308 f, 311 f; for a fuller account,
including statements given by the Indian delegates who walked out, see *Indian
Quarterly Register,* July-December 1928, Vol. II, pp. 293-95. A fortnight later,
at the 3rd Congress of the Labour and Socialist International, Diwan Chaman
Lall and R.R. Bakhale sought to elicit support for a resolution critical of the policy
of the Labour Party on the Simon Commission, and were stoutly supported by
the I.L.P. left winger John Paton. But opposition from the official delegates of
the Labour Party led to a compromise resolution being passed (*Indian Quarterly
Register,* n, 149, p. 285 f),

never be won by such divided allegiance."[153] Brockway, who had
sat on the platform as Iyengar made these remarks, tried in the following October at the Labour Party conference to criticize the party
executive for its Indian policy, but was defeated.[154] Ramsay Macdonald somewhat pompously criticized Indian nationalists who,
in his opinion, "were much less inclined to favour the Indian bottom
dog than they themselves were or their own representative in India
were."[155]

How deeply the two movements had become distrustful of the
bona fides of each other, by 1928, was also illustrated, tragically,
by the last months of Lala Lajpat Rai. A friend of Keir Hardie and
Josiah Wedgwood, a member of the I.L.P., Lala Lajpat Rai had
for some time past been getting bitterly disillusioned with the Labour
Party.[156] In the winter of 1927-28, he wrote scathing articles entitled,
"English Socialism a huge mockery" and "Labour Party under
Imperialistic Macdonald."[157] About a month before his death,
just before returning to the Punjab to demonstrate against the Simon
Commission (during which he was badly injured by the police)
Lala Lajpat Rai told Jawaharlal Nehru "that we should expect
nothing from the British Labour Party."[158]

It is no wonder that the tenure of the second Labour government
was characterized by a militant and uncompromising temper among
Left wing nationalists in India. It affected the Labour movement
as well as the wider political movement.

Two decisions of the Indian government taken before British
Labour's electoral victory in May 1929, split the Indian Labour move-
ment—the Meerut conspiracy case, and the appointment of a Royal
Commission to enquire into Indian labour conditions. Between
April and July 1929, on behalf of Jawaharlal, who was president
of the A.I.T.U.C. at that time, Reginald Bridgman of the League
Against Imperialism lobbied to get official support for the Meerut

[153]*Indian Quarterly Register,* n. 149, p. 280.

[154]Labour Party, *Annual Report* 1928, p. 171 f.

[155]*Ibid.,* p. 173.

[156]See the recollections of his friend, Wilfred Wellock, Labour M.P., in the
Lajpat Rai memorial number of the *People,* 13 April 1929, p. 29.

[157]These, published in the *Tribune* (Punjab) of 11 and 14 December, 1927,
have been reprinted in V.C. Joshi, ed., *Lala Lajpat Rai: Writings and Speeches*
(Delhi, 1966), Vol. II, pp. 366-8.

[158]J. Nehru, *An Autobiography* (London, 1936), p. 176.

prisoners from the general council of the T.U.C. The response was not encouraging.[159] Citrine, the secretary of the T.U.C., was then finalizing his report on Communist infiltration (which he submitted to the Belfast T.U.C. the following September), and he was convinced that the League Against Imperialism was a Communist organization controlled from Moscow.[160] Jawaharlal was irritated at Citrine's indifference, and wrongly suspected N.M. Joshi of poisoning the attitude of the British T.U.C. against the Meerut prisoners.[161] He later withdrew this accusation that Joshi had been working behind his back,[162] but there remained a difference in outlook between them. Joshi wrote to him:

> It is true that I do not take your view regarding the Meerut case, but I have not concealed that fact from you....But I am sure that I gave you no ground to expect active support in this matter.... I am very doubtful that even with my active support the right-wingers in the Trade Union Congress General Council would have done anything in this matter.[163]

As the Royal Commission on Labour was a culmination of the efforts of the A.I.T.U.C. since 1924 to get a comprehensive enquiry started on Indian labour, people like Joshi, Bakhale, Chaman Lall, V.V. Giri, Shiva Rao and others were willing to participate in it. The Communist members of the A.I.T.U.C. executive wrote from behind prison bars advocating a boycott, [164]and their view was shared by Left wing nationalists because, in the words of Subhas Bose, "boycott was then in the air."[165] At the Nagpur session of

[159]Leaflet "War on Indian Workers," May 1929 A.I.C.C., Misc. 12 (T.L. 144), 1929. Nehru-Bridgeman correspondence in A.I.C.C., F.D. 23 (T.L. 175 R), 1929-1930, pp. 47-139.

[160]Lovell and Roberts, n. 55, p. 112.

[161]J. Nehru to R.R. Bakhale, 24 September 1929 A.I.C.C., Misc. 16, (T.L. 159), 1929, p. 34.

[162]J. Nehru to Bakhale, 4 October 1929, A.I.C.C., Misc. 16 (T.L. 159), 1929, p. 11.

[163]N.M. Joshi to J. Nehru, 11 October 1929, A.I.C.C., F.D. 1 (ii), Part II (T.L. 143), 1929, p. 130.

[164]See their letter to the Assistant Secretary, A.I.T.U.C., 20 September 1929 A.I.C.C., Misc. 16 (T.L. 159), 1929).

[165]S,C. Bose, *Indian Struggle* (Bombay, 1964), p. 166.

the A.I.T.U.C. in December 1929 Jawaharlal decisively tipped the scale in favour of a boycott. Already in September he had publicly denounced the Labour Commission.[166] There was just a chance that after Lord Irwin's declaration on Dominion Status on 31 October, he might have reconsidered his decision to refuse coopera- tion with the British government, because he did sign the Delhi manifesto. This was, however, a reluctant acquiescence.[167] In his speech to the Nagpur session of the A.I.T.U.C. he questioned the sincerity of the Labour government and said, "Indeed the time has come when we should make it perfectly clear that we cannot coope- rate with any such Commission or with the British Government that appoints them."[168]

During these critical months from May to December 1929, Jawahar- lal appears to have been in touch mainly with Reginald Bridgman of the League Against Imperialism and not directly in touch with left Labour M.P.s like Fenner Brockway or James Maxton.[169] Before taking the plunge into civil disobedience at the Lahore session of the National Congress he was unable or unwilling to co-ordinate efforts at wringing the maximum concession from the British govern- ment by allying with the leftist I.L.P.-ers, quite a number of whom had been returned to parliament.[170] Yet the latter were anxious to help. Fenner Brockway repeatedly lobbied Wedgwood Benn for declaring a general amnesty (including the Meerut prisoners), and Benn was inclined to go part of the way with him in late October and November.[171] Brockway's main contact with India at this time

[166]J. Nehru, "Statement on the Whitley Commission," 20 September 1929, A.I.C.C., Misc. 16 (T.L. 159), 1929, p. 40.

[167]J. Nehru to Mahatma Gandhi, 4 November 1929, in J. Nehru, *A Bunch of Old Letters* (New York, 1960 ed.), pp. 76-8.

[168]Report of the Nagpur session of the A.I.T.U.C., *Indian Quarterly Register,* July-December 1929, p. 427.

[169]There are no letters either in his file of personal correspondence or in the A.I.C.C. files, between him and Brockway or Maxton, whereas there are quite a few with Reginald Bridgman.

[170]These included Brockway, J.F. Horrabin, Fred Longden, Ellen Wilkinson, James Maxton, John Scurr, Josiah Wedgwood, Wilfred Wellock, M. Brothers, D.R. Grenfell, Jennie Lee. Besides there were more moderate but genuine friends of Indian nationalism like George Lansbury, Pethick Lawrence, Graham Pole and the Rev. James Barr.

[171]Brockway, n. 137, pp. 202-4. The correspondence between Wedgwood Benn and the Indian government on Brockway's suggestion is in NAI, Home-Pol.,

was the weekly organ of the Servants of India Society, for which he wrote the *London Letter*. It is not known whether Jawaharlal and the "Congress Left" took any notice of the account of Brockway's efforts that were published in that organ between October and December, although in one of them there was a personal appeal to Jawaharlal.[172] Without any positive response from the Indian radicals, and with positive hostility coming from Indian official circles, and only half-hearted co-operation from Benn,[173] Brockway's efforts were doomed. Yet, after the Civil Disobedience movement had started, the I.L.P.'s attitude was different from the general disapproval with which the non-cooperation movement had been greeted in British labour circles ten years before. I.L.P. Left-wingers repeatedly criticized the Macdonald government for repression in India and wrote books explaining the Indian point of view.[174] They organized, under I.L.P. auspices a special India weekend in I.L.P. branches in August 1930.[175] One of them, Reginald Reynolds started the Friends of India Society to carry on propaganda to justify the Civil Disobedience movement, and to urge that without Congress participation the Round Table Conference would be worthless.[176]

1929, File 299). Also see an earlier account by Brockway in his *Indian Crisis* (1930), pp. 130-3. ..

[172]F. Brockway, "The Declaration and the Conference" (London Letter), *Servant of India,* 21 November 1929, contains the personal appeal to Jawaharlal. It was written on 30 October, after a talk with Benn, but reached India by mail three weeks later. To some extent Brockway's efforts were frustrated due to the time lag between his letters and their publication. On 27 November 1929 he wrote privately to S.G. Vaze about the parliamentary resolution on India that he was moving with Benn's permission, but the long article in which he expounded the theme of his resolution was published only on 19 December 1929, too late to have any effect. Brockway to Editor, S.G. Vaze, 27 November 1929 (NAI, Srinivasa Sastri papers—Correspondence (i) Ser. No. 534); *Servant of India,* 19 December 1929.

[173]See the references to note 171; also see Wedgwood Benn to Lord Irwin (private and personal), 24 December 1929 (NAI, Home-Pol. 1930, File 11/19).

[174]On one occasion Brockway was disciplined by the Speaker for insisting on moving a resolution on arrests in India. He wrote *The Indian Crisis* in 1930. An ex-I.L.P. journalist H.N. Brailsford visited India later in the year and wrote *Rebel India* (1931).

[175]I.L.P., *Annual Report* 1931, p. 19 f.

[176]Notes and documents on the "Friend of India" Society, London, by Intelligence branch (NAI, Home-Pol., 1931, File 117).

The image of the Congress as a left-wing organization was projected in Britain only by the I.L.P. in 1930-31. Alone of all British parties the I.L.P. took notice of and welcomed the Left-wing resolutions passed at the Karachi Congress.[177] The Communists, by their sectarian policy had isolated themselves both from the Congress left as well as from the British Labour Left. There was no love lost between the I.L.P. and the British Communist Party. All the same, unlike Walter Citrine,[178] the I.L.P. did not allow its dislike of Communist policy to deflect itself from the task of continuing to agitate for the release of the Meerut prisoners.[179]

The only group of Indian leaders who hopefully co-operated with the Labour government were either liberals like Sapru or Srinivasa Sastri or labour leaders like N.M. Joshi and B. Shiva Rao who had seceded from the A.I.T.U.C. to form the I.T.U.F. in December 1929. They used the forum of the British Commonwealth Labour conference in July 1930 to get support from the British T.U.C., so that special safeguards and electoral arrangements for labour could be considered in the constitutional talks at the Round Table Conference.[180] They were very disappointed at the rejection of universal suffrage at the first Round Table Conference and said

---

[177]I.L.P., *Annual Report* 1931, p. 124 f. The Labour Party conference of October 1930 saw a drawn battle between the resolution of Kenworthy approving the Labour government's policy of calling the Round Table conference and the amendment of the I.L.P. Left-wing critical of the government and calling for release of prisoners. The Left-wing leader A.J. Cook got the "previous question" carried both resolution and amendment were shelved. Brockway wrote, "I think this meant that whilst the Party is not prepared to censure its own government, it is uneasy about the policy being pursued and is not in the mood to give it wholehearted endorsement" (Labour Party, *Annual Report* 1930, pp. 216-20; Brockway, "The Labour Party and India," *Servant of India,* 30 October 1930, p. 526).

[178]Walter Citrine did inquire about the Meerut prisoners early in 1930 but was easily convinced by the official view on the procedure adopted to try the accused (NAI; Home-Pol., 1930, File 108).

[179]I.L.P., *Annual Report* 1931, p. 117. Brockway said that the Meerut trial was "as disgraceful as the Dreyfus and Sacco and Vanzetti trials." He tried, unsuccessfully, to raise the matter at the Labour Party conference in October 1931 (Labour Party, *Annual Report* 1931, p. 168 ff).

[180]Labour Party, *Annual Report* 1930, p. 308 gives the names of participants but no details. I am grateful to Shri B. Shiva Rao, who was one of them, for giving me his recollections of the details (Interview with Shri B. Shiva Rao by P.S. Gupta, 23 December 1968).

so.[181] Macdonald does not appear to have made any special efforts to meet their point of view, although he had repeatedly claimed to be more concerned for the Indian masses than the Indian nationalists.[182]

V

The eight years from the fall of the Labour government in August 1931 to the outbreak of war in September 1939, saw a gradual renewal of contacts and mutual understanding between sections of the British Left and the Indian Left. The process was on both sides influenced by new forces.

In India, the early thirties were years when senior political leaders were in jail and the government ruled through ordinances. Moderate Congressmen and Gandhiji were at a loss for political initiative and tried, through personal contacts, to influence opinion abroad.[183] At first the Communists remained in self-imposed isolation, while the Roy-ists and the Congress Socialists aimed, in their own different ways, to link up the socialist and labour movements with the movement for national independence. The A.I.T.U.C. under Roy-ist influence, was indifferent to the question of international affiliation and somewhat prejudiced against the I.L.O.[184] The leaders of the I.T.U.F. united with the railwaymen's union to create the N.T.U.F. but remained suspicious not only of Communists but also of Roy-ists and rejected the "Platform of Unity" drafted by M.N. Roy.[185] The government of India recognized only the N.T.U.F. for purposes of representation at the I.L.O.

[181]Indian Round Table Conference, *Proceedings, November 1930—January 1931* (Cmd. 3778) (London, 1931), p. 433.

[182]Macdonald, in his concluding speech, ignored the points raised by Joshi and Shiva Rao.

[183]*Vide* "Record of the Home members" interview with H.S.L. Polak of the India Conciliation Group, 18 March 1933 (NAI Home-Pol., 1933, File 79).

[184]See the article of the Royist Labour leader V.B. Karnik, "A clean reply to Mr Bakhale," *The Mahratta,* 14 May 1933, p. 11 (kept in N.M.J.P. file 4, second folder); I am also indebted to an interview with Shri Rajani Mukherjee, who was organizing secretary of the A.I.T.U.C. then, and is now an official of the Hind Mazdoor Sabha (Interview on 6 July 1969).

[185]R.R. Bakhale, "Trade Union Unity," *Servant of India,* 4 May 1933, p. 209 f. The authorship of the *Platform of Unity* is attested by Shri Rajani Mukherjee, who was actively associated with M.N. Roy, (Interview on 6 July 1969), and is hinted at by Karnik, n. 184.

In Britain, Macdonald's defection not only shook the Labour Party out of excessive complacency but led to the emergence of Lansbury as the leader of the party for the next few years. Some other pro-Indian Labour politicians and journalists like Brockway and Reginald Reynolds broke with the Labour Party when the I.L.P. disaffiliated from the former, taking some of its members with it, though not all.[186] In course of the thirties the I.L.P. became a dissident Marxist party, sharply critical of Stalinist Russia as well as the social democratic parties of the west for their alleged compromises with capitalism and imperialism.[187] More realistic left-wing Labour intellectuals like G.D.H. Cole started the New Fabian Research Bureau (NFRB) to give the Labour Party an armoury of socialist ideas.[188] As the danger of war grew by the mid-thirties, many left wing Labour Party members tried to unite all left forces for a radical policy at home and abroad, first by means of the Socialist League (sponsored by Stafford Cripps) and later by advocating the Popular Front and supporting the work of the Left Book Club. Apart from Cripps, the leading role inside the Labour Party executive in these moves was played by Harold Laski, Ellen Wilkinson, and D.N. Pritt. Other Labour Party leaders remained suspicious of Communist-Labour co-operation, which was reinforced by the purges carried out by Sta'in in Russia.[189]

Ever since Britain introduced Imperial Preference in 1931 and extended it to the Dominions and the colonies by 1933, trade within the empire increased at the expense of trade with countries outside the empire.[190] The Conservative Party welcomed the increasing interdependence of the Empire-Commonwealth, but the economic crisis of the early thirties made even some left wing Labour leaders think in terms of maintaining the integrity of the Empire-Commonwealth for the purposes of socialist planning.[191] In a world with

[186]Dowse, n. 3, pp. 179-84.

[187]*Ibid.*, Ch. 13, *passim.*

[188]M. Cole, *The Story of Fabian Socialism* (London, 1961), pp. 226-30.

[189]G.D.H. Cole, *A History of the Labour Party from* 1914 (London, 1948), Ch. IX, *passim;* C. Cooke, *The Life of Sir Richard Stafford Cripps* (London, 1957, Ch. X, *passim;* Kingsley Martin, *Harold Laski* (London, 1953), pp. 102-12; D.N. Pritt, *Autobiography: from Right to Left* (London, 1965), pp.97-104.

[190]A.K. Kahn, *Great Britain in the World Economy* (London, 1946), p. 244.

[191]Ben Tillett, in his presidential address to the Belfat T.U.C. of September 1929, had visualized the British Commonwealth being organized as an economic

a tendency towards autarchic combinations, and in a Britain faced with unemployment and hunger marches, such a view could easily encourage, as one Labour M.P. pointed out, a British variety of national socialism.[192] Fortunately, economic recovery had started by the middle and late thirties. It was based, as we now know, on a domestic boom in the building industry and the growth of new industrial products oriented to a high-wage economy. These growing sectors of the British economy were not dependent on the trade of the tropical colonies.[193] So the apprehensions of Sir Stafford Cripps that the British working class was fattening on imperial exploitation and that this might be an obstacle to the work for Indian independence,[194] was not entirely well founded. It explains also why hardheaded empirically minded trade union leaders like Ernest Bevin who were prepared to come to terms with capitalism at home,[195] became nevertheless fully committed to granting dominion status to India by the end of the decade, and personally lobbied for it in Churchill's war cabinet.[196]

In the various constitutional discussions prior to the enactment of the Government of India Act of 1935, Labour Party leadership showed itself to be more aware of nationalist sentiments and more purposefully determined to fight for provisions specifically in the interests of the Indian working classes and peasantry than Macdonald had done in the first and second Round Table conferences. In 1928, despite the universal boycott of the Simon Commission, the Labour members had remained in the Commission, but in 1932

unit comparable to the U.S.A. (Lovell and Roberts, n. 55, p. 111). In 1930 Ernest Bevin further developed the idea of a Commonwealth Economic bloc (Bullock, n. 55, Vol. I, pp. 440-6). George Lansbury, in explaining Labour's colonial policy, suggested reorganizing the British Empire like the way the Soviet Union had reorganized the Tsarist colonies (G. Lansbury, *My England*, London, 1934, p. 166 f).

[192]John Parker, "Socialism and the Problem of Nationalism," in G.E.G. Catlin, ed., *New Trends in Socialism* (London, 1935), pp. 222-5.

[193]H.W. Richardson, *Economic Recovery in Britian, 1932-1939* (London, 1967), *passim*.

[194]Sir Stafford Cripps, "The British Working-class and Indian Independence," *Congress Socialist*, 11 January 1936, p. 7 f.

[195]On Ernest Bevin's evolution see the perceptive comments of E.J. Hobsbawm, in his *Labouring Men* (London, 1964), p. 339 f.

[196]Bullock, *Life and Times of Ernest Bevin*, Vol. II, *Minister of Labour* (London, 1967), pp. 205-7.

when the Indian Liberals refused to participate in the constitutional talks any more, the Labour Party also refused to attend the third Round Table conference.[197]

In applauding the successful completion of the work of the Royal Commission on Labour "in the midst of the difficulties and struggles of the last two years," the Labour Party showed that it continued to believe that for "the Indian wage-earners the Party (sc. had) a special responsibility."[198] However, this did not lead it any more to encourage bureaucratic tutelage in opposition to nationalist forces. At the time of the publication of the White Paper of 1933, and again in the opening paragraphs of Attlee's draft minority report on the Indian Constitution in the Joint Select Committee in June 1934, the Labour front bench asserted that the Constitution should aim at establishing India "at the earliest possible moment as an equal partner with the other members of the British Commonwealth of Nations," and suggested steps which could expedite the process.[199] While making the expected obeisance to the achievements of the British rule in India, and "the devotion" of the British officials in "their tasks as servants of India," Attlee stressed the need to recognize "national consciousness in India," and to make constitutional provisions "for the living forces of Indian nationalism to be harnessed to the great tasks which confront any government in India."[200] Attlee had his doubts about the danger of putting "the Indian rural population and the urban wage-earners at the mercy of a politically dominant section in the possession of economic power," especially as "the Hindoo social system (sc. was) based on inequality."[201] His solution was to recommend in the constitution not only the abolition of special representation of landlords, university men, and commerical bodies, but also the increase of labour representation to a minimum of 10 per cent of the total number of seats as recommended by the N.T.U.F. In addition, adult suffrage was suggested for labour constituencies in the large

[197]Labour Party, *Annual Report* 1933, p. 73. For the reasons why the Liberals withdrew, see Dwarkadas, n. 33, p. 432.

[198]Labour Party, *Annual Report* 1931, p. 84.

[199]*Joint Committee on Constitutional Reform,* session 1933-34, Vol. I (Part II, Proceedings, London, 1934), para 3.

[200]*Ibid.,* paras 11, 19.

[201]*Ibid.,* para 12.

industrial cities, immediately, and within ten years the provinces were to have universal adult suffrage.[202] During discussion in the select committee, the four labour members pressed these suggestions, as well as the suggestions of abolishing the second chambers to the vote.[203] Considering that Attlee had signed the report of the Simon Commission with hardly any reservations, these efforts on his part were a step forward and a denial of a bi-partisan approach on Indian policy.

The leader of the Labour Party, George Lansbury, was less inclined than Attlee to stress the positive achievements of British rule. In a book expounding his political ideas he wrote, in the same year as Attlee's draft report, "These benefits of British rule are benefits paid for in hard cash, and well paid too. This tribute is almost entirely spent outside India....Whatever the Press may say, we do not in fact make India rich and contented."[204] Among Labour intellectuals who were influential in the N.F.R.B. there were, in the early thirties, crosscurrents of opinion. J.M. Keynes regarded the Indian White Paper as being, "broadly speaking, the utmost progress which (sc. could) be made at this stage," and criticized Kingsley Martin for his readiness "to inflame, rather than pacify Indian grievances against it."[205] Harold Laski, on the contrary, having participated in all the Round Table Conferences as an unofficial adviser to Lord Sankey, had shifted from the view that India "really (sc. was) not fit to govern itself,"[206] to a sympathetic understanding of the nationalist psychology, and a personal rapport with Gandhiji.[207] After working with Sankey in 1932, he concluded that Sankey's draft bill was so "cluttered up with all kinds of checks and balances" that

[202]Ibid., paras 36, 37.

[203]Ibid., paras 335, 347, 351.

[204]G. Lansbury, My England (London, 1934), p. 171.

[205]J.M. Keynes to Kingsley Martin, 23 April 1933, quoted in full in K. Martin, Editor: a Volume of Autobiography, 1931-1945 (London, 1968), p. 42. This must have been caused by the editorial approval given to a long letter a fortnight before from an "Indian," sharply criticising the White Paper. (New Statesman and Nation, 8 April 1933, pp. 442-43).

[206]Laski to Justice Holmes, 15 June 1930, quoted in M. de W. Howe, ed., Holmes-Laski Letters (London, 1953), Vol. II, p. 1261.

[207]Ibid., pp. 1264, 1301, 1332, 1335-36. On 3 December 1931 Gandhiji had a serious discussion with Labour Party intellectuals at the flat of J.F. Horrabin, M.P. At the end of it, Harold Laski, at Gandhi's request, summed up the various points of view. (Woolf, Downhill All The Way, pp. 228-30).

it would "reproduce the worst features of the worst modern Constitutions."[208]

Laski and Lansbury were closely associated with V.K. Krishna Menon. Menon was the pupil of the former and the publisher of the latter.[209] Thanks to Menon's efforts in the India League and the encouragement given to the League by Jawaharlal Nehru the non-Communist Labour Left was able to re-establish contact with the Congress and the Congress left in the early thirties. Menon had come to Britain in the late twenties after having worked in Madras with Mrs. Besant. He had therefore a link with the Commonwealth of India League associated with Graham Pole and H.S.L. Polak. In the early thirties Menon transformed it into the India League with a new commitment to Purna Swaraj.[210] As a result the League lost the support of some people like Polak,[211] but radical Labour M.P.s began to give Menon active support. The names of the members of its various committees included Brockway, Purcell, George Hicks, Lansbury, H.N. Brailsford, Wilfred Wellock, J.F. Horrabin—names which had been associated with the more radical moves by Labour leaders in the twenties.[212] Among those who started taking an active interest in India now were Bertrand Russell, Horace Alexander, and Dorothy Woodman, the last named providing a link with Kingsley Martin, editor of the increasingly influential journal *New Statesman and Nation*.[213] To these people Menon distributed Congress propaganda material, defeating government censorship. The chief of the Intelligence branch commented wryly:

We do all we can to prevent such information as is published

[208]Laski to Holmes, 12 July 1932, in Howe ed., n. 206, p. 1396.

[209]T.J.S. George, *Krishna Menon: A Biography* (London, 1964), p. 52. George Lansbury's *My England* (London, 1934), was part of a series which Menon was editing for the publishers Selwyn and Blount.

[210]George, n. 209, pp. 53-7.

[211]*Ibid.*, also see the Home department's dossier on Polak (NAI, Home-Pol., 1936, File 137).

[212]The names are taken from the printed notepaper of the India League for 1932, used in a letter from Menon to H.G. Haig, 10 October 1932 (NAI, Home-Pol. File 40/XII, p. 105).

[213]K. Martin, *Editor* (London, 1968), pp. 157-62, for the work of Dorothy Woodman in the Union of Democratic Control, and the links of the U.D.C. with the India League.

in Congress bulletins reaching England, but the energetic editor of the *Information Bulletin,* Menon...is quite cunning in arranging post boxes in England...a certain amount of this kind of propaganda reaches Mr Lansbury, and we have so far refrained from tapping the correspondence of the Leader of the Opposition of the House of Commons.[214]"

Till 1934, the India League agitated in Britain against the repressive ordinances, and, on constitutional questions, to secure radical amendments to the Government of India Bill but preferably to get support for the idea of an Indian Constituent Assembly framing India's future constitution. The most important achievement was to organize a tour of India by three British Labour politicians (of whom two were ex-M.P.s)—Ellen Wilkinson, Leonard Matters, and Monica Whateley. In June and July 1932, Pandit Madan Mohan Malaviya discussed details of the tour with C.F. Andrews and Horrabin, and gave £500 towards its expenses.[215] The delegates were not allowed to see the leaders who were in gaol,[216] but were able to study the political and Labour movements in different parts of the country.[217] The Indian government was so worried about the possible effects of this trip on British public opinion that the Under-Secretary of State for India urged them, before they left Britain, to keep "in close touch with officials," and promised "to write to prominent people, outside Congres circles, whom it would be worth their while to meet."[218] Later, in India, the government ruefully noted that despite the best efforts of the officials, the delegates were spending much of their time listening to the Congress and other left wing points of view.[219] When their report came out in March

[214]Note by H.W. Williamson, (D.I.B.), 14 March 1933 on a P.U.C. on the India League's work (NAI, Home-Pol., 1933, File 30/2).

[215]Telegram from Malaviya to Horrabin, 15 July 1932 (intercepted copy in NAI, Home-Pol., 1932, File 40/XII, p. 26); also Andrews to Malaviya, 22 July 1932 (NAI, Home-Pol., 1932, File 40/XII, p. 45) and Horrabin to Malaviya, 2 August 1932 (NAI, Home-Pol., 1932, File 40/XII, p. 41).

[216]R. Peel to M.G. Hallett, 5 August 1932, No. Pt J(S) 805/32 (NAI, Home-Pol. File 40/XII, p. 49 f).

[217]NAI, Home-Pol. File 40/XII, *passim.*

[218]Peel to Hallett, 5 August 1932, n. 216.

[219]See for example, H.S. Turnam to M.G. Hallett, 17 October 1932 (D.O. No. 1088, P.S.D.) (NAI, Home-Pol. File 40/XII, p. 134 f); Note by C.H. Everett,

1934, with an introduction by Bertrand Russell,[220] it was banned in India, because, according to the Chief of Intelligence, "The book as written contains more Congress propaganda than any volume seen by me." He admitted, however, that "very many of the allegations are or may be true."[221]

The book highlighted the suppression of political and civil rights in India, and warned the Labour Party against being led to underestimate the strength of nationalism through an overdose of the official point of view.[222] Having met all shades of Indian labour opinion, the delegates were able to appreciate both the non-Communist left who dominated the A.I.T.U.C. in 1932, as well as the N.F.T.U. under N.M. Jsohi.[223] They emphasized the fact that all trade union movements in India had a political colour—"indeed, in modern India no live movement can escape it."[224] This conclusion must have helped to disabuse some British Labour leaders of the belief that the N.T.U.F. contained the only genuine trade unionists. The delegates also added that the Communists "appeared to be in hostility to the Indian National Congress and to the labour organizations."[225]

This picture of the Indian labour movement probably explains why from March 1933 the British Labour movement launched a high-level agitation to get the Meerut prisoners released at once. The National Joint Council of Labour co-operated with a committee, set up by Leonard Matters, for the release of the prisoners. Unlike 1929, Citrine, Bevin, Morrison, and Attlee unanimously agreed with leftists like Swales, Grenfell, and Lansbury that "at a time when it (sc. was) more important than ever that the difference between British and Indian opinion should be reconciled...no wiser step

---

Superintendent of Police, C.I.D., 25 October 1932 (*ibid.,* p. 191). The Law Member, Sir B.L. Mitter, tried to argue a very pro-government and anti-Gandhi case to Ellen Wilkinson, giving the moderate Liberal point of view, and felt pleased with himself for "the opportunity of dealing a few direct blows at popular delusions" (Note by Sir B.L. Mitter, 30 October 1932, *ibid.,* p. 167a).

[220]India League, *Condition of India* (London, 1934).

[221]Note by H. Williamson, 23 March 1934, in NAI, Home-Pol. 1934 File 35/3, pp. 4-7.

[222]India League, n. 220, pp. 45, 47 f, 102, 118 ff.

[223]*Ibid.,* pp. 433-42.

[224]*Ibid.,* p. 441.

[225]*Ibid.,* p. 436.

could be taken by the government...than to grant all these men their unconditional freedom."[226] This belated gesture was successful. Thereafter, while the British T.U.C. kept in touch with the N.T.U.F. through the I.F.T.U., to which both were affiliated,[227] it did not interfere in the efforts towards reuniting the Indian labour movement. These efforts were to succeed in 1938, on the condition that the united Indian movement, while participating in the I.L.O., would not affiliate to any of the rival trade union internationals.[228]

The report of the India League delegation had been published three months before Attlee submitted his minority report to the Joint Select Committee. It may have exerted some influence on him. The Congress proposal of a constituent assembly was put across early in 1934 in the Labour press by Horace Alexander,[229] and by George Lansbury in his book *My England*.[230] The parliamentary Labour Party decided, after the rejection of Attlee's draft report by the Joint Select Committee, not to raise the Indian proposal for a constituent assembly in parliament but to press for other radical amendments during the second reading.[231] Even if these amendments were defeated, however, they would vote for the bill at the third reading, because otherwise the extreme Right wing Conservatives under Churchill, who wanted to constitutional change at all, would win.[232] This approach did not satisfy Labour's Indian lobby. They were more successful next year after the Government of India Act had been passed, at the party conference in October 1935. This conference accepted a resolution from the floor, "the freely elected representatives of the Indian people shall formulate a settlement of the problems of India, in the interests of the Indian masses." Though the mover of the resolution had criticized Attlee's draft report of the previous year, Attlee, on behalf of the national exe-

[226]Labour Party, *Annual Report* 1933, p. 19.

[227]*Ibid.*, p. 146 (Lansbury's statement); National Trade Union Federation, Circular No. 1 (11 October 1933), issued by R.R. Bakhale (N.M.J.P. File 3, p. 6); Interview with Shri B. Shiva Rao, 23 December 1968.

[228]V.B. Karnik, *Indian Trade Unions: A Survey* (2nd revised ed., Bombay, 1966), p. 80.

[229]H. Alexander, "India," *New Statesman and Nation*, 14 April 1934, p. 540.

[230]G. Lansbury, *My England* (1934), p. 172 f.

[231]Labour Party, *Annual Report* 1935, p. 84 f.

[232]*Servant of India*, 29 November 1934, p. 557 f, 565, and *ibid.*, 6 December 1934, pp. 573, 597.

cutive did not oppose the resolution, possibly because the Government of India Act was quite the reverse in letter and spirit from his draft.[233]

A typical representative of the younger generation of promising labour politicians, Anthony Greenwood, said, in the course of a speech on the above-mentioned resolution, "In India we have got growing up a virile and determined socialist movement. One-third of the members of the Congress party today are convinced socialists and members of the Congress Socialist Party."[234] This appreciation of the Congress as a potentially Left wing organization was enormously increased by Jawaharlal's visits to Britain in the course of the next four months. Thanks to contacts suggested by Ellen Wilkinson, C.F. Andrews and Horace Alexander,[235] he was able to meet Leonard Woolf (Secretary of the Colonial Sub-committee of the Labour Party),[236] Sir Stafford Cripps, Harold Laski, George Catlin,[237] and other members of the Labour Left, some of them left wing Fabians, others semi-Marxists. Nehru was able to convince all of them unlike the Swarajist leaders eleven years earlier, that the only way to help the Indian masses was to support the Congress and other left forces. In the twenties British socialists had had doubts about the working-class and agrarian base of the national movement, and their rationalism had rebelled against Gandhi's philosophy. (It is not surprising that those close to Gandhiji in British labour circles were mainly Quakers and pacifists). These doubts about the difficulties of combining the grant of self-determination with the promotion of socialism in the colonies recurred as late as 1937 in Attlee's book, *The Labour Party in Perspective*.[238] Nehru's *Auto-*

[233]Labour Party, *Annual Report* 1935, pp. 84-6, 240 ff.

[234]*Ibid.,* p. 241.

[235]Ellen Wilkinson to J. Nehru, 5 November 1935 (J.L.N.P., Correspondence, Wilkinson file, No. 1); C.F. Andrews to J. Nehru, 3 November 1935 (J.L.-N.P., Correspondence, Andrews file); J. Nehru to H. Alexander, 17 January 1936 (Nehru Library, Horace Alexander Papers, Accession 73, p. 37).

[236]Woolf, n. 103, pp. 230-2.

[237]Vera Brittain (Mrs Catlin), *Envoy Extraordinary* (London, 1965), p. 12.

[238]C. Attlee, *The Labour Party in Perspective* (London, 1937), pp. 228-29, 239-40, 245-6. Dr Ram Manohar Lohia took offence at Attlee's book and implied that Attlee should have openly recognized the fact that the Congress was a socialist organization (R.M. Lohia, "Indian Problem Misunderstood," *A.I.C.C. Foreign Department Newsletter,* No. 26, 30 September 1937, A.I.C.C., F.D. 11 K.W. (ii) T.L. 716-H, 1936, p. 25.

biography, published shortly after his visit, dispelled these doubts for many people. Ellen Wilkinson wrote to him, "The ignorance of even good 'lefts' on India is abysmal. I think...your socialist summing up will give a great impetus to the interests of the socialists in England." She particularly appreciated his criticisms of Gandhiji's policy on the agrarian question in India.[239] To a wider socialist reading public Brailsford wrote of the book, "Here is a man who is one of us, by his culture, his humanity, and his scientific vision. He aims at doing what Englishmen in India have boasted that they did but could not do. He is struggling to bring the social organization that reflects this culture of ours to a very backward people. But we are the obstacle."[240] The judgment of these two people about the likely impact of the book was further confirmed when Reginald Reynolds, requesting a foreword fom Jawaharlal for his book *The White Sahibs in India* (1937), wrote, "Your stock is very high over here just now—the *Autobiography* and your personal visits having done incalculable service to the Indian cause at this end."[241]

Nehru appreciated the work done by the I.L.P-ers associated with Reynolds' "Friends of India" group. Nevertheless, his visit convinced him that the most effective organization was the India League, because it had "some prominent men in it like Harold Laski" and as a result "it (sc. was) definitely socialistic in outlook (sc. and) of the three it (sc. was) the only really political organization."[242] About Menon he wrote, "I met him for the first time. He is very able and energetic and is highly thought of in intellectual, journalistic, and left wing Labour circles. He has the virtues and failings of the intellectual. I was very favourably impressed by him."[243]

Menon was able in 1936 to activize Sir Stafford Cripps' Socialist League effectively for a Left wing approach on the Indian constitutional problem. The League passed a long resolution on India, in which it urged that the next Labour government should seek "an agreement with Indian opinion through the Congress and the organi-

[239]Ellen Wilkinson to J. Nehru, 22 March 1936, in J. Nehru, ed., *A Bunch of Old Letters,* p. 177.

[240]*New Statesman and Nation,* 9 May 1936, p. 730.

[241]Reginald Reynolds to J. Nehru, 23 June 1936 (J.L.N.P., Correspondence, Reynolds file, p. 7 f).

[242]J. Nehru to Rajendra Prasad, 20 November 1935 (Intercepted copy of letter, the original of which was passed on, in NAI, Home-Pol., 1936, File 1/2).

[243]*Ibid.*

zation of workers and peasants as to the time of summoning and the
methods of conducting the Constituent Assembly."[244] Cripps urged
the delegates to help the India League in its efforts. Menon also
noted that "the official Labour party (sc. appeared) to have become
a little more receptive to what (sc. was) happening in India" and he
explained "in a general way...in their official organ the main trend
of Indian development...."[245] Unlike the late twenties, when Nehru's
British contacts were mainly through the League Against Imperialism
(which was effectively controlled by Communists), his British allies
were now active members of the left of the Labour party itself. A
year after the success of the Congress in the election of 1937, Horace
Alexander wrote a pamphlet about the Congress governments for
the New Fabian Research Bureau.[246]

What were the ideological effects of these renewed contacts with
the British Labour movement on the Indian non-Communist Left?
Indian socialists mostly thought in Marxist terms, as their writings,
bibliographical preferences, and lectures indicate. Acharya Narendra
Deva was avowedly Marxist and his differences with Communists
arose over their extra-territorial loyalty and their claim that they
alone were the correct interpreters of Marxism.[247] Lecture topics
suggested by Jaiprakash Narain to Ram Manohar Lohia abound
in phrases like "Development of Socialist thought culminating in
Marx and Lenin," "Fascism and the decay of Capitalism,"
and on world politics, Palme Dutt's book *World Politics* was
recommended.[248] Only a few leaders of the Congress Socialist party
show a greater influence of British democratic socialist tradition
in their intellectual evolution, influence of the writings of Laski,

[244]Intercepted copy in NAI, Home-Pol., 1936, File 32/8.

[245]V.K. Krishna Menon to J. Nehru, 5 June 1936 (Intercepted copy passed
on, NAI, Home-Pol., 1936, File 32/8).

[246]John Parker, M.P. to the Secretary, A.I.C.C., File F.D. 40.1, 1936, (T.L.
No. 970 F.).

[247]For a general account see Hari Kishore Singh, "Rise and secession of the
Congress Socialist Party of India, 1934-48," in Raghavan Iyer, ed., *South Asian
Affairs,* No. 1 (St. Antony's Papers No. 8), London, 1960 *passim*. Also see Acharya Narendra Deva, "Problems of Socialist Unity," 9 April 1938, reprinted in
his *Socialism and the National Revolution* (Bombay, 1946), p. 116.

[248]Jaiprakash Narain to Ram Manohar Lohia, 13 February 1937, A.I.C.C.,
Misc. Category file, 21 (T.L. 660), 1936-1938, pp. 461-3; Jaiprakash Narain to
Ram Manohar Lohia, undated (probably early 1937). A.I.C.C., F.D. 40, I (T.L.
970 F), 1936.

Cole, Tawney, or J.A. Hobson. These were Asoka Mehta, B.P. Sihna (of Bihar), and M.R. Masani.[249]

Given the political realities in India—the absence in the middle thirties of constitutional instruments of mass democracy which could be used for social change—the attraction of revolutionary Marxism (and even its Leninist variant) was natural. Subhas Bose criticized the Congress Socialist Party for not being sufficiently revolutionary, because they supported the proposal for a constituent assembly, whereas Lenin had dissolved the constituent assembly after the Bolshevik revolution.[250] The renewed contacts with the British Left were being made with people like Laski, Cripps, Ellen Wilkinson and others, who were at that time either supporting the Popular Front and/or organizing the Left Book Club. Thus the contacts strengthened rather than weakened the Marxist trend in Indian socialism. The books of the Left Book Club were banned in India, but copies were secretly circulated.[251] Only shortage of funds made Jawaharlal unable to follow up an idea of simultaneously publishing some of these titles in India by Indian publishers in the freer atmosphere of the Congress regimes after 1937.[252] The only person who appears to have thought of the New Fabian Research Bureau as a model for serious socio-economic studies to aid the Congress governments was Dr V.K.R.V. Rao.[253]

[249]Hari Kishore Singh, n. 247, p. 129 f; B.P. Sinha, "Why am I a Congress Socialist," *Congress Socialist,* 10 March 1935, p. 5 f; articles by Asoka Mehta in *Congress Socialist,* Vol. I, No. 10 (February 1935) and *Ibid.,* 8 August 1936.

[250]Subhas Bose, "Congress Socialist Party" (first published 15 March 1935), reprinted in Bose, *The Indian Struggle* (Bombay, 1964), p. 384.

[251]Home Political files show that the government, instead of directly banning them, resorted to their prohibition under the Sea Customs Act. Jawaharlal Nehru got copies through private channels (J. Nehru to Sasadhar Sinha, letters in 1936, J.L.N.P. Sasadhar Sinha file). In our own family, in the thirties, copies of the Left Book Club edition of Sidney and Beatrice Webb's *Soviet Communism,* and John Strachey's *Theory and Practice of Socialism* were acquired (P.S.G.). There is evidence of many such unofficial pipelines.

[252]Proposal between J.L. Nehru and Victor Gollancz to start an Indian Left Book Club to publish in India "Left Literature," in NAI, Home-Pol. 1938, File 41/13).

[253]"Are you thinking of any Economic Research Bureau, something on the lines of the New Fabian Research Bureau?" wrote Dr. Rao to Nehru. (V.K.R.V. Rao to J. Nehru, 9 July 1937, J.L.N.P. Correspondence, V.K.R.V. Rao file, p. 12 f). There may have been other socialists influenced by Fabian models, but in the A.I.C.C. and Nehru correspondence this is the only example of a conscious imitation of the Fabian technique.

In Britain, Marxists who dissented from the Comintern were mainly to be found in the I.L.P., now fast dwindling in membership and influence.[254] On Stalin's purges and on some aspects of the Spanish Civil War they had perceived the truth,[255] whereas Labour party supporters of the Left Book Club tended to keep their eyes half shut about these uncomfortable facts.[256] The I.L.P. went further. It rejected the idea of an alliance of imperialist powers with the Soviet Union within the framework of the League of Nations, as that would strengthen the ruling classes, weaken the colonial liberation movements by tying them to the great power interests of Britain, France, and the Soviet Union.[257] They were able, as a result, to get the support of some colonial leftists, like the Ceylonese "Trotsky-ites" and Jomo Kenyatta.

Among the Indian Left there was a fair degree of indifference to the diplomatic strategies of the popular front in Britain. The general approach of Subhas Bose to the prospects of a war in Europe, and the amendments to foreign policy resolutions of the A.I.C.C. proposed by the Congress Socialists, indicate this. At Fenner Brockway's request M.R. Masani had sent Kamladevi Chattopadhyaya to represent the Congress-Socialist Party at the "International Congress against War and Imperialism," organized under the auspices of the "Fourth International."[258] (At the same time Krishna Menon,

[254]Dowse, n. 3, pp. 193, 202.

[255]H. Pelling, *The British Communist Party* (1958), p. 104; Fenner Brockway's report on his journey to Spain and the experience of the P.O.U.M., June 1937 (A.I.C.C., F.D. 7 (T.L. 906-E), 1936-1938); George Orwell, *Homage to Catalonia* (London, 1938), *passim.*

[256]Kingsley Martin did not publish Orwell's reports. See his justification of this action in *Editor* (London, 1968), p. 215 f. In fairness, it must be said that the *New Statesman and Nation* took a critical line on the purges, while advocating an anti-Fascist alliance with the U.S.S.R. But the left Book Club did appear to be a little too pro-Soviet and pro-Communist. (See controversy in the *New Statesman and Nation*, 10 April 1937, p. 587 (letter by Allen Skinner), *Ibid.*, 17 April 1937, p. 632 f, *Ibid.*, 24 April 1937, p. 672 f, *Ibid.*, 1 May 1937, p. 712, *Ibid.*, 8 May 1937, p. 768.

[257]F. Brockway to M.R. Masani, 25 May 1936 (copy sent to J. Nehru, J.L. N P., Correspondence, Brockway file, No. 4); F. Brockway to J. Nehru, 20 June 1938 (*ibid.*, No. 8).

[258]Brockway to Masani, 25 May 1936. (n. 257); *Congress Socialist*, 29 August 1936, p. 4. T.J.S. George, in his book *Krishna Menon*, mistakenly says that the Brussels congress of the International Bureau of Revolutionary Socialist Unity was "Communist-inspired" (n. 209, p. 109). It was Trotsky-ite. The official Comin-

on behalf of the Congress had supported Romain Rolland's committee against war and Fascism, which had the support of the Popular
Front socialists and Communists).[259]

The Soviet purges disturbed Indian socialists too, and we have
record of Masani, Yusuf Meherally and Kamladevi Chattopadhyaya
discussing with Jawaharlal the possibility of the growth of "narrow
nationalism" in Russia.[260] Lohia still considered that "Soviet Russia
(sic was) the only great power which (sic. had) definitely discarded
imperialism...and (sic. was) reconstructing society in the interests
of workers and peasants." Yet he admitted to John Dewey that
his vindication of Trotsky against Stalin's charges was correct and
that these made "it all the more imperative that without for a moment
forgetting that Soviet Russia (sic. was) the only great non-imperia-
list and non-Capitalist power we should make strenuous efforts
to help bring about the rule of normal law."[261]

Indian socialist reactions to the Soviet purges made Krishna
Menon write an anxious letter to Nehru about the possible spread
of Trotskyite views in India. Nehru replied that "there (sic was)
no such thing here," but also expressed forcibly his misgivings about
the purge trials.[262] A few months later, when Nehru visited Britain,
Menon was in charge of his itinerary,[263] and Nehru spoke at success-

---

ern line was to support the other Congress organized by Romain Rolland and
others (See note 259).

[259]J. Nehru to F. Brockway, 21 June 1936 (J.L.N.P., Correspondence, Brockway file, No. 7); George, n. 209, p. 109. Harry Pollitt, on behalf of the British
Communist Party, and following the line of the 7th Congress of the Comintern,
attended this Congress *(New Statesman and Nation,* 19 September 1936, p. 386
letter from Harry Pollitt); also see *Critic's* (Kingsley Martin) comments on the
moderation of the Congress and the Communists' reluctance to take an extreme
stand in the interests of unity (*ibid.,* 12 September 1936, p. 343).

[260]Mohan Kumaramangalam to J. Nehru, 17 October 1937 (J.L.N.P. Kumaramangalam file) refers to a conversation between himself, Nehru, Masani, Mehe-
ally, and Kamladevi on this.

[261]Ram Manohar Lohia to John Dewey, 26 March 1938. A.I.C.C., F.D. 7
T.L. No. 906 E), 1936-38.

[262]J. Nehru to V. K. Krishna Menon, 11 November 1937 (J.L.N.P., Corres-
ondence, Menon file, No. 1). The letter from Menon to Nehru is not available,
but from Nehru's reply its purport can be inferred. Also see a letter Menon
wrote to Masani, probably about this time, deploring the "Trotsky-ite streak"
and the "campaign to isolate Russia." (George, n. 209, p. 92).

[263]"My programme in England is being fixed up by Krishna Menon in con

ful demonstrations on Spain, and on "Peace and Empire" along with most of the Labour left and some Communists.[264] I.L.P.-ers like Brockway, Reginald Reynolds and others complained that they hardly had an opportunity of meeting Nehru, and that Communist pressure had prevented the I.L.P. being represented at the welcome meeting given to Nehru.[265] Brockway felt, with a lot of justification, that the claims of the I.L.P. as a fighter for India were being neglected, and told Nehru, "I want to warn you very earnestly against the clever intrigue which is going on to capture you for the Communist Party."[266]

Possibly, without sharing the Communist viewpoint, Nehru and Menon considered that their most important task was to harness the growing volume of Labour Party opinion in favour of a popular front and alliance with the Soviet Union also to the cause of the anti-imperialist movement in India. Therefore getting involved in I.L.P Communist controversies could weaken the larger purpose.[267] In the same letter to Menon in which Nehru had been critical of the Mascow trials, he had ended the letter with the words "They are more or less academic questions which do not affect our actions."[268] A logical expectation from the alliance that Nehru was encouraging and Menon was forging between the India League and the Popular Front labour-ites was that should Britain become involved in wa

---

sultation with others," J. Nehru to Agatha Harrison, 28 April 1938 (J.L.N.P Correspondence, Agatha Harrison file).

[264]The Peace and Empire rally was on 15-16 July 1938. Speakers were Nehru Cripps, Ellen Wilkinson, Paul Robeson, Wilfred Roberts, M.P., Reginald Sorensen, M.P., etc. The rally on Spain was at Trafalgar square on 17 July 1938 with a large number of speakers ranging from the Young Liberals' representative to Communists like J.B.S. Haldane (AICC, Misc. 31 (T.L. 1067-P 1938).

[265]Reynolds to Nehru, 21 June 1938; 30 June 1938; 31 July 1938 (J.L.N.P Correspondence, Reynolds file). The letters show that had Nehru been able to spare time to see Reynolds, he would have had an opportunity to meet George Padmore, the African leader, George Orwell, and others.

[266]Brockway to Nehru, 6 August 1938 (J.L.N.P.—Correspondence, Brockway file, No. 13).

[267]Menon had begun to feel the dwindling significance of the I.L.P. in 1936 He wrote, "The internal war between Trotskyites and Stalinists to capture the shade of a once militant socialist movement is pathetic." (Congress Socialist 25 April 1936, p. 25).

[268]Nehru to Menon, 11 November 1937 (n. 262).

with the Fascist powers, the popular front, while supporting the
British war effort, would agitate for Indian freedom. The Indian Left
would reciprocate by helping an anti-Fascist Britain in the war
effort.[269] The events of September 1939 upset the whole strategy.
With the British Communists not supporting the war because of the
Soviet-German pact, the popular front idea in Britain was damaged.
With the British government refusing to listen to the Congress
request for a statement of war aims as it affected India, the prospects of the Indian left supporting the war receded. Though Kingsley
Martin campaigned vehemently through his paper in September
and October 1939 for a forward-looking policy on the part of Britain,[270] by and large, British Labour forgot India for the time being
to fight the battle for Britain. Meanwhile the Indian left was getting
psychologically prepared to fight Britain even when she was at war
with Fascism. The seeds of 1942 and the Indian National Army
were sown. Thus, in the short run, the strategy of the India League
had failed. In the long run, however, the fact that the third Labour
government, unlike its predecessors, recognized Indian independence,
showed that the strategy of sustained work inside the Labour party,
carrying on and radicalizing the tradition started by Mrs. Besant,
was well worthwhile.

VI

Most Indian non-Communist Labour and socialist leaders, who have
been studied in these pages, were more influenced by the Russian
revolution and by varieties of Marxist thought than by the models
provided by the experience of the British labour movement. This
was not because they were enamoured of Bolshevik theory and prac-

[269]India League propaganda was careful to combine agitation for complete
independence with a pledge to "have the closest contacts...with all progressive
countries, including England, if she has shed her imperialism." (India League,
Indian National Congress—Foreign Policy Resolutions and Views, March 1937),
p. 10, kept in A.I.C.C., Misc. 31 (T.L. 1067-P), part 2, 1938).

[270]*New Statesman and Nation,* 30 September 1939, pp. 448-49. He suggested
bringing national leaders into the Viceroy's Council and making Nehru "Pre-
mier in fact if not in name." Also see *ibid.,* 14 October 1939, p. 510. When
finally Linlithgow gave an indefinite reply to the Congress, he wrote, "The
Viceroy's reply...has missed an opportunity that comes only once in a generation" (ibid., 21 October 1939, p. 537).

tice, or of the Comintern. Nationalism inoculated them against the latter, and their organizational methods were in fact more characteristic of mass democratic institutions than of a conspiratorial vanguard organized under "democratic centralism." What really prevented the British labour movement and these Indian leaders from being on the same wave length were the assumptions which guided the actions of the leadership of the Labour Party between 1921 and 1931. The belief in progress towards independence only by stages, the assumption that the timing of constitutional changes should be guided entirely by the exigencies of the British parliamentary situation, the acceptance of a bi-partisan approach in many fields of foreign and colonial policy,[271]—all these, however justified in the context of British politics, projected an image of benevolent patronage which no self-respecting Indian nationalist could stomach. The record of the first Labour government and the support given by the Labour Party to the Simon Commission strengthened this impression.

Many members at the policy-making level in the Labour Party took their duties as trustees for the Indian masses seriously. The sincerity of the intentions of people like Graham Pole, H.S.L. Polak, Lord Oliver, Wedgwood Benn, or Clement Attlee need not be questioned. The role of trustees, however, was to be played by having steady empirical adjustments within the framework of the existing imperial bureaucracy. To be sure, the two ex-I.C.S. officers who were advisers to the Labour Party—Sir John Maynard, an expert on the agrarian problem, and G.T. Garratt, the historian,[272] were men of a different cast of mind from the average Indian civilian. Yet because of their specialist knowledge of Indian social injustices they were unable to give unequivocal support to all aspects of the Congress agitation, especially in the twenties.[273]

To Indian nationalists, the bureaucracy was simply bolstering up a great deal of Indian social privilege and British capitalist strength, and so the gradualist approach of the Labour party policymakers did not appeal to most of them. They were attracted to those British labour leaders who had some Marxist or semi-Marxist tendencies,

[271]Fischer, n. 1, pp. 323-30 for a useful summing-up of these ideas.

[272]Woolf, n. 103, p. 223.

[273]See G.T. Garratt, *An Indian Commentary* (London, 1928), pp. 150 f, 155. The second edition of the book (1930) was more sympathetic to the Congress.

people who made a connexion, however crudely, between the misery of the Indian masses and the fact of Imperial rule. In the twenties these were people like George Lansbury, Fenner Brockway, and A.A. Purcell. In the late thirties intellectual mentors were to be found among the writers of the Left Book Club.

In this situation, in the twenties, co-operation with Communists did not appear reprehensible or dangerous to Indian leaders, especially as the only Indian M.P. in the House of Commons was the Communist Saklatvala. Pro-Indian British Labour leaders (again with the exception of Brockway and Purcell) would have preferred this not to happen, and instead they hoped to create replicas of the Fabian Society or the British Labour Party on Indian soil. In the heydays of Annie Besant's Home Rule movement this might have been possible. As the paths of the Labour Party leadership and the Indian National Congress diverged in the twenties, the chances became thinner.

The British labour influence was most successful in trade union organization and legislation. Despite the split of 1929 and despite the challenge of Royist and Communist leadership, the N.T.U.F. maintained its position in the thirties. The personal integrity of N.M. Joshi and their life long devotion to the cause of labour enabled them to win the respect of even those who found their political positions too moderate.

NEHRU AND SOCIALISM IN INDIA
1919-1939

P. C. JOSHI

"The *avatars* of today are great ideas which come to
reform the world. And the idea of the day is social equality.
Let us listen to it and become its instruments to transform
the world and make it a better place to live in."

Jawaharlal Nehru, 22 September 1928.

AN ANALYSIS OF Nehru's contribution to socialism requires first of
all a brief review of the various trends of thought and practice which
existed in India before the advent of Nehru on the political scene.

I

THE GENESIS OF THE SOCIALIST IDEA

India's conquest by the British led not only to the loss of her
political freedom; it also brought to light India's social and economic
inferiority to the West, thus posing a challenge to her total identity.
The failure of the 1857 Mutiny further confirmed what had already
been demonstrated earlier—the vast gulf which separated the van-
quished from the victor in terms of material and social progress.
India was defeated because she had lagged behind on account of
her grave internal weaknesses. The lesson of the Mutiny was not
lost on sensitive Indians nor on the Indian society as a whole. This
constituted the starting point of the new wave of Indian nationalism
during the period following the Mutiny.

The Mutineers had no clear conception of a new identity for India.
They only dreamed of expelling the British from India and restoring

the pre-British pattern of life. In contrast, underlying the new wave of Indian nationalism was the quest for a new national identity. The pioneers of this nationalism were not backward-looking like the Mutineers. They clearly perceived that the challenge of the West could not be met by merely working for the restoration of the pre-British society; it could be met only by understanding the basic causes of Indian backwardness and the secret of the dynamism of the Western societies. Thus they were inspired not by the idea of a return to the past; theirs was the vision of a new India which had shaken off the burden of the past and regenerated itself by emulating the Western countries. Many of them even believed that British rule had been a boon in as much as it had sown the seeds of change and progress in India which had been static and stagnant before the coming of the British. The future of India lay not in opposing the implantation of these seeds of progress. On the contrary, Indians must exert pressure on the British for accelerating the very processes which had been set into motion by them and which held the promise of Indian regeneration.

Even though the representatives of the new nationalism were more advanced in their social outlook as compared to the Mutineers, they reflected mainly the urges and aspirations of the narrow-minority of the Indian upper middle classes. As a result, gradually they were out of tune with the growing nationalist spirit and the urge for more effective resistance against alien rule which was fast developing in the country; they also failed to offer any programme which could capture the imagination of the vast masses which were gradually awakening to a new consciousness. Further, these nationalists had only imbibed the rational, liberal and utilitarian outlook of the first phase of the Western renaissance and their approach to the Indian problem was inspired as well as circumscribed by this outlook. The new intellectual currents in the West, specially the socialist critique of the ascendant capitalist order, remained foreign to their thought and consciousness.

Among the thinking sections in the West the early enchantment with the triumphs of the Industrial Revolution had already yielded place to a critical appraisal of the new industrial society that had replaced the mediaeval society. The critics observed that, far from putting an end to the exploitation of man by man, the new society had only replaced one type of exploitation by another. It was characterized by the relentless exploitation of the industrial proletariat which had emerged as a result of expropriation of peasants from land and artisans from their handicrafts. Thus having been deprived of control over its means of subsistence, the proletariat now was at the mercy of the new men of wealth, the capitalists, who had accumulated vast economic power resulting from technological innovations accompanying the Industrial Revolution. The growing confrontation between the new classes of haves and have-nots and the accumulation of wealth at one pole and of misery at another had provided the social background for the genesis of the socialist idea as well as the socialist movement in the Western countries.

New thinkers and reformers had appeared who advocated the necessity of the replacement of the capitalist society by a "just society," a socialist society. The most important of them was Marx who had emerged as the most formidable critic of the new industrial-capitalist society and as the philosopher of socialism. He had presented for the first time in 1848 a full statement of "scientific socialism" in his *Communist Manifesto*. This statement had been exercizing a tremendous impact on sensitive minds in different parts of the world. In the countries where the new industrial society had already taken firm root, this doctrine had become the inspirer of working class movements with more well-defined, anti-capitalist aims and with greater confidence in the justice and victory of their cause. In the other types of countries like Russia which were still far behind the West but were in the process of making a transition to the new type of society, this doctrine had led to sharp questioning whether it was at all desirable or necessary to go the West European way. Thus Russia had become the centre of a powerful revolutionary movement of workers and peasants committed to the goal of socialism. In 1917 occurred the Socialist Revolution and the capture of power by the socialist revolutionaries, under the leadership of Lenin who initiated the reconstruction of an economic and social order on non-capitalist lines.

In the third group of countries like India which were under colonial domination, these historical developments both in West Europe and Russia made a tremendous impact in two ways. The Russian Revolution first of all demonstrated that an oppressive and tyrannical regime could be overthrown by the common, ordinary people if they were awakened and organized. The Revolution also posed and answered another question which was most pertinent to the Indian situation. What path should a backward country follow in order to achieve development without the evils associated with it in West Europe? Is it at all desirable or necessary to follow the West European way or did there exist paths of development other than the capitalist? In the peculiar situation in which India was placed, the Russian example seemed to provide a unique possibility of rejecting Westernism without rejecting the concept of progress and therefore it made a great impact on the Indian elite. The challenge to the ideas of early nationalists was thus imminent from new trends both outside and inside the country.

Within the country, Gandhi emerged on the crest of the new urge for anti-British resistance and the wave of anti-Westernism. There was never perhaps a more complex and puzzling figure in Indian history who was at once both backward-looking and forward-looking and the creator as well as the container of a vast revolutionary ferment. It was the merit of Gandhi that he evolved a form of resistance against the British which transgressed the limits of constitutionalism accepted by the early nationalists and which drew vast millions into the fold of the freedom struggle. He brought about a shift in the social base of the nationalist movement from the urban middle classes to the village-dwelling peasantry and in the focus of the nationalist cause from the richer classes to the *Daridranarayan*.

In sharp contrast to the early nationalists, an outstanding feature of Gandhi's political personality was his ability to communicate with the common people of India in a language which was intelligible to them. He interpreted new social goals and aims to them through the categories and concepts of traditional culture and attacked the forces of conservatism in Indian (specially Hindu) society not on the basis of the concepts and ideas imported from the West but on the basis of the fundamental principles of Indian tradition itself. But where Gandhi was at once revolutionary as well as conservative was in his anti-Westernism. He was both more patriotic and revolutionary when he questioned the blind craze of the Indian elite for the westernization of India and when he drew pointed attention to the idolatory of wealth, the exploitation and misery of the masses, and the "alienation" that had followed the triumph of capitalism in the West. He warned that if India followed the West European ideal of economic progress and its path of industrialization, the consequences would be much worse in India. In Gandhi's view, it was bound to result in greater misery to the masses than before. But when he came to the solution of the Indian problem, he advocated a return to the Indian way. He upheld the perspective of the reconstruction of Indian society not on Western lines as the early nationalists were advocating nor on the basis of blind attachment to past tradition as the revivalists were advocating but on the basis of the reformation of the Indian tradition as required by the changing times.

Gandhi recognized that private property was at the root of exploitation of the masses and the inequality that prevailed in Indian society but he did not agree with the socialist method of intensification of class conflict and socialization of private property for removing this inequality; instead he offered the concept of "trusteeship" as the better method of resolving class conflict without class hatred and violence.

This historical background of Indian nationalism—its main trends and currents—is necessary for an appropriate appraisal of Nehru's contribution to socialism during 1919-39. It may be said that Nehru's thinking on socialism evolved and crystallized into a pattern in the course of his confrontation with West-oriented nationalists, Gandhi and the Gandhites, Hindu and Muslim revivalists and, finally, the Indian socialists. From the early nationalists Nehru imbibed the modernization ideal—the concept of progress and the passion for science and technology. But he rejected their advocacy of the West European path of development. From Gandhi he imbibed the passion for uplift of the *Daridranarayan* and his critique of the acquisitive and competitive way of life characteristic of western capitalism but he rejected Gandhi's anti-Westernism. He contributed socialism as a synthetic concept which sought to combine the vital impulsions of Gandhian thought viz. the concern for the masses and for a moral and ethical approach to life into the modernization ideal itself. Nehru's socialism therefore was the fruit of synthesizing of various trends of thought at the level of the ideal. In its synthetic quality lay its main appeal.

II

In this background Nehru's contribution to socialism in India can be analyzed under three heads: (1) the socialist vision, (2) the socialist model, and (3) the socialist mobilization.

THE SOCIALIST VISION

The distinctive contribution of Jawaharlal Nehru lay in imparting *a socialist vision* to the Indian nationalist movement and in presenting an integrated view of the struggle for national liberation on the one hand and the fight for social and economic emancipation on the other. As Nehru himself observed, "he was by no means a pioneer in the socialist field in India."[1] Indeed, much before Nehru proclaimed his commitment to socialism, there were individual socialists and socialist groups in India who "had gone ahead blazing a trail"; they had been organizing youth leagues and forming trade unions and *Kisan Sabhas* as part of the broad aim of building up a socialist movement in India. One of the most important features of the political scene, however, was the cleavage between the nationalists and the socialists The former, organized in the Indian National Congress were wedded to only one goal: that of freedom from foreign rule. They regarded the consideration of any other goal as divisive and disruptive for a united struggle for freedom. The socialists, on the other hand, did not deny in principle the primacy of the struggle for political independence; but they were inclined to look with suspicion on a nationalist movement the leadership of which, instead of being wedded to the goal of emancipation of the oppressed and the exploited, had the vision of reproducing in India either a western-type of capitalist society or a reformed model of the traditional society. Again, the socialists were inclined to distrust a nationalist leadership which tried to keep the workers and the peasants on the fringes of the national movement, which tended to render the nationalist organization merely as a pressure group for extracting concessions from the British rather than a broad and militant movement for total national liberation and as a precursor to a social and economic revolution. Some socialists went so far as to characterize the nationalist movement led by the Congress as totally "reactionary" and to equate Indian nationalism with Fascism. (M.N. Roy asserted in unmistakable terms that "Indian nationalism...is identical with Fascism"). Others did not go so far but even then characterized the movement as a "reformist" movement with a dual character, progressive in so far as it opposed the British but reactionary in so far as it sought to

[1]Dorothy Norman, *Nehru: The First Sixty Years* (Bombay 1965), Vol. I, p. 139.

resist the broadening of the social base of this movement or the interpretation of political freedom in terms of the economic and social emancipation of the masses.[2]

In short, there was no meeting point of these two currents of nationalist struggle for freedom and of the socialist struggle for economic and social emancipation. At times, the two currents came into sharp clash with each other with harmful consequences for both. It was Gandhi who for the first time tried to provide a bridge between the two currents by linking up the cause of *Swarajya* with the cause of the *Daridranarayan*. But Gandhi spoke a language unintelligible to the socialists who failed to distinguish between the substance of the Gandhian approach and the form in which it was presented by Gandhi. Another reason for the lack of any communication between Gandhi and the socialists was that Gandhi failed to provide either a rational, philosophical basis for his approach, or a revolutionary programme concretizing the conception of the unity of *Swarajya* and the emancipation of the *Daridranarayan*. Thus, far from emerging as a unifier, Gandhi continued to be an enigma and an irritant for the socialists. Some socialists saw in him a "Jonah of the Indian revolution" who was the "mascot of the bourgeosie"[3] and some others regarded him as a "mediaeval fascist."[4] Thus the schism between nationalism and socialism remained.

It was the unique contribution of Nehru to provide a bridge between these two processes of nationalism and socialism. He questioned the underlying premises of the prevailing ideas both of the old nationalists and the socialists and presented a rational view of the interdependence of national and class factors in the ferment which had been gathering in India specially after the entry of Gandhi on the political scene. In this way he sought to provide a basis for the unification of the two streams of *national* struggle for political freedom and the *mass* struggle for social and economic freedom.[5]

Nehru explained how both the national ferment and the class ferment originated from common sources. The national ferment originated on the basis of the fundamental conflict between the Indian

[2]Revolutionary Movement in the Colonies and Semi-Colonies—*Thesis Adopted by the Sixth Congress of the Communist International 1928*, pp. 25-8.

[3]Rajni Palme Dutt, *India Today and Tomorrow* (New Delhi, 1955), p. 156.

[4]M.N. Roy, *Jawaharlal Nehru* (Bombay, 1945), pp. 9-16.

[5]Jawaharlal Nehru, *India's Freedom* (London, 1962), pp. 20-34.

national interest and the British colonial interest. But an inseparable part of the colonial structure was the retrograde and oppressive economic structure, particularly the feudalistic land system which crushed the masses. In fact, even if the British left India and the alien government was replaced by a native government, this would only mean a change of rulers without a change in the basic condition of the masses so long as there was no change in the economic structure existing in India. The national struggle for political freedom was, therefore, by the very nature of objective circumstances developing also into a struggle of the masses against the oppressive economic and social system buttressed by British rule. In other words, the nationalist movement which originally started merely as an anti-British movement dominated by the upper classes was gradually getting transformed by the very logic of events, into a mass movement against both foreign and indigenous vested interests.

Nehru perceived very clearly what other socialists could not—a qualitative change in the very character and social basis of the nationalist movement. Nehru was also ahead of the socialists in having a clear view of the revolutionary role which Gandhi had played in this, despite the limitations of his ideology. He admitted that:

> ...Gandhi, functioning in the nationalist plane, does not think in terms of the conflict of classes, and tries to compose their differences. But the action he has indulged in and taught the people has inevitably raised mass consciousness tremendously and made social issues vital. And his insistence on raising the masses at the cost, wherever necessary, of vested interests has given a strong orientation to the national movement in favour of the masses.[6]

In Nehru's view, "in this respect (of linking up *Swarajya* with the cause of the masses) Gandhi was always ahead of the nationalist movement."[7] Far from being an enemy, as the socialists imagined, of the socialist movement, he was its most powerful, even if unconscious, ally. As a result of his efforts and of the pressure of events in India and the world, "Indian nationalism had been powerfully pushed towards social changes and today it hovers, somewhat

[6]*Ibid.*, pp. 66-8.
[7]*Ibid.*, p. 67.

undecided, on the brink of a social ideology." Nehru thought that it would be sheer blindness if the socialists kept harping on the *reformist* and *bourgeois* character of the national movement instead of trying to accelerate and strengthen the emerging mass orientation of the nationalist movement favourable to socialism.[8] It was for the socialists to provide a new "social ideology" and a new vision the need of which had arisen within the national movement itself.

In Nehru's view, this ideology can only be a socialist ideology and the vision can only be that of a "socialist" India. Nehru thus rejects a capitalist perspective for India.[9] This view of Nehru was based not only on his value-preference, that is to say, his preference for socialism as the realization of a just and humane society; he derived support for this view also from his interpretation of the trend of historical development itself. In Nehru's concept of socialism are blended the two conceptions of socialism (*i*) as a utopia, and (*ii*) as an "objective necessity" dictated by the very logic of economic and social development in the world. His thinking in this respect bears the distinct impress of three important trends of western thought—humanism, Utopian socialism and Marxian "scientific socialism."[10] In the typical Utopian and humanist strain, he shows his preference for a society in which man is not exploited by man, in which wealth is for man and not man for wealth and in which the acquisitive and competitive spirit is replaced by the spirit of service and co-operation. At the same time in conformity with the ideas of scientific socialism, he considers the abolition of private property in the means of production or the abolition of classes as a necessary condition for a socialist society. On this point he is categorical as is shown by his polemical dialogue with Gandhi. He criticizes the "muddled humanitarianism" of those who show great concern for the masses and even call themselves socialists but are scared at the very mention of any attack on private property. Where Nehru is not very categorical is on the question of the method and means of achieving socialism in the sense of abolition of classes. He does not appear inclined to accept the "dictatorship of the proletariat" as a necessary part of socialism or the transition to socialism.[11]

[8]Dorothy Norman, n. 1, pp. 175 and 281-2.

[9]*Ibid.*, pp. 177-82.

[10]*Ibid.*, pp. 371-83.

[11]*Ibid.*, pp. 450-51 and 128-37

He is inclined to regard such "dictatorship" only as a Russian phenomenon determined by conditions prevailing there and not as a universal necessity. On this question, Nehru seems to lean more towards the Fabian view of socialism than towards the classical view of Marx or Lenin.

It is necessary to emphazise that Nehru neither propounded nor conformed to any single socialist theory or doctrine. His conception of socialism was synthetic to the point of being eclectic; it is best to characterize it therefore as a *vision* which is as much socialist as humanist. The key elements of this vision, are: (1) A deep sympathy for the underdog and a passion for equality between man and man;[12] (2) the idea that "the economic system should be based on a humane outlook and must not sacrifice man for money"; that "it is for the benefit of the labourer who works on it that the industry must be run and for the peasant that land must produce food";[13] (3) the view that private property in the means of production resulting in exploitation of one class by another is incompatible with (1) and (2) and therefore it must give way to social ownership of the means of production; (4) the view that socialism should not just be equated with social ownership of property but that it should imply a new relation between man and man, a vast "psychological transformation" involving a new spirit of service and co-operation in place of the spirit of acquisition and self-aggrandisement.[14]

Nehru's thinking implies a clear distinction between the universalistic *content* of socialism which should guide socialists in all countries and the specific *form* of socialism which would differ from country to country in accordance with the economic, social, cultural, and political conditions of each country. What Nehru seems to regard as universal is the socialist vision and not any particular economic and political form evolved by any country, or for that matter, the form evolved by the Russians in the context of their own conditions.[15] In a message to Indian socialists in December 1936, Nehru posed two questions which required thinking by those who were interested in socialism in India. "One is how to apply this (socialist approach) to the Indian conditions. The other is how to

[12]*Ibid.*, p. 450.
[13]*Ibid.*, p. 203.
[14]*Ibid.*, pp. 433-4.
[15]*Ibid.*, pp. 626-7 and 450-1.

speak of socialism in the language of India."[16] In another context, he emphasized that socialists should avoid the tendency to apply the concepts of European socialism or Russian communism blindfold in India without due regard to facts and conditions.

In concrete terms he explained that socialists and communists in India are nurtured on literature dealing with Europe where the national factor was absent and the class factor was relevant mainly in relation to industrial workers. But "in India, nationalism and rural economy were the dominating considerations and European socialism seldom deals with these."[17] Even in Russia the national factor was absent and though pre-war Russian conditions were a much nearer approach to India, there was a vast difference between the two in many respects. Indian socialism therefore could never be a carbon-copy of Russian socialism; it has to be suited to Indian conditions. What should then be the form or model of socialism for India?

Here Nehru makes a distinction between a short-term programme on the basis of which the Indian National Congress should try to mobilize the masses for the national movement and a long-term model of socialism which could be put into effect only after the achievement of freedom. It is Nehru's thinking on the long-term model of socialism which is of interest for us in this paper.

THE SOCIALIST MODEL

Nehru's ideas on the socialist model can be discussed under three heads: (1) the economic model of socialism, (2) the political model, and (3) the ideological model of socialism.

In this connection, it must be emphasized that from Nehru's writings and speeches covering the period 1919-1939, we have a clearer idea of Nehru's socialist vision than of his view of the socialist model appropriate to Indian conditions. In fact, stimulus to thinking on the economic model of socialism was provided by the formation of the National Planning Committee towards the end of 1938 under the chairmanship of Nehru himself. Thus before 1938, one finds the gradual crystallization of a *general view* rather

[16]Pattabhi Sitaramayya, *The History of the Indian National Congress* (Bombay, 1947), Vol. II, p. 15.

[17]Dorothy Norman, n. 1, pp. 282-3.

than a concrete outline of the economic model. This general view itself is of considerable significance in as much as it represents an attempt to examine the pre-Gandhi and the Gandhian approach to the Indian economic problem and to present a new perspective on Indian economic development.

Economic Form of Socialism

Nehru first traces the genesis of the Indian economic problem—the poverty and backwardness of India—to the economic domination of Britain which reduced India into a producer of raw materials and a market for its industrial goods. During the same period when Britain advanced to the position of the leading industrial country of the world, India underwent a process of "passive industrialization" which resulted in the destruction of her handicrafts, the over-pressure of population on land and the deliberate thwarting of her industrial development.[18] Nehru felt that the earlier nationalists had exaggerated the beneficial influence and underplayed the depressive effects of the British rule.[19] The solution of the Indian economic problem was thus incompatible with the continuance of British rule, even if the British agreed to grant some measure of political freedom to India within the framework of the Empire. More importantly, as and when India regained freedom, she would have to catch up fast in order to overcome this legacy of mass poverty and backwardness left by the British. The only solution for this lay in utilizing modern science and technology for accelerating the progress of industrialization on which depended also the prospects of agricultural development.

Here Nehru made a sharp break from the two fundamental tenets of the Gandhian economic ideology—the rejection of modern economic progress along with scientific technology and the emphasis on small industry as the way out for India. Nehru argued that the evils of the Western industrial society did not emanate from industrialism or the big machine which were only tools available to man "to be used for good or evil"; the evils were a "necessary consequence of industrial development on *capitalist* lines."[20] In order to avoid these evils it was not industrialism which had to be given up but industrial

[18]*Ibid.*, p. 310.
[19]*Ibid.*, Vol. II, pp. 544-56.
[20]*Ibid.*, pp. 156-7.

progress had to be planned on socialist lines. Nehru attacked the idealization of the "simple peasant life" by Gandhi and argued that it represented a "throw-back into primitiveness" at the very time when modern civilization with its scientific and technological advance had created the grand prospects of providing freedom from want and hunger to the masses who had suffered for long. Nehru characterized Gandhi's emphasis on the *Khadi* movement and small hand-operated industry as "an intensification of individualism in production" and as "a throwback to the pre-industrial age." In his view, these could not be taken seriously for the solution of any vital present day problem and may produce a mentality which may become an obstacle to growth in the right direction. At the same time, he maintained that small industry should remain an important part of the industrialization programme in order to provide relief and employment to the people for the period of transition till employment in modern industry becomes available on a large scale. Modern industrialization and the fullest utilization of science and modern technology is therefore an inseparable part of the economic perspective underlined by Nehru for India.

What is Nehru's view of the institutional framework for economic development? First of all, in contrast to the early nationalists, Nehru rules out the capitalist form as unsuitable for Indian conditions and pleads for the adoption of the socialist form of development. He argues that capitalism is caught in a crisis even in the industrially developed countries and it is also threatened by the "upheaval of the weak and the oppressed."[21] There is no doubt that "capitalism is a young and growing force in the East." But in the East also "even before capitalism had established itself, other forces inimical to it, have risen to challenge it. And it is obvious that if capitalism collapses in Europe and America, it cannot survive in Asia."[22] Nehru also speaks in glowing terms of the success of the socialist experiment in the Soviet Union. But on the question of the nature of the socialist economic form in India, Nehru offers only general statements up to 1938, favouring social ownership of industry and peasant ownership in land followed by cooperativization. During the pre-1938 period, his thinking is not only general but also shows a great fascination for the socialist form adopted by Russia

21*Ibid.,* pp. 262-3.
22*Ibid.,* p. 314.

for its economic development. His ideas on this question, however, crystallized into a definite pattern in the course of his discussions with the members of the National Planning Committee. As a result of these deliberations, he acquired a better perception of the Indian conditions and began to think in terms, not of immediate adoption of the socialist form, but of a pattern of development which would "inevitably lead us towards establishing some of the fundamentals of the socialist structure."[23] Here one can see in an embryonic form the conception of a mixed economy as the Indian model of transition to socialism which later constituted the hard core of the Five Year Plans evolved under the guidance of Nehru after the advent of freedom. State ownership of defence and the key industries and public utilities, the utilization of private enterprise in industry but the regulation of its scope and activity in the over-all national interest, abolition of landlordism and introduction of peasant farming in small holdings as a transitional measure leading to co-operatives, a socialized system of credit and an overall planning of the national economy to ensure both justice as well as efficient utilization of national resources—these were the key elements of the Indian economic model as it took a more definite shape through the work of the National Planning Committee. Nehru explains that this was not socialism in its pure form but this form would lead the country in the direction of socialism in as much as "it was limiting the acquisitive factor in society, removing many of the barriers to growth and thus leading to a rapidly expanding socialist structure." Further, "it was based on planning for the benefit of the common man, raising his standard greatly, giving him opportunities of growth and releasing an enormous amount of talent and capacity."[24]

Political Form of Socialism

On the question of the political form of socialism, again, there are certain general observations available from Nehru rather than an exposition of any political theory or doctrine. These observations, however, give a fairly clear idea of his view of the political structure associated with socialist transformation in India. He is categorical and firm in his view that India should have a democratic state structure with maximum regard for democratic freedoms—freedom of

[23]*Ibid.*, p. 693.
[24]*Ibid.*, pp. 693-4.

speech and organization and individual liberty. Indian socialist transformation, he suggests, should be based on a wide consent of different sections of Indian society and even on "a large measure of cooperation of some at least of the groups who were normally opposed to socialist doctrine." He is hopeful that a free national government which is both strong and popular would be capable of introducing fundamental changes in the social and economic structure. He is, therefore, keen to avoid the path of regimentation and concentration of power for bringing about basic changes. At the same time, he clarifies that democracy should not provide a sanction for the status quo and if social change through the method of consent was not possible on account of the resistance of the vested interests, the use of coercion in the limited context should not be ruled out. Nehru thus seems committed to explore the possibility of socialist transformation through a democratic political structure; his view therefore stands in sharp contrast to the classical view which stresses the necessity of "dictatorship of the proletariat" as the political form inevitable for transition to socialism.

Ideology of Socialism

Nehru repeatedly emphasized that socialism is not just an economic doctrine but a philosophy of life which involved a profound "change in habits, instincts, values and motivations." He also posed the problem of giving the socialist ideology an Indian form so as to make it meaningful to the common people of India. He was aware of the fact that European socialism originated in an entirely different social context and it addressed itself to the industrial proletariat. In India, on the other hand, the national factor was of great significance and the bulk of the population lived in villages and was illiterate. In this context, he stressed the need of "speaking of socialism in the language of India," through the idiom and categories which were current coin among Indian people. What would be the ingredients of this Indian socialist ideology and the motivational system of Indian socialism in the context of India's past traditions and present requirements? Even though Nehru was perhaps the first among Indian socialists to have realized the need of an Indian ideological form of socialism, he did not devote much thought to it and did not make any appreciable contribution to the development of such an ideology.

SOCIALIST MOBILIZATION

What is the social force for the realization of socialism and for mass mobilization behind a socialist programme? On this question, there occurred a sharp divergence and cleavage between Nehru and other socialists. E.M.S. Namboodiripad has aptly summed up that "the essence of that conflict (between Nehru and other socialists) consisted in their different approaches to the question of the political instrument through which the struggle for socialism is to be conducted."[25] So far as Nehru was concerned, he believed that the Congress could serve as the instrument of achieving both national freedom and socialism.[26] In his Presidential address to the All-India Trade Union Congress at Nagpur as early as in 1929, Nehru expressed the view that "...bourgeois as the outlook of the National Congress was, it did represent the only effective revolutionary force in the country. As such, labour ought to help it and cooperate with it and influence it, keeping, however, its own identity and ideology distinct and intact." Nehru hoped that "the course of events and the participation in direct action would inevitably drive the Congress to a more radical ideology and to face social and economic issues." He noted that "the development of the Congress during recent years has been in the direction of the peasant and the village. If this development continued, it might in course of time become a vast peasant organization, or at any rate an organization in which the peasant element predominated."

Thus Nehru did not contemplate the building up of a socialist organization independent of the Congress. In the early stages of his political life, his objective was to provide a link between the forces of nationalism as represented by the Congress and the forces of socialism as represented by socialist groups and mass organizations existing outside the Congress. He hoped that as a result of the unification of these two forces "the National Congress (would) become more socialistic and proletarian and organized labour (would) join the nationalist struggle."

In the later stages, he saw the possibility of pushing forward the Congress itself in the direction of socialism. He observed that after

[25]E.M.S. Namboodiripad, *Economics and Politics of India's Socialist Pattern* (Delhi, 1966), p. 56.
[26]Dorothy Norman, n. 1, p. 176.

the mass awakening brought about by Gandhi, the Congress was becoming more and more the vehicle both of the *national* urge for political independence and the *proletarian* urge for social change. The Congress had become in this way "the most effective and radical organization in the country and it is easier to work great changes in the mass mentality through it rather than through any other means." It was not necessary therefore to think of any other organization for the goal of socialism. Nehru was not unaware of the influence exercized by vested interests and by those indifferent and hostile to socialism in the Congress organization. He believed, however, that with greater influence exercised by the masses on the Congress, and with the increasing participation of the socialists in the affairs of the Congress, the resistance to the socialist orientation of Congress programme and activities could be neutralized. From the Presidential platform he pleaded for more vigorous and active organization of the workers and peasants, and affiliation of their organizations with the Congress so as to counter the middle class domination of the Congress leadership.[27] In short, Nehru was firmly committed to the role of the National Congress itself as the main instrument of socialist transformation in India.

III

CONCLUSION

The foregoing pages present a broad outline of Nehru's contribution to socialism in India during 1919-39. This is the period which is noteworthy for the rise and maturation of Nehru as a socialist and, at the same, as the most outstanding leader of the national movement, next only to Gandhi. We have here a glimpse of the socialism of Nehru the nationalist fighter, rather than of Nehru the ruler or nation-builder. This explains the qualities of dynamism and receptivity in Nehru's thinking during this period which are not found in any period later. These qualities distinguished Nehru from other nationalist leaders who were far less receptive to the new currents of thought and far more rooted in a conservative outlook. What distinguished Nehru from fellow socialists, however, was the spirit

[27]*Ibid.*, pp. 469-70.

of questioning some of the basic elements of classical socialist ideology in the light of Indian realities.

In the history of socialism in India, the period intervening between
the two World Wars will always be treated as crucial. It was then
that the socialist idea gained a foothold in the Indian soil and the
conception of a new India was gradually enlarged and transformed
in the mind of the elite into the vision of a socialist India. It is also
during this period that the intellectual framework of Indian socialism
was evolved in a rudimentary form. In bringing about this turn in
Indian nationalism, an outstanding role was played by Jawaharlal
Nehru.

The socialist model for India was a creative concept which represented a departure from the classical capitalism of the West and
classical socialism of Russia. Oscar Lange, the Polish Marxist scholar,
has aptly characterized it as the conception of the Third Way—of
a "national revolutionary pattern" which is non-classical in its
character and content.

This era will be regarded as important from another point of
view in as much as the seed of the basic weakness of the non-classical
conception of socialism was also sown during this period which
has stubbornly persisted to this day.

The first weakness was that the socialist vision remained broadly
confined to the educated elite as their shining ideal; it was not given
an ideological or institutional form so as to ensure the identification
and involvement of the masses. The elite could not communicate
this ideal to them in a language understood by them, as Gandhi
conveyed his ideas through living symbols and categories. Nor could
this socialist elite evolve a style of work and a way of life (as Gandhi
did) which could bring it into intimate touch and communication
with the common people. The result was that the idea which stirred
the elite was not internalized as part of the consciousness of the
masses.

The other weakness, related to the first, was the apathy of Nehru
and his like-minded followers to the painstaking work of socialist
organization specially at the grass roots. Nehru even during this
period, when he was a fighter rather than a ruler, was in the habit
of functioning as an inspired individual, the hero of the masses,
rather than their organizer or as an educator of socialist cadres
from among the masses. The contrast with Gandhi is so evident

even in this sphere. Nehru set the example even for other individuals subscribing to his ideas who did not possess his "charisma" but who also abstained from doing the humdrum spadework for socialism.

These weaknesses would have mattered less had the socialists of the classical tradition realized the revolutionary potential of the non-classical approach and strengthened it by supplying the necessary communication with the masses and the force of socialist organization. But this did not happen as these socialists looked at Nehru through the prism of classical socialism and thus saw only his limitations and not his possibilities.

Thus occurred the chronic schism between idea and organization the beginnings of which can be seen even during this eventful period for Indian socialism. Fired by a "grand idea," Nehru tirelessly carried on a national campaign for socialism and evoked wide response for a change in the socialist direction. But he did not create the supporting socialist organization. So the response remained only amorphous and diffused and could not assume any solid, organized shape. On the other hand, other socialists who had more intimate links with some sections of the masses and an independent socialist organization failed to transform the socialist idea from an intellectual postulate into a mobilizing force. On account of a doctrinaire bias, their socialism lacked an emotive power and a national appeal. The consequences of this gap between idea and organization and between different trends of socialism had serious repercussions not only during this period but in the entire history of Indian socialism in the subsequent period.

BOOKS CONSULTED

Pattabhi Sitaramayya, *The History of the Indian National Congress*, Vol. I (Madras, 1935) and Vol. II (Bombay, 1947).

Dorothy Norman, *Nehru : The First Sixty Years*, Vol. I and II (Bombay, 1965).

G.D. Overstreet and M. Windmiller, *Communism in India* (Bombay, 1960).

Michael Brecher, *Nehru : A Political Biography* (London, 1959).

Jawaharlal Nehru, *The Discovery of India* (Calcutta, 1956).

M.N. Roy, *Jawaharlal Nehru* (Bombay, 1945).

Revolutionary Movement in the Colonies and Semi-Colonies—*Thesis Adopted by the Sixth Congress of the Communist International, 1928.*

Rajni Palme Dutt, *India Today and Tomorrow* (New Delhi, 1955).

E.M.S. Namboodiripad, *Economics and Politics of India's Socialist Pattern* (Delhi, 1966).

G.D.H. Cole, *Socialism in Evolution* (London, 1938).

K.S. Shelvankar, *The Problem of India* (London, 1940).

T.B. Bottomore and M. Rubel, *Karl Marx: Selected Writings of Sociology and Social Philosophy* (London, 1963).

N.K. Bose, *Selections from Gandhi* (Ahmedabad, 1948).

Jawaharlal Nehru, *India's Freedom* (London, 1962).

Jawaharlal Nehru, *A Bunch of Old Letters* (New York, 1960).

Bipan Chandra, *The Rise and Growth of Economic Nationalism in India* (New Delhi, 1966).

K.P. Karunakaran, *Continuity and Change in Indian Politics* (Delhi, 1964).

R.H. Tawney, *Religion and the Rise of Capitalism* (London, 1948).

P.C. Joshi, ed., *Rebellion 1857: A Symposium* (New Delhi, 1957).

B.B. Misra, *The Indian Middle Classes* (London, 1961).

Irfan Habib, "Marxist Interpretation", *Seminar* Past and Present, 1962.

N.V. Sovani, "Ranade's Model of the Indian Economy," *Artha Vignan,* Vol. IV, 1962.

K.M. Panikkar, *The Foundations of Modern India* (London, 1963).

Raymond Aron, *Industrial Society* (London, 1967).

D.P. Mookerji, *Modern Indian Culture* (Bombay, 1942).

D.P. Mookerji, *Diversities* (New Delhi, 1958).

SOCIALISM AND FOREIGN POLICY THINKING, 1919-1939

BIMAL PRASAD

As IS WELL known, the Russian Revolution (1917) elicited much favourable comment in India, particularly in the columns of the leading newspapers and periodicals. This naturally led to an increased awareness of socialism which was not completely unknown in India before, and to the growth of a feeling of admiration for the Soviet Union as the first Socialist State in the world. Such awareness and feeling received a further fillip from the foundation of the All-India Trade Union Congress in 1920 and the Communist Party of India in 1925. Nevertheless, until 1927, Socialism did not occupy any significant place—in fact, any place, in the mainstream of our nation's thoughts on foreign policy.

This statement can best be tested by a reference to the attitude of the leaders of the Indian National Congress towards the Soviet Union before 1927, for it does not seem unfair to imagine that specially during those days foreign policy thinking influenced by Socialism would include admiration for the Soviet Union, for obvious reasons. At the outset it may be noted that at no time was there any support for the British policy towards the Soviet Union. In 1920, Gandhi spoke of the futility of attempting to crush Bolshevism in Russia by force of arms,[1] thus implying a criticism of the Western policy at the time. Gandhi also refused point blank to support the British contention that the Soviet Union had aggressive designs against India. "I have never believed in the Bolshevik menace," he wrote in 1921.[2] This was a significant statement in the context of the Afghan war and the British propaganda that behind Afghanistan lay the Soviet Union with its aggressive designs upon India.

[1] *Young India* (Ahmedabad), 10 March 1920.
[2] *Ibid.*, 4 May 1921.

But such statements were in line with the old Congress tradition of not believing in any menace from Russia, coming down from the nineteenth century when the Tsars ruled over that country, and should not be considered relevant for the present discussion.

On the other hand, there was occasional criticism of the Soviet regime during this period, for its reliance on violent means. This was natural, in view of the stress on non-violence, which had become a recurrent theme of the speeches of the Congress leaders at that time. Thus C.R. Das, in his presidential address of 1922, remarked that the shape which the Russian Revolution had then assumed was due to the attempt to force Marxian doctrines and dogmas on the unwilling genius of Russia. "Violence," he emphasized, "will again fail. If I have read the situation accurately, I expect a counter revolution. The soul of Russia must struggle to free herself from the socialism of Karl Marx. It may be an independent move-ment, or it may be that the present movement contains within itself the power of working out that freedom."[3]

The purpose behind this observation was not to run down the Soviet regime, but to make a point in support of Gandhi's insistence on non-violent means for achieving India's independence. Never-theless, it can be taken as broadly indicative of the thinking of the top Indian leadership regarding the Soviet Union. In 1924, while referring to the Soviet Union, Gandhi left no doubt about his dislike of the new political system. "I am yet ignorant," he said, "of what exactly Bolshevism is, I have not been able to study it. I do not know whether it is good for Russia in the long run. But I do know that in so far as it is based on violence and denial of God, it repels me."[4] At the time of the annual Congress session of 1924, a resolution expressing deep sense of sorrow at the passing away of Lenin could not be carried because of the opposition of the leadership. Gandhi, who presided, went so far as to declare that if it were constitutional for him to rule that resolution out of order, he would not take a second to do so. While he based his objection on a technical ground, namely, that the resolution lay beyond the scope of the activities of the Congress[5]—his attitude indicates a definite coolness and reserve towards the Soviet Union.

[3] Report of the Thirty-Seventh Indian National Congress (Patna, 1923), p. 29.
[4] Young India, 11 December 1924.
[5] Tribune (Lahore), 1 January 1925.

II

By 1927, however, there was a radical change in the situation and Socialism did become an important factor influencing Indian thinking on foreign policy. This came about chiefly as a consequence of the experiences and reactions of Jawaharlal Nehru, particularly during his sojourn in Europe in 1926-27. In February 1927, he actively participated, as the accredited representative of the Indian National Congress, in the International Congress against Imperialism held at Brussels. As a member of its Presidium he delivered one of the opening addresses on the first day. When the Brussels Congress set up the League Against Imperialism, Nehru was included among the five honorary presidents of its council, the others being Albert Einstein, Romain Rolland, Madame Sun Yat-sen and George Lansbury. Nehru was also elected a member of the Executive Committee.[6] The Brussels Congress greatly influenced him and through him the Indian National Congress.

Communists had played an important part in the Brussels Congress as also in the League Against Imperialism. However, these organizations were not exclusively communist. It is revealing of Nehru's mind at that time that, while refuting the allegation that the League Against Imperialism was a wholly Communist organization, he openly admitted that it had Communists in its ranks and did not consider it necessary to be apologetic about it. "Communists," he wrote, "are undoubtedly the greatest opponents of Imperialism today and as such their co-operation is welcome, but in no sense do they dominate the League."[7] This was understandable, for though not himself a Communist, he had become strongly sympathetic to the world Communist movement of the time, largely as a result of his association with the Brussels Congress and the League Against Imperialism. "As between the labour world of the Second International and the Third International," he writes, "my sympathies were with the latter. The whole record of the Second International from the war onward filled me with distaste, and we in India had sufficient personal experience of the methods of one of its strongest

[6]Jawaharlal Nehru, "Report on the International Congress against Imperialism held at Brussels," *The Indian National Congress, 1927* (Madras, 1928), pp. 61-78.

[7]*Congress Bulletin,* 22 March 1929.

supports—the British Labour Party. So I turned inevitably with goodwill toward Communism, for, whatever its faults, it was at least not hypocritical and not imperialistic."[8]

With Nehru's sympathy for Communism on the world plane went an enthusiastic, though not uncritical, admiration for the Soviet Union. He was immensely attracted by the momentous changes taking place there.[9] This attraction further increased as a result of his visit to the Soviet Union, at the invitation of its Government, in November 1927, on the occasion of the tenth anniversary celebrations of the Russian Revolution. It was a family visit: the group included Nehru's wife and younger sister and was headed by his father, Motilal Nehru. This short visit, lasting only three or four days, had a great impact on the Nehrus. Even though Motilal Nehru, an old lawyer, found it hard to understand the collectivist ideas prevailing in the Soviet Union,[10] he was definitely impressed by what he saw.[11]

Whatever that may be, there was no question that the visit just thrilled young Jawaharlal Nehru. "I must confess," he wrote a few months later, "that the impressions I carried back with me from Moscow were very favourable and all my reading had confirmed those impressions, although there is much that I do not like or admire."[12] For several months, after his return to India towards the end of 1927, the subject suggested for his talk, especially at student gatherings, was almost invariably Soviet Russia, and he gladly responded.[13] On the basis of his impressions and readings, he also contributed a number of articles on the Soviet Union and they were published in a book form in 1929. He wrote of the fascination of that "strange Eurasian country, where workers and peasants sit on the throne of the mighty." He emphasized that in their own self-interest Indians must try to understand the new forces operating in the Soviet Union. For one thing, the problems faced by India and the Soviet Union were similar in several respects. Both were largely

---

[8]Jawaharlal Nehru, *Toward Freedom* (New York, 1941), pp. 125-6.

[9]*Ibid.,* p. 126.

[10]Krishna Hutheesingh, *With No Regrets* (New York, 1945), p. 57.

[11]Jawaharlal Nehru, n. 8, p. 127.

[12]Jawaharlal Nehru, *Soviet Russia, Some Random Sketches and Impressions* (Bombay, 1949; first published 1929), p. 34.

[13]*Ibid.,* p. 1.

agricultural countries, with only a slight degree of industrialization and both suffered from poverty and illiteracy. If the Soviet Union succeeded in finding a satisfactory solution for her problems, the task in India would become much easier. For another, the Soviet Union was India's neighbour, a powerful neighbour, which might be friendly to India and cooperate with her, or, be a thorn in her side. In either case, it was essential for Indians to know the Soviet Union well, so that they might be able to shape their policy correctly.[14]

Nehru looked forward to the establishment of friendly relations between the two countries. Much of the talk about Soviet designs upon India, he thought, was nothing but British propaganda and Indians must remain wary of it. Economically, India was too similar to the Soviet Union to be of any use to her. The latter wanted to build up her industries and for that purpose needed capital and expertize none of which she could get from India. Normally the Soviet Union and India should live as good neighbours with the fewest points of friction. The continuous friction that the British Government had with the Soviet Union was not between India and the Soviet Union as such, but between Great Britain and the Soviet Union. This was due to the age-old rivalry between Britain and Russia, which India had no reason to inherit. That rivalry was based on the greed and covetousness of British imperialism, and Indian interest surely lay in ending that imperialism and not in supporting or strengthening it.[15]

Indeed, the continued rivalry between Britain and Soviet Russia immensely added to the popularity of the latter in India, for, it highlighted her position as a great anti-imperialist power. Besides, Soviet Russia's treatment of her neighbours in Asia shone by contrast to Britain's treatment of those countries. The nature of the Indian image of the Soviet Union comes out vividly in a speech delivered by Nehru in 1928:

And Russia, what of her? An outcaste like us from nations and much slandered and often erring. But in spite of her many mistakes she stands today as the greatest opponent of imperialism and her record with the nations of the East has been just and generous. In China, Turkey and Persia of her own free will she gave up her

[14]*Ibid.*, pp. 2-3.
[15]*Ibid.*, p. 131.

valuable rights and concessions, whilst the British bombarded crowded Chinese cities and killed Chinamen by the hundred. In the city of Tabriz in Persia, when the Russian Ambassador first came, he called the populace together and on behalf of the Russian nation tendered formal apology for the sin of the Tsars. Russia goes to the East as equal, not as a conqueror or a race proud, superior. Is it any wonder that she is welcomed?[16]

Nehru's enthusiasm for the Soviet Union was not without its effect on Gandhi. In 1928, Gandhi provided space in three successive issues of his paper for Nehru's articles favourably commenting on the system of education in the Soviet Union.[17] In the same year, while addressing the students of the Gujarat Vidyapeeth, Gandhi referred to Bolshevism in such a way as to reveal a warmth for the Soviet experiment. Of course, he said that he did not fully understand Bolshevism and declared that the Bolshevik regime, in the form in which it then existed, could not survive, as in his opinion, nothing enduring could be built on the basis of violence. Having said this, he added that there was no questioning the fact that "the Bolshevik ideal has behind it the purest sacrifice of countless men and women who have given up their all for its sake, and an ideal sanctified by the sacrifice of such master spirits as Lenin cannot go in vain, the noble example of their renunciation will be emblazoned for ever and quicken and purify the ideal as time passes."[18]

III

The growing fascination for socialism and for the Soviet Union in the immediate post-Brussels period was accompanied by strident anti-imperialism. Even in the pre-Brussels phase the Congress had expressed its sympathy with the nationalist movements in Asian countries and also shown interest in the concept of an Asian federation. But such sympathy and interest grew stronger and became much more noticeable after 1927. This should not appear surprising in view of the fact that the Brussels Congress provided the first

[16]Jawaharlal Nehru, *Before and After Independence*, J.S. Bright, ed., (New Delhi, n.d.), p. 66.
[17]*Young India,* 9, 16 and 28 August 1928.
[18]*Ibid.,* 15 November 1928.

opportunity for direct contact among the leaders of the various Asian countries.

In particular, the Indian feeling of a close bond with China now became much stronger than before. One of the resolutions passed at the Brussels Congress was in the form of a joint declaration by the Indian and the Chinese delegates. It referred to the most intimate cultural ties that had united the two countries for more than three thousand years before the advent of British rule in India and emphasized the need for their revival. Further, it condemned the British use of Indian men and money against the Chinese people and expressed the hope that the Indian leaders would coordinate their struggle with that of the Chinese, thus simultaneously engaging British imperialism on two of its most vital fronts, providing active support to the Chinese and assuring the final victory of both India and China.[19]

In India, this was followed by an increased interest in the national struggle of the Chinese people. The All India Congress Committee conveyed its sympathy to them and protested against the despatch of Indian troops to their country through a resolution adopted in 1925.[20] After the Brussels Congress, it adopted a similar resolution in May 1927, affirming its sympathy with the Chinese people and demanding withdrawal of the Indian troops from their country.[21] Further, it decided to send an ambulance corps to China as a gesture of goodwill, but this could not materialize as the Government of India refused to grant the necessary passports.[22] At its annual session in December 1927, the Congress again passed a resolution sending its warmest greetings to the Chinese people and strongly criticizing the use of Indian troops against them. It also advised Indians not to go to China as agents of the British Government to fight or work against the Chinese people, "the comrades of the Indian people in their just struggle against Imperialism."[23] The success of the Chinese nationalists during the following years greatly pleased the Congress, and in its next session it congratulated the people of China on their having ended the era of foreign domination.[24]

[19] Jawaharlal Nehru, n. 6.
[20] *The Indian National Congress,* 1925 (Allahabad, 1926), p. 4.
[21] *The Indian National Congress,* 1927, p. 4.
[22] *Ibid.,* p. 54.
[23] *Report of the Forty-Second Indian National Congress* (Madras, n.d.), p. 3.
[24] *Report of the Forty-Third Indian National Congress* (Calcutta, n.d.), p. 94.

The increased interest of the Congress in Asian countries was not limited to China. The annual Congress session of 1927, while demanding withdrawal of the Indian troops from China, also asked for their withdrawal from all foreign countries and the British colonies, wherever they might be.[25] In 1928, the Congress warmly assured the people of Egypt, Syria, Palestine, and Iraq of its full sympathy with them in their struggle to free themselves from the grip of Western Imperialism which, in its view, was also a great menace to the Indian struggle.[26] Next year, the turmoil in Afghanistan over the reforms sought to be initiated by King Amanullah, excited the interest of the Congress. All Congressmen, wrote Jawaharlal Nehru, had been following with the keenest anxiety the recent happenings in Afghanistan and had felt deep sympathy for her gallant King.[27] A few days after this was written, the Working Committee noted with anxious concern the recent troubles in that country and wished success to the progressive elements.[28]

With this strengthening of interest in the freedom movements, came a desire for closer association with the Asian countries. From the presidential rostrum of the Congress, C.R. Das in 1922, Mohammad Ali in 1923, and S. Srinivasa Iyengar in 1926, had supported the idea of setting up a federation of Asian nations. Nehru reported that at the Brussels Congress representatives from the Asian countries evinced a strong desire for establishing a closer bond among them, but no practicable formula could be devised. It was generally felt that the League Against Imperialism would offer a meeting ground for the time being and enable them to remain in touch with each other. In addition, national organizations in the Asian countries could also foster direct contact among themselves through exchange of publications and visits.[29]

Against this background, M.A. Ansari again brought up the subject of an Asian Federation in his presidential address to the Congress in 1927. He declared that the only hope of success in checking the forces of European Imperialism and capitalism lay in the Eastern nations coming closer and taking a more intimate interest in the

[25]*Report of the Forty-Second Indian National Congress*, p. 94.
[26]*Report of the Forty-Third Indian National Congress*, p. 94.
[27]*Congress Bulletin*, 27 January 1929.
[28]*Ibid.*, 14 February 1929.
[29]Jawaharlal Nehru, n. 6.

problems facing them, and expressed the hope that common cultural
and economic interests would facilitate the consummation of the
scheme of an Asian Federation.[30] It was, however, difficult to accomplish much under the then existing circumstances. Asian leaders
found it difficult even to visit India. Two leaders from French Indo-
China, after braving great difficulties, succeeded in coming to the
annual Congress session of 1928 as fraternal delegates, but Madame
Sun Yat-sen was refused a visa both in 1927 and 1928.[31] Nevertheless,
the Congress was so fascinated by the idea of an Asian Federation
that, in 1928, it directed its Working Committee to correspond with
the leaders of other Asian countries and take other steps to hold
in India the first session of a "Pan-Asiatic Federation" in 1930.[32]
It seems that all that was intended by it was to hold an Asian conference or congress. No such conference was indeed held until 1947.

Another aspect of the impact of the Brussels spirit was the growth
of a feeling of solidarity with the anti-imperialist and progressive
forces and movements throughout the world. The Indian struggle
now began to be viewed as part of a world struggle against imperialism. Of course, as early as 1922, C.R. Das, in his presidential
address, had advised Indians to keep themselves in touch with world
movements and with the lovers of freedom all over the world.[33]
Not until after the Brussels Congress, however, did this become
a recurrent theme in the pronouncements of the Congress leaders
or affect their action. Nehru described the Brussels Congress as
"the outward symbol of the intense desire for mutual cooperation
all over the world." He wanted the Indian National Congress to be
associated with the League Against Imperialism, one of the grounds
being that we could not "in our own interest and in the interest
of the rest of the world, afford to remain isolated from the rest of
the world."[34] Nehru's suggestion was accepted and the Congress
in 1927 decided to affiliate itself with the League Against Imperialism as an associate member.[35] The new world outlook of the
Congress came out clearly, in a resolution, adopted by it in 1928.

[30]*Report of the Forty-Second Indian National Congress*, p. 22.
[31]*Congress Bulletin*, 27 January 1929.
[32]*Report of the Forty-Third Indian National Congress*, p. 92.
[33]*Report of the Thirty-Seventh Indian National Congress*, p. 32.
[34]Jawaharlal Nehru, n. 6.
[35]*Report of the Forty-Second Indian National Congress*, p. 3.

This declared that the Indian struggle was part of the general world struggle against imperialism and, hence, desired that Indians should develop contacts with other countries and peoples who were also combating imperialism. The Congress also decided to open a Foreign Department in its office to develop such contacts.[36]

IV

Sympathy with the Soviet Union and the feeling of solidarity with the anti-imperialist forces throughout the world, led to a deep distrust of Britain's foreign policy and to a tendency to view international developments from the Soviet stand-point. In his report on the Brussels Congress, Nehru referred to the worsening relations between Britain and Soviet Russia and between Britain and China. He apprehended danger from the drift in Anglo-Russian relations and warned of the possibility of the outbreak of war.[37] If this did happen, he wrote elsewhere, Britain would be wholly responsible for it, for the whole basis of British policy, according to him, was to encircle Russia by pacts and alliances with a view to crush her ultimately and the object of the Locarno treaties and the efforts to improve Anglo-German relations was the isolation of Russia.[38]

Nehru also apprehended that if war broke out, Britain would fight largely with Indian blood and treasure and would thereby seek to strengthen still further her hold over India and other Asian countries. Such a war, however, could be avoided if Indians made it clear in advance that they would in no way co-operate with the British war efforts. This was the burden of Nehru's argument in support of the resolution on war danger which the Congress passed at his suggestion, for the first time in 1927. This resolution declared that the Indian people had no quarrel with their neighbours and wanted to live with them in peace. Further, Indians must have the right to decide whether to participate in any war or not. If the British Government embarked on any warlike adventure, the resolution went on, and made an attempt to involve India in it, it would be the duty of the Indian people to refuse to take any part in such a war.[39]

[36] *Report of the Forty-Third Indian National Congress*, p. 91.
[37] Jawaharlal Nehru, n. 6.
[38] Jawaharlal Nehru, n. 12, pp. 129-30.
[39] *Report of the Forty-Second Indian National Congress*, pp. 4-11.

The Congress reiterated this stand in the following year and declared that the Indian people would not allow themselves to be exploited by Britain to further her imperialist aims.[40]

The same Brussels Congress which went a long way in drawing Nehru towards the Soviet Union also for the first time made him fear the rise of American imperialism and its alliance with British imperialism for the creation of an Anglo-Saxon bloc to dominate the world. This apprehension came through his contacts with the Latin American delegates to the Brussels Congress. In his report on that Congress, Nehru wrote:

> Most of us, especially from Asia, were wholly ignorant of the problems of South America, and of how the rising imperialism of the United States, with its tremendous resources and its immunity from outside attack, is gradually taking a strangle-hold of Central and South America. But we are not likely to remain ignorant much longer; for the great problem of the near future will be American Imperialism even more than British Imperialism which appears to have had its day and is crumbling fast. Or, it may be, and all indications point to it, that the two will unite together in an endeavour to create a powerful Anglo-Saxon bloc to dominate the world.[41]

V

The Congress did not pay much attention to world affairs from 1930 to 1935. Up to 1934, with a short interval in 1931, it was preoccupied with the Civil Disobedience Movement which involved the breaking of laws and bearing the consequences. Its offices were closed and the leaders and workers were put in prison. When the movement was suspended in 1934, it naturally took some time before the Congress could resume its functions on all fronts in full vigour. This was specially true of its interest in world affairs, as its guiding spirit in that field, Jawaharlal Nehru, was still absent from the scene, first in prison and then in Europe by the sick-bed of his wife. The Congress resumed its interest in world affairs when Nehru returned to India to take up the presidentship of the Congress in April 1936.

[40]*Report of the Forty-Third Indian National Congress,* p. 95.
[41]Jawaharlal Nehru, n. 6.

A Foreign Department was set up in the office of the All-India Congress Committee in the following months and put under the charge of Ram Manohar Lohia, one of the leaders of the Congress Socialist Party. Within six months, the Foreign Department established contact with over four hundred individuals and organizations in foreign countries. It also regularly sent bulletins and press notes on world affairs to Indian newspapers.[42] In fact, it will not be wrong to say that between 1936 and 1939, there was scarcely any important international development to which the Congress did not react and hardly any problem for which it did not offer a solution.

Behind this upsurge of interest in world affairs, we find the impact of socialism on foreign policy thinking, which came largely through Jawaharlal Nehru. During 1932-33 when he was in prison he spent most of the time pondering over world events and seriously analyzing the world situation as it had emerged from the crisis of 1929. The more he studied this subject, the more fascinated he grew. "India with her problems and struggles," he observed, "became just a part of this mighty world drama, of the great struggle of political and economic forces that was going on everywhere, nationally and internationally."[43]

In that struggle, Nehru's sympathies went increasingly to the Communist side. He disliked much in Soviet Russia including suppression of all contrary opinion, regimentation of life and violence, but the capitalist world also was not free from violence. Whereas the violence of the capitalist world seemed inherent, that in Soviet Russia aimed at a new order based on peace and real freedom for the masses. Besides, Russia was forging ahead while the capitalist world lay benumbed under the dead weight of the past. In particular, Nehru was impressed by the reports of Soviet progress in Central Asia. In short Nehru inclined towards the Soviet Union, the example set by Soviet Russia appeared to him as a bright and heartening phenomenon in a dark and dismal world. Even if Soviet Russia blundered or failed, her performance would not affect the soundness of Marxist theory, which lighted many a dark corner of his mind and gave a new meaning to history. It was the scientific

[42]Indian National Congress, *Report of the General Secretary, April-December* 1936 (Allahabad, 1936), pp. 29-40.
[43]Jawaharlal Nehru, n. 8, p. 228.

outlook of Marxism that appealed to him. Above all, Marxism seemed to have been proved right by the Great Depression.

Reading and reflection went on side by side. Nehru studied carefully the developments in the Soviet Union, Germany, Great Britain, France, Spain, Italy, Central Europe, the United States, Japan and China and tried to understand their problems. While Marxism made him feel that in spite of failure and set-backs the world was moving towards the desired consummation, he viewed many events in the world, particularly the rise of Fascism and Nazism, with utter dislike, pain, and abhorrence. "Worse still," he writes, "was the sight of intelligent men and women who had become so accustomed to human degradation and slavery that their minds were too coarsened to resent suffering and poverty and inhumanity. Noisy vulgarity and organized humbug flourished in this shifting moral atmosphere, and good men were silent."[44]

Nehru took the opportunity presented by the brief respite from prison to share his thoughts with his countrymen through a series of articles on the national and international situation which were subsequently published in a pamphlet entitled *Whither India*. He emphasized that it was only in a world perspective that the Indian problem could be properly understood. The troubles in the world were largely owing to the inherent conflicts of a decaying capitalism. As the capitalist order decayed, it had to face increasing challenge from labour. As the latter grew strong, the possessing classes joined together to fight the common enemy. This led to the rise of Fascism as well as the "so-called national governments," but as neither offered any solution to the problem of inequitable distribution of wealth, they were bound to fail. Roosevelt's New Deal, though it appeared to Nehru as the only instance of an attempt in the capitalist world towards lessening inequalities of wealth by State action, likewise, failed to impress him. Carried to its logical conclusion, he prophesied, the New Deal would lead to a form of State Socialism, but it was far more likely to fail and lead to Fascism. Not only did Capitalism lead to Fascism, but also to Imperialism. This, in turn, led to conflicts over the distribution of colonies, raw materials and markets, and to conflicts between the imperialist powers on the one hand and the nationalist and working class movements of colo-

[44]*Ibid.*, pp. 228-31.

nial countries on the other. Recurrent crises and wars were the inevitable results of these conflicts.[45]

Nehru made his position clear in a statement issued to the press on 18 December 1933. He declared that fundamentally the choice before the world then was one between some form of Communism and some form of Fascism, and he was all for the former. From the point of view of methods and approach to the ideal, he might not agree with everything that the orthodox Communists had done. According to him, these methods would have to be adapted to changing conditions and would vary in different countries. But the basic ideology of Communism and its scientific interpretation of history were sound.[46]

VI

When Nehru became the President of the Congress in April 1936, these views became the foundation of the Indian Nationalist outlook on world affairs. In his presidential address, Nehru devoted a good deal of space to an analysis of the world situation and called upon the Congress to identify itself with the nationalist and socialist forces in the world struggling against Imperialism and Fascism, the two faces of decaying capitalism:

> Thus we see the world divided into two vast groups today—the imperialist and fascist on one side, the socialist and nationalist on the other. There is some overlapping of the two, and the line between them is difficult to draw, for there is mutual conflict between the fascist and imperialist powers and the nationalism of subject countries had sometimes a tendency to fascism. But the main division holds, and if we keep it in mind, it will be easier for us to understand world conditions and our place in them. Where do we stand then, we who labour for free India? Inevitably we take our stand with the progressive forces of the world which are ranged against fascism and imperialism.[47]

[45]Jawaharlal Nehru, *India and the World: Essays* (London, 1936), pp. 51-61.
[46]Jawaharlal Nehru, *Recent Essays and Writings on the Future of India, Communism and Other Subjects* (Allahabad, 1934), p. 126.
[47]*Report of the Forty-Ninth Session of the Indian National Congress* (Allahabad, n.d.), pp. 9-12.

The Congress followed the lead given by Nehru and between 1936 and 1939, extended its sympathy and support to all victims of fascism and imperialism in Abyssinia, Spain, China, Palestine (Arabs), and Czechoslovakia. Subhas Chandra Bose, who became president of the Congress in 1938, wanted the Congress to follow a foreign policy based more on considerations of national interest than on emotional or ideological considerations. In his presidential address,[48] he suggested that in the field of foreign policy the Congress should not be influenced by the international politics of any country or its form of government. People in every country, whatever their political views, sympathized with the Indian aspiration for freedom. The Congress should take a leaf out of Soviet diplomacy which did not hesitate to make alliances with non-socialist states and had not declined sympathy or that the Congress should tone down its utterances against the militarist and expansionist activities of Italy, Germany and Japan. Nehru, however, continued to be so influential in the affairs of the Congress that Bose's advice went unheeded. Indeed, even while Bose was president, the Congress took several notable steps in line with the policy of active opposition to both fascism and imperialism everywhere. Bose understood the strong sentiment in the Congress behind the steps and although he did not approve of it, yet he did not protest against it; rather on the contrary, he publicly associated himself with it as president of the Congress.[49]

Throughout this period between 1936 and 1939, a strong support for the Soviet Union remained implicit in the policy of the Congress. It did not show itself in the resolutions of the Congress on foreign affairs and was not shared by all the top leaders or perhaps even by a majority of them. It was, however, very much a part of the thinking and utterances of Nehru, the man largely responsible for shaping the Congress policy on foreign affairs. In his presidential address in April 1936, he admitted that much had happened in the Soviet Union which had pained him greatly and with which he disagreed. He made it clear that he looked upon "that great and fascinating unfolding of a new order and a new civilization as the most promising feature of our dismal age." If the future was full of hope, it was

[48]*Report of the Fifty-First Indian National Congress* (Ahmedabad, n.d.), p. 190.
[49]Jawaharlal Nehru, *The Discovery of India* (New York, 1946), p. 428.

largely because of Soviet Russia and what it had done. In fact, he
was convinced that if some world catastrophe did not intervene,
this new civilization would spread to other lands and put an end to
the wars and conflicts which capitalism generated.[50]

By 1939, this enthusiasm for the Soviet Union diminished. Nehru
confessed that he had been considerably upset by the mass trials
and purges there. Though he believed that the trials had been generally *bona fide* and that there had definitely been a conspiracy against
the Soviet regime, he could not reconcile himself to such happenings;
they indicated ill-health in the body politic, necessitating an ever-
continuing use of violence and suppression. Nevertheless, the
progress made by the Soviet Union continued to impress him. Moreover, any doubts he might have had about internal developments
did not extend to Soviet foreign policy. This, according to him,
had been consistently one of peace and unlike the policies of England and France, of fulfilling international obligations and supporting the cause of democracy abroad. The Soviet Union stood as the
one real and effective bulwark against Fascism in Europe and Asia.
Without her, Fascist reaction would triumph everywhere and democracy and freedom would become dreams of a past age.[51]

VII

During 1936-39, socialism not only strengthened natonalist India's
opposition to both Fascism and Imperialism and contributed to
the support of the Soviet Union, but also conditioned, to a considerable extent, the Congress attitude to the war issue. On this issue,
the Congress, to use the phrase of Nehru, followed "a dual policy."[52]
This dual policy was the result of the interplay of Socialism and
Nationalism. On the one hand it strongly criticized the aggressive
action of Italy, Germany and Japan, extended moral support to
their victims, showed its readiness to join hands with other peoples
in the preservation of peace and freedom, and associated itself with
the international peace movement in which communists and non-
Communists both participated, with the former playing the key role.
On the other hand, it insisted on the immediate recognition of Indian

[50]*Report of the Forty-Ninth Session of the Indian National Congress*, p. 20.
[51]Jawaharlal Nehru, *Where Are We?* (Allahabad, 1939), pp. 55-6.
[52]Jawaharlal Nehru, n. 49, p. 428.

independence and repeatedly declared that imperialism itself was one of the greatest causes of war and so it must disappear if peace was to be preserved or Fascism defeated.

Thus, when Romain Rolland, Honorary President of the World Committee for the Struggle against War and Fascism, invited the Congress to participate in the World Congress for Peace to be held at Brussels in September 1936, it readily accepted his invitation and assured him of its full sympathy and cooperation in the great work of ensuring peace in the world. At the same time, it also declared its conviction that lasting peace could be established only with the removal of the underlying causes of war and the ending of the domination and exploitation of one nation by another.[53] Nehru, in his message to the Peace Congress, emphasised that imperialism itself was the negation of peace.[54] V.K. Krishna Menon, who attended the World Peace Congress on behalf of India, echoed the Nehru line. "We cannot," he said in the course of his speech at Brussels, "hope to stop war—aggression and conquest in the future—if at the same time we do not examine the character and results of the conquest under which we live."[55] The next session of the Indian National Congress, held in December 1936, reiterated its whole-hearted support for the efforts of the World Peace Congress to ensure peace, but also re-emphasized that imperialism itself was a continuing cause of war.[56]

The question which concerned the Congress more intimately was the attitude to be adopted if Britain became involved in a war. On this question, the dual policy outlined above, led it to adopt an attitude which was somewhat contradictory. On the one hand, it strongly criticized the British Government for not effectively opposing the aggressive actions of Germany, Italy and Japan. On the other hand, with equal vehemence it declared that if the British Government did decide upon such opposition and took the risk of war, it would not support Britain unless India was immediately declared independent. This contradiction was inherent in the situation and, as mentioned above, was the result of the interplay

[53]*Report of the Forty-Ninth Session of the Indian National Congress* pp. 44-5
[54]All India Congress Committee, *Foreign Department Newsletter*, 10 September 1936.
[55]*The Hindu* (Madras), 18 September 1936.
[56]*Indian National Congress, 1936-1937*, p. 85.

of socialism and nationalism. In particular, it arose from Nehru's crusading zeal aginst Fascism on the one hand and his eagerness to hasten India's march towards independence on the other.

Even before 1936, the Congress Socialist Party had adopted a strong line on the war issue. The Party's policy resolution at the organizing conference in Bombay in 1934, declared that it was necessary for the Congress to define its opposition to India's participation in any war in which Britain might be involved, to prepare the Indian people to resist the utilization of Indian men, money and resources in such a war, and to use the crisis created by British involvement to secure independence.[57] The leaders of the Party repeatedly tried in vain as in 1934 and 1935 to get this line adopted by the Congress as a whole.[58] The Congress did not pass any resolution on the war issue during those years. Nehru was absent, and the other top leaders of the Congress did not at that time care much for the socialists.

With Nehru's return from Europe in 1936, the situation changed and the Congress began to give increasing attention to the war issue. Most of the resolutions on this subject were drafted by Nehru and they expressed the dual aims described above. Thus the Lucknow Congress (April 1936), in a unanimous resolution recalled the stand of the Madras Congress (1927), which had for the first time opposed Indian participation in any war without the consent of her people. In its view, the danger of war had now become more evident because of the growth of fascist dictatorships, the Italian invasion of Abyssinia, the continuing Japanese aggression in Manchuria and North China, the rivalries and conflicts of the imperialist powers, and the feverish growth of armaments. In case of war, the resolution continued, an attempt would inevitably be made to drag in and exploit India to her manifest disadvantage and for the benefit of British imperialism. The Congress, therefore, reiterated its old resolve to resist such an exploitation and to oppose Indian participation in any imperialist war.[59]

The next Congress which met in December 1936, noted that the

[57]Nripendra Nath Mitra, ed., *The Indian Annual Register,* 1939, II (Calcutta, n.d.), p. 296.

[58]Thomas A. Rusch, *The Role of the Congress Socialist Party in the Indian National Congress, 1931-1942* (Ph.D. Dissertation, Chicago University; Typescript), pp. 418-9.

[59]*Report of the Forty-Ninth Session of the Indian National Congress,* pp. 46-7.

fascist powers were forming alliances and grouping themselves for war with the object of establishing their domination over the world. It recognized the necessity of facing this world menace in co-opera-tion with the progressive nations and people who were dominated over and exploited by Imperialism and Fascism, but declared that in the event of war there was grave danger of Indian men, money and resources being utilized for the purposes of British imperialism. It, therefore, considered it necessary to warn Indians of this danger and to prepare them to resist it.[60]

The annual Congress session which met in February 1938, held Britain largely responsible for the rapid deterioration in the inter-national situation which had been caused by her steady support of Fascist Germany, Spain, and Japan. Such a policy was encouraging the drift to an imperialist world war. India could not be a party to such a war and would not allow the use of her men and money in the interest of British imperialism. Nor could India join any war without the express consent of her people.[61] At its next annual ses-sion (March 1939), the Congress passed a similar resolution, dis-sociating itself completely from British foreign policy, which it described as one of deliberate betrayal of democracy and repeated breach of pledges which had emerged ending the system of collective security and cooperation with governments, which were avowed enemies of democracy and freedom.[62]

It soon became clear, however, that contrary to the earlier Con-gress expectations Britain was heading towards a war with Germany. Any doubt that might have existed before was removed by the stiffening of British policy after Czechoslovakia was overrun by the Nazis in March 1939. Now the Congress modified its earlier stand of total opposition to collaboration with Britain in any war and declared that such a collaboration was possible, in the fight against Fascism. At the same time, the Congress made it clear that such a contingency could be thought of only if India herself was made free. Already at the time of the Munich crisis, Nehru had writ-ten (in the last week of September 1938) that an India with her freedom assured to her and working for the establishment of a demo-

[60]*Indian National Congress, 1936-1937*, p. 88.
[61]*Report of the Fifty-First Indian National Congress*, pp. 199-200.
[62]*Report of the Fifty-Second Indian National Congress* (Jabalpur, n.d.), pp. 151-2.

cratic State would be a pillar of strength to freedom and democracy elsewhere, and would throw in her weight and resources, in war or peace, for the defence of democracy. She would most willingly join hands with others to defend Czechoslovakia, to combat Fascism, and to work for a settlement which would do away with the injustices of the past and the present and lay the foundation of a true world order.[63] After the overrunning of Czechoslovakia by Hitler's forces, Nehru reiterated this line. "For us in India," he wrote on 18 April 1939, "our path is clear. It is one of complete opposition to the Fascists; it is also one of opposition to Imperialism. We are not going to throw in our resources in defence of an empire. But we would gladly offer those very resources for the defence of democracy, the democracy of free India lined up with other free countries."[64]

On 1 May 1939, the All-India Congress Committee reaffirmed its determination to oppose all attempts to involve India in a war or to use Indian resources in such a war without the consent of the Indian people.[65] As war seemed likely to break out any day, the Congress Working Committee thought it fit to restate its policy at some length in the second week of August 1939. It declared that in the world crisis its sympathies were entirely with the people who stood for democracy and freedom, but it also recalled Congress opposition to all attempts to impose a war on India without the consent of her people. In protest against the despatch of Indian troops to Egypt and Singapore, it called upon the Congress members of the Central Legislative Assembly to refrain from attending the next session of that body. It also advised the Congress Ministries in the provinces not to assist in any way the war preparations of the British Government and to remain prepared to give up office, if the Congress is faced with such a contingency.[66]

VIII

To sum up, socialism did not have a place in the mainstream of

[63]Jawaharlal Nehru, *The Unity of India, Collected Writings, 1937-1940*, Second ed., (London, 1942), p. 300.

[64]*Ibid.,* p. 304.

[65]*Indian National Congress 1930-1940* (Allahabad, n.d.).

[66]*Ibid,*

Indian thought either on foreign policy or any other subject in the beginning of the period of this survey. But this situation changed gradually. From 1927 onwards, socialism became one of the important factors which influenced the foreign policy thinking of our leaders, especially Jawaharlal Nehru. His participation in the Congress of Oppressed Nationalities held at Brussels in 1927 was of cardinal importance from this point of view. It can be said that this event marks a landmark in the evolution of Indian outlook on foreign policy.

Socialism influenced Indian foreign policy thinking in various ways. As a result of Nehru's interest in Socialism, his interest in world affairs became more pronounced. The Indian struggle for freedom appeared to him more and more as a part of a world struggle against Imperialism and, later on, Fascism. This imparted a more strident anti-imperialist note to the proceedings of the Indian National Congress with reference to world affairs and deepened the interest of the Congress in the freedom struggles in Asian countries and in developing close relations with them. It also made Nehru for the first time apprehensive of the growth of American imperialism, and what is even more significant, of the possibility of the emergence of a joint Anglo-American bloc to dominate the world.

Above all, the Indian attitude towards the Soviet Union became extremely cordial and this also influenced the general Indian approach to world problems. The Congress first showed interest in the problem of preventing a world war, or, at any rate, India's participation in it, largely as a result of the feeling that Britain was preparing for a war to crush the Soviet Union. Later, the Congress began to approach the war issue more and more from the point of view of using it for pressing the demand for independence. While doing so, it never lost sight of international considerations, among which the importance of strengthening the anti-Imperialist and anti-Fascist forces always occupied the most important place. And right up to 1939, the Soviet Union was considered as the outstanding leader of such forces.

THE IDEOLOGICAL DEVELOPMENT OF THE REVOLUTIONARY TERRORISTS IN NORTHERN INDIA IN THE 1920's*

BIPAN CHANDRA

THE REVOLUTIONARY TERRORISTS of northern India during the 1920's became popular heroes in their own life time and have remained so since then. But their popular image was and is that of heroic youths, saturated with the emotions of abstract or "pure" nationalism and burning with the desire to sacrifice themselves "at the altar of the motherland." Their critics had, of course, harsher things to say about them. But both the admirers and the critics continue to believe that these daring young men had no social ideology, no thought to guide their actions, or that, in other words, they were mindless patriots. The revolutionary terrorists were fully aware of this widely prevalent view. As one of their many public declarations noted: "There are few to question the magnanimity of the noble ideals they cherish and the grand sacrifices they have offered, but their normal activities being mostly secret, the country is in the dark as to their present policy and intentions."[1] To remove this lacunae they published and distributed over the years, many statements and pamphlets, some of which were carried in the national press. Many of them are now available, though many more have yet to be traced. In addition, several excellent autobiographies have been published more recently by several of the participants in the

---

*The Words "Revolutionary Terrorists" have been used in the absence of a better term. No criticism or value judgment is implied in the use of the terms. The alternative was to describe them as "Armed Revolutionaries," as some of the Hindi writers do.

[1] *The Manifesto of the Hindustan Socialist Republic Association,* distributed at the Lahore Session of the India) National Congress, December 1929 (hereafter referred to as the Manifesto). Source: *History of the Freedom Movement, Phase III,* B 38/3.

revolutionary movement. There is now hardly any excuse for the persistence of the old belief.

II

The Revolutionary Terrorist movement of the 1920's in northern India was the product of several new factors in the situation. Of course, it arose on the shoulders of the previous revolutionary movements such as the attempts of Rash Behari Bose and Shachindranath Sanyal during the First World War, the Hardinge Bomb Case, the Ghadar Movement, the Manipuri Conspiracy and the First Lahore Conspiracy Case. There was also the background of the terrorist movements in Bengal, Maharashtra and Europe.

More immediately, it was the product of the Non-Cooperation Movement and its abiding impact on Indian politics. Nearly all of the important members of the new revolutionary movement had taken active part in the Non-Cooperation Movement, and had shared in the heady enthusiasm generated by the unprecedented popular upsurge and the hopes raised by Gandhi's promise of winning freedom within a year. Among the participants in the non-violent *Satyagraha* were, for example, Jogesh Chandra Chatterjee, Chandrashekhar Azad, Bhagat Singh, Sukhdev, Jatin Das, Bhagwati Charan Vohra, Yashpal, Shiv Varma, Dr Gaya Prasad and Jaidev Kapur. But the failure of the Non-Cooperation Movement shattered the high hopes raised earlier. Among the youth who had followed the call of Gandhi and abandoned their schools and colleges and even their homes, there was deep dissatisfaction with the manner in which the movement had been withdrawn. Their sense of gloom was heightened by the replacement of Hindu-Muslim unity forged in common struggle by an orgy of communal riots and an atmosphere poisoned by mutual communal hatred. These idealist youth could not see anything wrong with Chauri Chaura. Nor could they appreciate a conception of politics and morality which would fell a powerful popular movement with a single blow. Nor were they satisfied with the two substitutes that the national leadership offered them: parliamentary politics of the Swarajists or the so-called constructive programme of the No-changers. The more these young people pondered over the prevailing pessimism and frustration, the more they found fault with the basic strategy of the dominant nationalist leadership and the Gandhian political ideology underpinning it. Their rejection of Gandhism made them search for alternatives. This search led them to socialism on the one hand and revolutionary terrorism on the other. They embraced both, as had been done half a century earlier by the revolutionary Russian youth.

The third event to influence them, though very vaguely in the beginning, was the upsurge of the working class after the First World War. This new social force was watched carefully by many of the older as well as the emerging leaders of the Revolutionary Terrorist movement. They could see the revolutionary potentialities of the new class and desired to harness it to the nationalist revolution.[2] The influence of the working class was strongly felt in 1928 when a strike wave spread over the country.[3]

A major influence on the young revolutionaries was the Russian Revolution and the success of the young socialist state in consolidating itself against heavy internal odds and powerful external enemies. This also led them to study Marxist literature and other books on socialism. The older generation revolutionary terrorists had started discussing the Soviet Revolution and Communism as early as 1924.[4] Gradually more information regarding the Soviet Union trickled down to India. Literature on the Soviet Union was easily accessible at Lahore and was eagerly devoured at the Dwarkadas Library, founded by Lala Lajpat Rai.[5] It had an immediate impact. Bhagat Singh and Sukhdev began to look upon the Soviet Union as the state nearest to their ideal.[6] Soviet Union's growing impact was also revealed by the attention paid by the public (as opposed to the secret) wing of the revolutionary movement in popularizing the Soviet Union. This public wing, the Naujawan Bharat Sabha, celebrated along with radical Congressmen, "Friends of Russia

[2]Shachindranath Sanyal, *Bandi Jiwan,* in Hindi (Delhi, 1963), pp. 237 ff; Virendra Sandhu, *Yugdrastha Bhagat Singh,* in Hindi (Delhi, 1968), p. 138; Yashpal, *Sinhavalocan,* in Hindi (Lucknow, 1951), Vol. I, p. 138; Ajoy Ghosh, *Articles and Speeches* (Moscow, 1962), p. 15.

[3]Yashpal, n. 2, p. 138.

[4]Jogesh Chandra Chatterjee, *In Search of Freedom* (Calcutta, 1967), Sanyal, n. 2, pp. 314 ff.

[5]Yashpal, n. 2, p. 96.

[6]J.N. Sanyal, *Sardar Bhagat Singh* (Lahore, 1931), p. 26; H.R. Vohra's evidence, *Tribune,* 30 November 1929. Also see Ajoy Ghosh, n. 2; p. 15.

Week" in August 1928. In the same month, the Sabha organized a meeting to eulogize the Russian Revolution.[7] The revolutionaries behind bars also carried on similar propaganda. On 24 January 1930, the Lahore Conspiracy Case prisoners celebrated the "Lenin Day" in the court and sent greetings to Moscow.[8] Similarly, in November 1930, they sent greetings to the Soviet Union on the anniversay of the Revolution.[9]

An important aspect of the Soviet influence was the eagerness of the terrorist revolutionaries to take monetary and other help from the Soviet Union and to send Indians there to get training in the arts, methods, and organization of the revolutionary process. In 1926, Ashfaqullah of the Hindustan Republican Association (HRA) was planning to go to Russia when he was arrested in the Kakori Conspiracy Case.[10] In 1928, Bejoy Kumar Sinha was deputed by the newly founded Hindustan Socialist Republican Army Association (HSRA) to go to the Soviet Union.[11] Later Chandrashekhar Azad made vain attempts to send Yashpal and Surendra Pandey to the Soviet Union.[12] The influence of the Russian Revolution was a major factor not only in spreading socialist ideas among the revolutionaries but also in weaning many of them away from purely terrorist ideas.[13]

The young terrorist revolutionaries also established contact with the small communist groups which were sprouting up all over the country. Particularly in the Punjab, but also at Kanpur and Allahabad, they maintained close contact with the communists.[14] During the years 1928-1930, the communist groups and the terrorist revolutionaries worked together in the Naujawan Bharat Sabha.

Gradually, the revolutionary groups and individuals began to emerge out of the mood of frustration and stagnation. Their attempt to create an all-inclusive organization led to the formation of the Hindustan Republican Army in 1924 under the leadership of the

---

[7]Note on the N.B. Sabha by Rai Bahadur Bhagwan Dass of C.I.D. dated 27 May 1929, Home (*Political*) *Proceedings*; F. 130 and K.W., 1930, pp. 40-1.

[8]See *Tribune*, 26 January 1930.

[9]Ajoy Ghosh, n. 2, p. 25.

[10]J.C. Chatterjee, n. 4, pp. 247 and 391.

[11]Interview with B.K. Sinha.

[12]Yashpal, n. 2, Vol. III, pp. 49 and 59.

[13]J.N. Sanyal, n. 6, p. 26.

[14]Interview with Sohan Singh Josh and P.C. Joshi.

"old-timers," i.e. Shachindranath Sanyal, Jogesh Chandra Chatterjee, and Ramprasad Bismil.[15] The programme and ideology of the HRA, of which youngsters such as Bhagat Singh, Shiv Varma, Sukhdev and Azad were members, were an amalgam of the old and the new. The HRA helped the young revolutionaries make a transition to an advanced programme. It also enabled them to maintain continuity with the older tradition.[16] The result was a revolutionary programme with an advanced revolutionary socialist outlook which still tried to incorporate within it individual or group armed actions of a terrorist nature. The new programme emerged fully when the group of young revolutionaries met at Ferozeshah Kotla grounds on 9 and 10 September 1928, created a new leadership, and gave their party a new name with a difference—The Hindustan Socialist Republican Association (Army).[17]

III

The new generation terrorist revolutionaries were men of ideas and ideologies.[18] Their ideas were, of course, rapidly developing and cannot be studied except in motion, so to speak. Moreover, as is true of any other movement with a distinct set of ideas, these ideas were not equally coherently articulated by all the participants. Some naturally assumed the role of ideologues. Such was, for example,

[15]J.C. Chatterjee, n. 4, pp. 20, 208-9 J.N. Sanyal, n.6, p. 12.

[16]The continuity with the older generation of revolutionaries was always stressed by the younger revolutionaries. See, for example, Sukhdev's letter in *Young India,* 23 April 1923, p. 82. Similarly, Bhagat Singh constantly held up the image of Kartar Singh Sarabha before himself. Shachindranath Sanyal's *Bandi Jiwan* Part I, was a virtual textbook in their ideological and propaganda work. Similarly, the Lahore Conspiracy Case prisoners made it a point to send a condolence message on the death of Shyamji Krishna Varma, *Tribune,* 8 April 1930.

[17]According to Yashpal, Prof. Jai Chandra Vidyalankar and J.N. Sanyal were deliberately kept out as representing the older spirit and the participants in the meeting were determined to have a new aim for their movement and a new path for their organization. See Yashpal, n.4, p. 145.

[18]The important role of ideas in the movement was recognized early in 1925 by the leaders of the HRA. One of the qualifications laid down for a district organizer was : "He must have the capacity to grasp political, social, and economic problems of the present day with special reference to his motherland." *The Constitution of the HRA,* in J.C. Chatterji, n.4, p. 341.

clearly the role of Bhagat Singh and Bhagwati Charan Vohra—two men of exceptionally powerful intellect and capacity to translate their ideas into the written word. Other ideologues of the movement were Shiv Varma, Bejoy Kumar Sinha, Sukhdev, and later Yashpal. These men (except Yashpal who came into the movement later) were also responsible for adding the socialist objectives to the aims of the movement. But what is equally important is that others discussed these ideas, grasped them, and accepted them with a full sense of responsibility. Chandrashekhar Azad, for example, was not merely a military leader. He made others read and explain to him books in English till in the end he was able to grapple with their ideas himself. He followed every major turn in the field of ideas and endorsed them only after full discussion and self-conviction.[19] The draft of *The Philosophy of the Bomb* was written by Bhagwati Charan at the instance of Azad and after a full discussion with him.[20]

At the level of the ideologues, the revolutionary ideas were clearly articulated and brilliantly expounded, as even a cursory reading of the documents cited below would show. The young revolutionaries took particular care to be clear and distinct in their exposition for they were fully aware that the revolutionaries had "all along been, either deliberately or due to sheer ignorance, misrepresented and misunderstood." They wanted to let the people "know the revolutionaries as they are."[21] Of course, their ideas became much less clear as they came to be expressed by the less educated and less articulate members of the party, as is evident from a perusal of the *Atshi Chakkar* leaflets written by Inderpal's group.

IV

The greatest advance that the revolutionary terrorists made was in the definition and development of their aims and objectives. The

[19]Yashpal, n. 2, pp. 148-9. Ajoy Ghosh is wrong in stating that Azad did not care much for new ideas. He makes this mistake mainly because he was behind bars in the crucial years of Azad's growth as a leader. What is true is that Azad accepted the superiority of some other comrades as ideologues and was fully conscious of his limitations in this respect.

[20]Yashpal, n.2, Vol. III, pp. 66-7.

[21]*The Philosophy of the Bomb.*

questions they sought to answer at the ideological plane were: What were the aims of their struggle against the foreigners? What sort of change in society and policy were they aiming at? What sort of social order and state structure would replace the present ones? And, at the purely intellectual level, they succeeded in postulating the development and organization of a mass movement of the exploited and suppressed sections of society led by the revolutionary intelligentsia for the reconstruction of society on the basis of a new social order—the socialist system based on the abolition of class distinctions and class domination.

The following sections would trace this development in their thought in greater detail. But at the outset, it is necessary to contradict the impression that all the major shifts in revolutionry thinking occurred during the period of their imprisonment and mainly as a result of the opportunities for serious study that they got while in prison. In fact, the basic ideological formulations of Bhagat Singh were made in the early period of his incarceration on the basis of his earlier reading and thinking—and he had made a great deal of progress in this respect in the pre-1929 period. Moreover, he had read Karl Marx's *Capital* in addition to other Marxist, socialist, and revolutionary literature. This is not to deny that continuous development occurred in the thinking of the revolutionaries due to fresh experiences, study or discussion. But while those who were in jail accomplished all this inside the jail, others who escaped arrest did so outside. For instance this was the case with Bhagwati Charan, Chandrashekhar Azad, and Yashpal. The most mature work of the revolutionary terrorists in terms of theory, *The Philosophy of the Bomb,* was produced by those who had managed to evade arrest.

V

The first major commitment of the revolutionary terrorists was to liberate India from foreign rule and to transform Indian society through a revolution. This commitment found a capsuled expression in the slogan, "*Long Live Revolution*" or "*Inquilab Zindabad.*"

Their commitment to revolution was moreover total. To them, revolution was not a mere historical accident or curiosity. It was not merely the demand of a particular historical situation in India.

It was "the inalienable right of mankind."[22] More, it was the eternal principle of human progress. A perpetual process of revolution was needed if human society was not to stagnate and if it was not to be overpowered by the dark forces of decay. It was, therefore, the very embodiment of humanist principles. According to the Manifesto of the HSRA (1929):

Upheavals have always been a terror to holders of power and privilege. (But) Revolution is a phenomenon which nature loves and without which there can be no progress either in nature or in human affairs. Revolution is not a philosophy of despair or a creed of desperadoes. Revolution may be anti-God but is certainly not anti-man. It is a vital living force which is indicative of eternal conflict between the Old and the New, between Life and Living Death, between Light and Darkness. There is no concord, no symphony, no rhythm without Revolution. The music of the spheres of which poets have sung, would remain an unreality if a ceaseless Revolution were to be eliminated from the space. Revolution is Law, Revolution is Order and Revolution is the Truth.

The revolutionaries were not afraid of chaos or anarchy which so frightened the middle class intelligentsia of the time. The task of destruction was essential before regeneration could occur. *The Revolutionary* published by the HRA in January 1925 had proclaimed: "Chaos is necessary to the birth of a new star and the birth of life is accompanied by agony and pain." The Manifesto of the HSRA (1929) fully endorsed this view.

Revolution also implied a total struggle—a struggle without compromises, a struggle in which the victory had to be total. *The Philosophy of the Bomb* ended with the declaration: "We ask not for mercy and we give no quarter. Ours is a war to the end—to victory or Death."

Such glorification of revolution and willingness to make great sacrifices at its altar were, of course, not peculiar to the period under discussion. These were, in fact, inherited from their predecessors. Where first the leaders of the HRA, and then Bhagat Singh and his

---

[22]Bhagat Singh's and Dutt's statement of 6 June, 1929.

comrades took a giant step forward was in broadening the scope, the definition of revolution.

Bhagat Singh and others repeatedly disclaimed that revolution was to be identified with violence or with "the cult of the pistol and and the bomb." These were the mere means of bringing about revolution.[23] Revolution was no longer to be seen as a mere political act. That is why a rebellion was not a revolution though it might lead to it.[24] Revolution had a deeper, wider social content. Its aim now was to regenerate society, to change the social order based on "manifest injustice."[25] Revolution was "the spirit, the longing for a change for the better."[26] It was the people's desire to change their political and economic condition.[27] Bhagwati Charan defined revolution further as "Independence, social, political, and economic."[28] A fuller statement of their position was made in Bhagat Singh's and Dutt's statement of 6 June 1929:

By revolution we mean the ultimate establishment of an order of society which may not be threatened by such (social) breakdowns and in which the sovereignty of the proletariat shall be recognized and as a result of which a world federation should redeem humanity from the bondage of capitalism and misery of imperial wars.

Starting with this view of the revolutionary process, the revolutionary terrorists were no longer satisfied with the mere prospects of the achievement of complete national independence. Even national freedom had to be seen as a means to a new social order. Initially this yearning found expression in the HRA's proclamation in 1925 that it stood for "the abolition of all systems which make the exploitation of man by man possible."[29] Later revolutionaries also railed against exploitation. The poster put up at Lahore after the assassination of Saunders in December 1929, declared that the

[23]Bhagat Singh's and Dutt's letter to the Modern Review, *Tribune*, 24 December 1929; *Manifesto*; Bhagat Singh etc. n. 22.
[24]Bhagat Singh's and Dutt's letter, n. 23.
[25]Bhagat Singh etc., n. 22.
[26]Bhagat Singh's and Dutt's letter, n. 23.
[27]Bhagat Singh quoted in N.K. Nigam, *Balidan* in Hindi (Delhi, n.d) p. 41.
[28]*The Philosophy of the Bomb,* n. 21.
[29]J.C. Chatterjee, n. 4, p. 338.

revolutionaries were working "for a revolution which would end exploitation of man by man."[30] The goal was reiterated in the Red Leaflet thrown in the Central Assembly on 7 April 1929.[31] With slightly greater sophistication, *The Philosophy of the Bomb* invited the readers to help establish "a new order of society in which political and economic exploitation will be an impossibility."

From this egalitarian demand, the next step—the demand for a socialist society—was quickly taken. Socialism became the official goal of the revolutionary terrorists of northern India when they met at Delhi on 9 and 10 September 1928, for reorganizing their party, the HRA. Here, Bhagat Singh proposed that the name of the party be changed to the Hindustan Socialist Republican Association (Army). He was given powerful backing by Sukhdev, Bejoy Kumar Sinha, and Shiv Varma. His proposal was carried in the end.

The change in name was not just a gesture. It was taken after full debate and discussion. Several participants had objected on the ground that the older name had acquired a great deal of prestige due to its association with leaders like Ramprasad Bismil, Shachindranath Sanyal and Jogesh Chandra Chatterji. But they were convinced in the end that the change was essential to denote the changed social, economic, and political character of the struggle they were about to initiate.[32]

Nor was the injection of socialism as a goal into the revolutionary movement really sudden. The HRA had already taken some vague steps in the direction. At the HRA Council meeting, held at Kanpur on 3 October 1924, it had been decided "to preach social revolutionary and communistic principles."[33] The HRA's publication, *The Revolutionary*, had proposed the nationalization of the railways and other means of transport and communication and the large-scale industries such as steel and ship-building. For other private and small scale business enterprises it had suggested the organization of co-operative unions.

Gradually, more and more revolutionaries had come under the influence of socialist ideas. In 1924, Jogesh Chandra Chatterjee had

[30]Quoted in Gopal Thakur, *Bhagat Singh: The Man and His Ideas* (New Delhi, 1952) p. 9.

[31]*Tribune*, 10 April 1929.

[32]J.N. Sanyal, n. 6, pp. 28-9.

[33]*Proceeding of the HRA Council meeting*, 1924.

become a proponent of socialism.[34] Young revolutionaries both in the Punjab and U.P. were taking keen interest in socialism.[35] Many of them were in touch with "Communist" groups.[36]

The goal of socialism was not based on vague and woolly notions or youthful impetuosity. A great deal of intensive reading and discussion had gone into the making of their ideology. At Lahore, Bhagat Singh had helped the Dwarkadas Library acquire a unique collection of literature on revolutions, particularly those of Russia, Ireland, and Italy. He himself had read about them during the years 1924-27. He had organized several study circles with the help of Sukhdev and others and carried on intensive political discussions.[37] J.N. Sanyal, his co-prisoner in the Lahore Conspiracy Case, made in 1931 the following evaluation of Bhagat Singh as an intellectual:

Bhagat Singh was an extremely well-read man and his special sphere of study was socialism....Though socialism was his special subject, he had deeply studied the history of the Russian revolutionary movement from its beginning in the early 19th century to the October Revolution of 1917. It is generally believed that very few in India could be compared to him in the knowledge of this special subject. The economic experiments in Russia under the Bolshevik regime also greatly interested him.[38]

The socialist intellect of Bhagat Singh got a chance to grow and develop in prison. The story of his intellectual endeavours has been narrated at length by his niece Virendra Sandhu.[39] In Jail, Bhagat Singh wrote several books of which the four prominent ones were *Autobiography, The Door to Death, The Ideal of Socialism,* and *The Revolutionary Movement of India.* Unfortunately all the manus-

[34]J.C. Chatterjee, n. 4, p. 242.

[35]Yashpal, n. 2, p. 96; Ajoy Ghosh, n. 2, p. 36. As early as 1924, Lala Lajpat Rai publicly described Bhagat Singh as a Russian agent and complained that Bhagat Singh wanted to "make me into a Lenin." V. Sandhu, n. 2, p. 316.

[36]Many of them, including Bhagat Singh, might also have been influenced by the Kanpur Bolshevik Conspiracy Case since they were present in Kanpur at the time.

[37] J.N. Sanyal, n. 6, p. 15.

[38]*Ibid.,* p. 103.

[39]V. Sandhu, n. 2, pp. 234-5, 237, 262, 285 and 306.

cripts have been lost.[40] Similarly, Bhagwati Charan and Sukhdev had made extensive study of socialist ideas. Later, Yashpal emerged as a serious student of the subject. He had not only read R. Palme Dutt's *Modern India* but also translated it into Hindi.[41]

What is equally important, Bhagat Singh and others actively promoted the education of party members in the theories of socialism. They were fully aware of the great role that scientific ideology could play in the revolution. Before the Lahore High Court, Bhagat Singh had pointed out that "the sword of revolution is sharpened at the whetstone of thought."[42] In jail, he had described Gandhi as "a kind-hearted philanthropist" and pointed out that "it is not philanthropy that is needed, but a dynamic scientific social force."[43] Consequently, when, after the Delhi Conference, the Party office was shifted to Agra, Bhagat Singh immediately built up a small library with economics as the core subject. Here the members were constantly urged to read and discuss socialism and other revolutionary ideas.[44] Bhagwandas Mahour, a virtual teenage member at the time, has narrated how Bhagat Singh urged him to read Marx's *Capital* and other books.[45]

It may, however, be stated that Bhagat Singh and his friends were not great scholars of socialism or Marxism but they were no mere novices either. They had travelled some way and were gradually feeling, studying and thinking their way towards a scientific socialist understanding of the problems of the Indian Revolution.[46] For instance, Bhagat Singh grasped that socialism as a system is not the product of a mere subjective longing for a desirable system but far more the objective product of the necessity of the social circumstances.[47] Writing to Sukhdev who was tormented by doubts, and who along with Bhagat Singh was awaiting the execution of the death sentence, Bhagat Singh remarked:

[40]*Ibid.*, pp. 237 and 306.
[41]Yashpal, n. 2, Vol. II, p. 11.
[42]V. Sandhu, n. 2, p. 196.
[43]J.N. Sanyal, n. 6, p. 106.
[44]*Ibid.*, pp. 32-3; Yashpal, n. 2, Vol. I, p. 170.
[45]Bhagwandass Mahour in Banarsi Das Chaturvedi, ed., *Yash Ka Dhrohar*, in Hindi (Delhi, 1968), 2nd edition, pp. 27-8.
[46]Yashpal, n. 2, p. 145, Mahour, n. 45, p. 26.
[47]Last message of Bhagat Singh, see Appendix 5, to Vishwanath Vaishampayan, *Amar Shahid Chandrashekhar Azad,* in Hindi, Parts 2-3 (Banaras, 1967), p. 306,

If we had not entered the field, would it have meant that no revolutionary action would have occurred? You are wrong if you think so. It is true that we helped to a large extent change the (political) atmosphere. At the same time, we are mere products of the necessity of our times. I would even say that the creator of Communism, Marx, was in fact not the creator of this ideology. It was the Industrial Revolution in Europe which produced many persons of a particular way of thinking. Marx was just one of these men. In his situation Marx undoubtedly helped impart a particular motion to the movement of his times. I and you have not created the socialist or communist ideas in this country. On the other hand, they are the result of the impact on us of our time and circumstances. Undoubtedly, we have contributed in a simple and humble manner to the propagation of these ideas.[48]

Furthermore, the extent of their socialist understanding is clearly brought out by their concrete understanding of what constituted a socialist society and its points of departure. After all it was on this question that the HRA had been transformed into the HSRA. While the HRA had held up as its immediate object the establishment of a Federal Republic of the United States whose basic principle would be adult suffrage,[49] the HSRA had by its very name proclaimed the goal of establishing a Socialist Republic.

VI

The leadership of the HSRA clearly grasped that socialism was a product of the historical process and that therefore, as a system it was the antithesis of capitalism. The first achievement of the socialist system would, therefore, be the ending of capitalism. This was made clear by Bhagat Singh and Dutt in their statement of 6 June 1929 as well as in their statement before the High Court. *The Philosophy of the Bomb* was equally definitive. It had proclaimed, "The revolution will ring the death knell of capitalism."

It was recognized that socialism would represent a new correlation

---

[48]Quoted in V. Sandu, n. 2, p. 241. It is interesting that Bhagat Singh looks upon himself mainly as a propagator of the ideas of socialism rather than as a great freedom fighter.

[49]*The Revolutionary,* published by HRA, 1925.

of class force in society. The entire socialist ideology was based on class analysis of society. Socialism would be based on the emancipation of the hitherto exploited classes of society, the workers and peasants, and the domination of their interests in the economy, society, and polity.[50] The 6 June statement of Bhagat Singh and Dutt gives even a clearer exposition of this view. After pointing out that the revolution of their conception would change the "present order of things which is based on manifest injustice," their statement goes on to explain:

> Producers or labourers, in spite of being the most necessary element of society, are robbed by their exploiters of the fruits of their labour and deprived of their elementary rights. On the one hand, the peasant who grows corn for all starves with his family. The weaver who supplied the world market with his textile fabrics cannot find enough to cover his own and his children's bodies. Masons, smiths, and carpenters, who rear magnificent palaces, live and perish in slums, and on the other hand, capitalist exploiters, parasites of society, squander millions on their whims.... Radical change, therefore, is necessary, and it is the duty of those who realize this to reorganize society on a socialistic basis.[51]

The leaders of the HSRA also raised the concrete question as to who controls the state power as distinct from the question of exploitation and class interests. Socialism, they said, also represented a new state structure in which power rests in the hands of the workers and peasants.[52] At the same time, socialism could not be established till the existing state apparatus, under the control of the exploiting classes, was captured by the socialist revolutionary forces. In a message from prison in October 1930, Bhagat Singh said:

> We mean by revolution the uprooting of the present social order.

---

[50] *The Philosophy of the Bomb*, n. 21.

[51] Bhagat Singh etc., n. 22.

[52] *Rules and Regulations of the Naujawan Bharat Sabha*, Punjab, 1 May 1928. *Meerut Conspiracy Case*, 1929, English translations of Urdu exhibits, Exhibit no. p. 205 (T); Reports on the Naujwan Bharat Sabha, *Home (Political) Proceedings*, F. 130 & K.W. (1930), p. 40 and p. 10 of K.W.; *The Philosophy of the Bomb*, n. 21.

For this, capture of state power is necessary. The state apparatus is now in the hands of the privileged class. The protection of the interests of the masses, the translation of our ideal into reality, that is the laying of the foundation of society in accordance with the principles of Karl Marx, demand our seizure of this apparatus.

What was to be the state form under socialism? Here the revolutionaries accepted the notion of the "Dictatorship of the Proletariat." The revolution will "establish the Dictatorship of the Proletariat" declared the *Philosophy of the Bomb,* "and will forever banish social parasites from the seat of political power."[53] In the course of the court hearings, Bhagat Singh and his co-prisoners made every effort to popularize the notion that the revolution of their conception was closely linked with the fortunes of the working class and its leadership function. On 13 June 1929, Bhagat Singh and B.K. Dutt met the court judgement in the Assembly Bomb Case with the twin cries of "Long Live Revolution" and "Long Live the Proletariat."[54] During the Lahore Conspiracy Case trial, all the prisoners used to shout three slogans on their arrival in the court: "Long Live Revolution," "Long Live Proletariat," and "Down, Down with Imperialism."[55]

VII

The growing socialist consciousness also enabled the revolutionary terrorists to constantly link capitalism and imperialism. Their understanding of imperialism and foreign rule went far beyond emotional nationalism. They began to see the close link between capitalism and modern imperialism, between capitalist economic exploitation and the enslavement of nations.[56]

Within India, foreign rule was seen as a form of class rule or as

[53]Bhagat Singh, etc., n. 22.

[54]*Tribune,* 14 June 1929

[55]See the *Tribune* report of the case during 1929-1930. See, for example, the *Tribune* of 6 October 1929.

[56]See Bhagat Singh etc. n. 22, *The Philosophy of the Bomb,* and the *Last Message of Bhagat Singh* in Vaishampayan, n. 47.

the rule of foreign capitalists.[57] Socialism was then seen as a specific remedy that would, by putting an end to class rule and economic exploitation bring about true independence.[58] This understanding pervades all revolutionary terrorist documents of the period and was, of course, inherent in the slogans where freedom was linked with the ending of exploitation of man by man. For example, *The Manifesto of HSRA* said: "The hope of the proletariat is, therefore, now centred on Socialism which alone can lead to the establishment of complete Independence and the removal of all social distinctions and privileges."

Once the socialistic outlook enabled them to see the class-based character of all society including Indian society, the revolutionary terrorists ranged themselves squarely against the domestic exploiting classes also. They denounced the domination of Indian capitalists and landlords as strongly as the rule of foreign capital and declared that the abolition of the former was as basic to the revolution as the abolition of the latter. According to *The Manifesto of the HSRA:*

> The position of the Indian proletariat is, today, extremely critical. It has a double danger to face. It has to bear the onslaught of Foreign Capitalism on the one hand and the treacherous attack of Indian Capital on the other: the latter is showing a progressive tendency to join forces with the former. Bhagat Singh wrote in a message from the prison: 'The peasants have to liberate themselves not only from foreign yoke but also from the yoke of landlords and capitalists.'[59]

His message of 3 March 1931 was even more explicit: the struggle in India would continue so long as "a handful of exploiters go on exploiting the labour of the common people for their own ends. It matters little whether these exploiters are purely British capitalists, or British and Indians in alliance, or even purely Indians."[60]

[57]Furthermore, in their 6 June statement, Bhagat Singh and Dutt referred to the "economic structure of exploiters of whom the Government happens to be the biggest in the country."

[58]*The Philosophy of the Bomb,* n. 21.

[59]Quoted in Gopal Thakur, n. 30, p. 39.

[60]See Vaishampayan, n. 47, part 2-3, p. 304. Also see *The Philosophy of the Bomb,* n. 21.

It may be noted that the revolutionary terrorists did not make a detailed class analysis of Indian society. There was no concrete analysis of the rural society; no discussion of the structure of Indian capitalism or its complex relationship with imperialism. They even failed to draw a clear distinction between the landlords, zamindars, and money-lenders and the industrial capitalists. It seems that to them capitalism was the epitome as well as the symbol of economic exploitation. What stands out, however, is their firm grasp of the class approach to society, their commitment to socialism, their anti-imperialism, and their recognition of the leading role of the working class. It was therefore not fortuitous that the overwhelming majority of the revolutionary terrorists turned to Marxism and Communism once their own movement reached a dead-end.[61]

VIII

As practical revolutionaries, the leaders of the HSRA also dealt with the question: who would fight for the revolution or who would bring it about, or, in other words, what was to be the social base of their movement? On the question of the social base of the revolution, the leadership of the HSRA was very clear at the programmatic or theoretical plane. Their movement was to be based on the common people, the workers and peasants, the youth, and the radical intelligentsia. *The Philosophy of the Bomb* was explicit on this question. The appeal was addressed to "the youth, to the workers and peasants, to the revolutionary intelligentsia." The manifesto of the Naujawan Bharat Sabha (1928), was also clear on the point: "The future programme of preparing the country will begin with the motto 'Revolution by the masses and for the masses'."[62] One of the major objectives of the Sabha, as laid down in its Rules and Regulations, was the organization of workers and peasants.[63] The Sabha also decided to open branches in villages in order to emphasize the importance of work in the rural areas.[64] The Kanpur meeting of the HSRA's Central Council in January 1930, in which, among

[61]See Mahour n. 45, p. 10; Yashpal, n. 2, Vol. II, pp. 263-4.

[62]Quoted in Gopal Thakur, n. 30, p. 39.

[63]Rules etc. of Naujawan Bharat Sabha, n. 52, p. 35. Also see J.N. Sanyal, n. 6, p. 25.

[64]Home (Political) Proceedings, F, 130 & K.W. (1930), p. 10 of K.W.

others, Chandrashekhar Azad, Bhagwati Charan Vohra, Yashpal, and Kailashpati participated, decided to intensify the work among the students, peasants, and workers, and to form for the purpose, a separate section of the party organization to be headed by Seth Damodraswarup as President and Bhagwati Charan as Secretary.[65] Similarly Bhagat Singh declared in 1931 that "our main task should be the organization of peasants and workers."[66]

The role of the common people in the struggle was emphasized from another angle also. The HSRA's leaders were convinced that the capitalists and upper classes were showing a tendency to join the foreign power and were likely to abandon the freedom struggle half-way through.[67] Only the common people could then be relied on, and had the strength to carry forward the struggle for freedom. As Bhagat Singh put it: "The nation can wage a successful struggle only on the strength of organized workers, kisans, and the common people."[68] This emphasis on revolutionary work among the peasants and workers, and recognition of their revolutionary potentialities, was not new in the revolutionary terrorist movement, though the emphasis on their being the social base of the revolution was. Earlier, in 1924, the HRA had also decided that "to start labour and peasant organizations suitable men must be engaged on behalf of the Association to organize and control labourers in the different factories, the railways, and the coal-fields."[69]

This was, however, all in theory or at the programmatic level. In practice, little effort was made to organize the common people or to do even elementary political work among them. The Naujawan Bharat Sabha did take part in one or two agrarian agitations in 1928 and issued a few exhortations to the peasants to organize themselves.[70] The Sabha had only one village branch in Morinda in Ambala and two *tehsil* branches at Jaranwala and Talagang, and

[65]Kailashpati's evidence, *Proceedings of the Delhi Conspiracy Case,* Vol. I, p. 229; Yashpal, n. 2, Vol. II, pp. 153-4.

[66]Quoted in Gopal Thakur, n. 30, p. 39.

[67]*The Manifesto*, Bhagat Singh, quoted in Gopal Thakur, n. 30, p. 39.

[68]Quoted in Gopal Thakur, n. 30, p. 39.

[69]*Constitution of the HRA,* in J.C. Chatterjee, n. 4, p. 342. This seems to have been the result of Shachin Sanyal's first hand experience of the effectiveness of labour as a political force. See S. Sanyal, n. 2, p. 237.

[70]Home (Political) Proceedings, F. 130 and K.W. (1930), pp. 38 ff. And these may be ascribed to the *Kirti-Kisan* component of the Sabha.

these were all inactive.[71] The activities of the Sabha were, for all
practical purposes, confined to the cities and their middle and lower
middle class sectors.[72] Similarly, Ajoy Ghosh and a few others
worked with labour at Kanpur, perhaps under the impact of communist workers.[73] Kailashpati, the approver in the Delhi Conspiracy
Case and earlier a member of the Central Council of the HSRA,
noted in his evidence that while the Council decided in January
1930 to intensify work among the workers, peasants and students,
no one was assigned to work among the peasants.[74]

In reality, the HSRA failed to do any political work among the
common people; it had hardly any link or contact with them, not to
speak of its organizing their class power and leading them in class
struggles. It was virtually cut off from the classes which it had accepted in its programme as the social base of the revolutionary movement. This was one of the most important weaknesses of the HSRA.

The fact of the matter was that the main appeal of the HSRA was
to the radical nationalist youth. In theory, the youth had a double
role to play. They were to act as the conveyors of the revolutionary
socialist message to the workers and peasants,[75] and they were also
to be the direct fighters for revolution. In practice, the leadership
of the HSRA placed almost its entire reliance for political work on
the youth: the youth was to be the vanguard of the revolution. The
wide participation and even leadership of the workers and peasants
remained the goal, but it could not yet be so in practice because it
was believed the workers and peasants were yet "passive," "dumb,"
and "voiceless."[76] The youth must, therefore, be the real builders
of the revolution, they must act on behalf of the people and arouse
them through their work and sacrifices.[77]

[71]*Ibid.,* K.W. p. 13

[72]*Ibid.,* pp. 36 ff,

[73]Lalit Kumar Mukherjee's Evidence in the Lahore Conspiracy Case, *Tribune,*
7 December 1929.

[74]Kailashpati's evidence, n. 65, p. 299.

[75]Bhagat Singh's and Dutt's Message to the Students' Conference at Lahore,
Tribune, 22 October 1929; Kailashpati's Evidence, n. 65, p. 299.

[76]*Peaceful and Legitimate,* an HSRA pamphlet, *Copies of the Exhibits in Lahore
Conspiracy Case (II), History of the Freedom Movement,* Phase II, Region III,
6/3 Exhibit P.N. Also see Bhagat Singh etc., n. 22.

[77]*Peaceful and Legitimate*: Bhagat Singh etc,. n. 22. Bhagat Singh, quoted
in V. Sandhu, n. 2, p. 323, Yashpal, n. 4, Vol. II, p. 12.

The political appeal of the revolutionary terrorists was at its emotive best when made to their real and immediate audience. According to *The Philosophy of the Bomb*, "The revolutionaries already see the advent of the revolution in the restlessness of youth, in its desire to break free from the mental bondage and religious superstitions that hold them." In 1929 *The Manifesto of the HSRA* made an appeal to the youth delineating before them their historical mission which in its passion, lyricism, and emphasis on the idealism of youth, reminds one of the appeals of the founders of the 4 May Movement in China. The following extract from the appeal indicates the type of emotion that the revolutionary terrorists tried to generate and on which they themselves relied in making their immense sacrifices:

> The future of India rests with the youths. They are the salt of the earth. Their promptness to suffer, their daring courage and their radiant sacrifice prove that India's future in their hands is perfectly safe....Youths—Ye soldiers of the Indian Republic, fall in. Do not stand easy, do not let your knees tremble....Yours is a noble Mission. Go out in every nook and corner of the country and prepare the ground for future Revolution which is sure to come....Do not vegetate. Grow! ...Sow the seeds of disgust and hatred against British Imperialism in the fertile minds of your fellow youths. And the seeds shall sprout and there shall grow a jungle of sturdy trees, because you shall water the seeds with your warm blood.[78]

In practice also, all the revolutionary terrorist public activities, all their propaganda, including the "propaganda by death," were directed towards the youth. The youth from the lower middle class constituted the real social base of the movement. Almost the entire membership of the HSRA was drafted from this section of society.[79]

One reason for this emphasis on youth was the understanding that the task of the present generation of revolutionaries was not to make the revolution but to prepare for it. Bhagat Singh looked upon himself as the precursor of the revolution. Revolution would

[78]Also see an eulogy to youth by Bhagat Singh, quoted in V. Sandhu, n. 2, p. 323.

[79]Yashpal, n. 2, p. 139, Vol. II, p. 232; K.N. Nigam, n. 27, p. 11.

be started only when the ideas of socialism and revolution had gained popularity. Then the masses could make the revolution. Only the youth had the intelligence, the sensibility, the freedom from domestic worries, and the sense of sacrifice and heroism to perform the former task. Hence the primacy of youth in the preparatory phase of the revolution.

Yet another factor made the revolutionary terrorists rely on the youth. The most important form of propaganda, they believed, was "propaganda by action," or through terrorist and other heroic actions. Their actions did not constitute the revolution but such actions were immediately necessary to prepare for the revolution. Thus they faced a dialectical contradiction. Even before the revolution, which the masses would make, men were needed to perform revolutionary actions. In other words, to arouse the revolutionary tendencies of the masses, people with revolutionary consciousness and with capacity to sacrifice their lives were needed. As it were the lower middle class youth alone filled the bill.[80] But the revolutionary consciousness was, to start with, purely nationalist. And these youth could, therefore, be used mainly for nationalist actions. This was another contradiction that the leaders of the HSRA faced. In theory they had become totally committed to socialism, but in practice they could not go beyond nationalism.

IX

The revolutionary terrorists never succeeded in "taking off" politically. They got stuck at what they themselves saw as the first, preliminary step. They failed to get the support of the masses for their party as distinct from getting popularity as hero-figures devoid of distinct ideology and political personality. This is amply testified to by the perpetual and extreme poverty which engulfed them all the time. Nor did they succeed in organizing a single mass revolutionary action or even a minor armed group action against the Government. Thus their few successful individual political or terrorist actions remained suspended in the air as it were, and in terms of their own programme, were more or less failures. After all, they themselves viewed such actions as a means of moving the people on to the revolu-

[80]Yashpal, n. 2, Vol. II, p. 262.

tionary path and of getting wider support and membership for mass revolt and armed struggle. In fact, they could not even find the ways and means of establishing contact with the masses. Consequently governmental action decimated their ranks and they failed to replenish them. Throughout 1930 not a single dramatic "action" could be organized. All the carefully prepared plans of Chandrashekhar Azad came to nothing. Interral squables began to divide the heroic band, squables which still find their echo in fierce controversy in the Hindi press. The party had to be dissolved and soon scattered into small, rapidly diminishing groups. Even the lion-hearted Chandrashekhar Azad, who had borne repeated blows of fortune with fortitude, began to lose hope, though he went on planning "actions" up to the end. The revolutionary terrorist movement in north India virtually came to an end with his death in February 1931.

The HSRA had failed in its other political aims also. It had come into existence primarily as a reaction to, and in opposition to the dominant Gandhian leadership of the national movement. In the short period of its existence, it had frontally confronted this leadership and its ideology. One of the aims of their programme of "propaganda by deed" was to wean the masses and youth away from Gandhism. They claimed to be revolutionaries precisely in opposition to the non-revolutionary, compromising leadership of Gandhi. Yet, with all their great popularity in 1929, 1930 and 1931, they failed to provide an alternative leadership to Gandhi. Of course, they failed to achieve their aim of establishing revolutionary socialist hegemony over the national movement or to give it a revolutionary turn. By and large, the national movement remained stuck in the Gandhian grooves.

One of the aims of the HSRA was to popularize the idea of socialism and to spread socialist consciousness in the ranks of the nationalist youth. It does not seem the HSRA achieved much success. The vast majority of their admirers remained unaware of the depth of their commitment to socialist ideology. This was, of course, partially due to the suppression by the Government of all their writings. Nor was there any other source except the Naujawan Bharat Sabha at Lahore, their own underground distribution of the *Philosophy of the Bomb* (though only once on 26 January 1930), and occassional publication of their message in the *Tribune* and other papers through which their views could be spread. It was only in the Punjab that the HSRA and the Naujawan Bharat Sabha became, to some extent, carriers of socialist ideas. Their ideas, and the prestige of their sacrifices behind those ideas, could perhaps have become powerful instruments in the spread of a revolutionary socialist consciousness in the later years if the communist and socialist parties had so utilized them. But for some strange reasons, these parties failed to do so.

The immediate objective of the revolutionary terrorists was to spread revolutionary consciousness in the country. Bhagat Singh said to Shiv Varma just before facing the gallows, "At the time of my joining the revolutionary party I thought that if I could spread the slogan 'Long Live Revolution' to every corner of the country, I would have received the full value for my life...I think no one's life can be worth more."[81] And, undoubtedly, Bhagat Singh achieved this ambition. But universal acceptance of this slogan and the great admiration that the self-sacrifices and struggles of the revolutionary terrorists aroused in the country cannot be said to have given the nationalist consciousness a revolutionary turn. Undoubtedly, the Left movement in the country as well as the peasants' and workers' organizations and movements were to make this slogan a battle cry. But as commonly understood, this slogan soon came to symbolize merely the nationalist desire to achieve independence.

The great success of the revolutionary terrorists was in arousing the anti-imperlialist consciousness. They succeeded in arousing the country and in winning the love and respect of their countrymen, but for the cause of nationalism. This was no mean success. But the fruits of their success were gathered by the traditional Congress leadership which they had denounced as bourgeois and middle class and which they had hoped to replace, but which was actually and actively heading the anti-imperialist struggle. In other words, their great and real success came in a field and bore consequences which were very different from those they had desired. This led to an interesting historical paradox. While nearly ninety per cent of the revolutionary terrorists later gave their allegiance to Marxism or Communism, their own youthful deeds and slogans became the inheritance of Left Congressmen wedded to Gandhian leadership.

Basically, their failure can be expressed in a series of contradic-

81Quoted in V. Sandhu, n. 2, p. 238.

tions between their ideology and their work. While in theory they were committed to socialism, in practice they could not go beyond nationalism. While in theory they desired mass action and armed struggle, in practice they could not rise above terrorist or individual action. While in theory they wanted to base their movement on the masses—the peasants and workers—in practice they could only appeal to the urban lower middle class or petty bourgeois youth. While in theory they wanted to create and lead a mass movement, in practice they remained a small band of heroic youth. While in theory their small organization was to serve as a "foco," a cell around which would gather the rising revolutionary forces of the country, in practice they found it difficult and in the end impossible even to maintain the integrity of the original group itself.

Two other aspects of their failure may, however, be kept in view. Their failure was not merely that of not linking their practice with their theory; it was also that of not integrating nationalism and socialism at the theoretical and programmatic plane. In their programme, they hoped to accomplish at one stroke the nationalist as well as the socialist revolutions. Since the historical conditions were clearly not favourable to such a conjunction, in practice this meant keeping the socialist consciousness and the nationalist consciousness in two separate compartments with the result that either the former was subordinated to the latter or it got separated from the latter. This contradication also took another form. While the leadership of the HSRA was rapidly advancing in its acceptance as well as grasp of socialist ideas, its rank and file remained disinterested in theory and functioned almost entirely at the level of revolutionary nationalist consciousness.[82]

Reliance on the radical youth of the middle and lower middle classes while talking of a revolution of the masses seems to be the historical dilemma of all political situations, programmes, and parties, where a revolutionary situation exists, where the starting of a revolution on howsoever tiny a scale appears to be the only way out of political stagnation, where the time and facilities (legal conditions etc.) for propaganda and organization do not exist, and where, at the same time, revolutionary consciousness and personnel do not yet

[82]See Mahour, n. 45, pp. 27-8; Yashpal, n. 2, Vol. II, p. 262, Inderpal's and Madan Gopal's Evidence in the Second Lahore Conspiracy Case; and Vaishampayan, n. 47.

exist among the common people either due to political backwardness, official suppression, or prolonged subjection to non-revolutionary political influence. The leadership of the HSRA went wrong in not trying to rapidly change the situation and combine their activity with mass organization and mass revolt or armed action. They failed to develop organized armed action, on howsoever small a scale, against the Government, as distinct from its officials. And this was in spite of the fact that at the theoretical plane the revolutionary terrorists' approach towards revolution was more correct, and from the beginning they planned to start an armed struggle which would rapidly lead to mass revolt, the overthrow of imperialism, and establishment of a socialist republic. But they hardly got the time to put their ideas into practice. Nearly all of them were arrested or killed within a matter of two or three years and even within that period they were constantly hounded by a most stable and efficient administrations. One of their major mistakes perhaps lay in thinking that revolution could be initiated by a handful of young men in a period when the bourgeois nationalist leadership yet retained vigour enough to fight against imperialism though by non-revolutionary means.

Another mistake of the revolutionary terrorists lay in the belief that propaganda by deed or by death, by daring young men could lead to the creation of a revolutionary socialist movement. This was believing blindly in the spontaneous generation of political forces and even revolution. Only this belief could have made them send their most outstanding leader to take part in a "propaganda by death" deed. But where were the political forces—parties, groups, individuals in the country which could take advantage of the sentiments released and aroused by their immense sacrifices? In fact, there did not exist even the political mechanism to explain to the people what they were dying for. On the other hand, they seemed to believe that their sacrifices, accompanied by their death-defying statements, would affect people's minds, educate them, and lead them to organize themselves. Consequently, their revolutionary thought hardly reached the people. To the people they appeared as simple heroic figures who defied death for their country. They merely generated a nationalist consciousness. The very bourgeois nationalist leadership which they had desired to replace through exposure of its pro-capitalist character harnessed their names and sacrifices to make popular their own brand of nationalism.

This is not to deny that propaganda by deed could be a powerful weapon of political education. But that would be so only when it became a part of an organized movement, peaceful or violent. It was not that the brilliant leadership of the HSRA was not to some extent aware of this elementary political fact. That was why Bhagat Singh, Bhagwati Charan, Ram Krishan, Dhanwantri, and Ehsan Illahi devoted, at one stage or the other, the major part of their energies in the work of the Naujawan Bharat Sabha. The only city where the great sacrifice of Bhagat Singh and his comrades created a political movement among the Left was Lahore, and this mainly because the Sabha was there to build upon their struggle inside the jails. Similarly, Azad and Yashpal made desperate efforts in 1930 to create a political organization which could take their political message to the people. But such efforts were puny and often abortive and in no case matched the immense propaganda by deed.

In a way a profound personal and political tragedy was being enacted at that time. As the socialist ideological horizons of the leadership of the HSRA were being broadened, they could see the correct road ahead.[83] But they were too close to their terrorist past. In fact, that past formed a part of their present for these young men had traversed decades in a few months. When they wanted to make a break, as in the case of the Assembly Bomb Case, they made it within the shell of the old way. Their very commitment to heroism prevented them from making a total break with terrorism. In the last stages, in the latter part of 1930 and 1931, they were mainly fighting to keep the glory of the heroic sacrifice of their comrades under sentence shining as before. The vision of the coming revolution had receded in the face of the hard knock that the political reality had given them. In the end, one finds Bhagat Singh grappling with the problem of how to convey the correct understanding of politics to the young men outside, without appearing to have reconsidered his politics under the penalty of death. The socialist within him had finally overcome the terrorist. He desperately tried to convey this change without abandoning the sense of heroic sacrifice which he had imbibed from terrorism.[84] Outside, Chandrashekhar Azad

[83]The present writer would agree with Bhagat Singh when he wrote in February 1931 that already before his arrest in 1929 he had abandoned terrorism. See V. Sandhu, n. 2, p. 244.

[84]*Ibid.*

waited stoically for a martyr's death while he made desperate efforts, including virtually begging for the intervention of the non-revolutionary leaders, to save the lives of Bhagat Singh, Sukhdev and Rajguru. By then he had realized what their lives were worth. For this exchange, he was even willing to suspend revolutionary action for the time being. At the same time, he sought to send two of the few remaining intellectual members, Yashpal and Surendra Pandey, to the Soviet Union to learn the art of mass organization and revolution-making. For he had realized, as others had done, that the way of the revolutionary terrorists had failed and that broad-based mass movements alone could pave the way to revolution.[85] This realization was, of course, becoming a part of their consciousness for several years now.

X

In conclusion it can be said that the revolutionary terrorists succeeded in arriving at a socialist understanding of society, the state, nationalism, imperialism, and revolution. On the other hand, the total mechanism of revolutionary political action and organization escaped them. All the time they kept intact their revolutionary consciousness.

[85]Mahour, n. 45, p. 117; Nigam, n. 27, p. 104; A. Ghosh, n. p. 31. Frank recognition of their failure and their willingness to choose the alternative path is, of course, a rare example of intellectual and political integrity in the history of revolutionary movements.

AGRARIAN MOVEMENTS IN BENGAL AND BIHAR, 1919-1939

BINAY BHUSHAN CHAUDHURI

THE INDIAN NATIONAL Congress ceased to be an "upper class club" and started functioning as a mass organization only in 1920, though there were instances of mass-participation earlier. The usual studies of this development, however, often fail to give us the whole story. The "mass" is taken as an undifferentiated whole, and the distinctiveness of the different groups composing it from the point of view of their socio-economic positions largely deriving from their differing places in the social relations of production, is often ignored. Emphasis is consequently laid mainly on how the mass participation strengthened the Congress organization. What remains insufficiently stressed is the fact that the patriotic masses had their own immediate interests to look after, a concern occasionally leading the members of such groups to co-operate for combined actions in defence of their interests. Such actions involved them in particular relations with the dominant nationalist leadership, and at certain stages, came into conflict with the strategies of this leadership for struggle against British rule.

This paper is an attempt to study such actions of one of the groups, the peasantry of Bengal and Bihar in the period between 1919 and 1939—their aspirations and struggles in the context of particular economic and political developments, the interaction of their "social radicalism" and the mainstream of the nationalist movement, and the extent of their success.

Peasant movements were, however, by no means an entirely new development in the period under review. In fact, the strength and extent of such movements before have been greatly underestimated.[1]

[1] I have elsewhere made a detailed study of the peasant movement in Bengal and Bihar in the second half of the 19th century. "Agrarian economy and agra-

Combined peasant resistance could be traced right from the beginning of British rule. It became increasingly strong in the second half of the 19th century, particularly in Bengal. The revolt of the Pabna peasants in 1873, sparked off a series of similar revolts in other districts. The resistance was most widespread during the period of the controversy over the Bengal Tenancy Bill (1879-85), which was finally enacted in 1885. The Bill aroused in the peasants extravagant expectations, and they construed it as a moral approval of their stand by the Government. All sorts of rumours were circulating: the despotic power of zamindars would soon be gone forever, and with it the scare of enhancement of rent; the rent-rate would be reduced everywhere and legislation would deprive zamindars of all powers to enhance it. As long as the peasants had nothing to hope for, they remained tame. Hope now made rebels of them.

The Bihar peasants also rebelled from time to time, though such uprisings were mostly confined to the indigo cultivators and the tribal people.

I

The novel features of the peasant movement in the period under review mainly relate to its organization. Peasant associations (Kisan Sabhas) were created nearly in every district under a unified command. Certain strata of the peasantry which previously remained largely inactive or aloof, increasingly participated in the kisan movement. Moreover, the initiative of the peasants now remained sustained over a much longer period than before.

The peasant organizations which already existed were far from adequate for building up a sustained movement. The peasant associations were mostly local groups, because the peasant rebellions arose mainly out of particular local grievances. Some movements did spread outside the localities. The rebellion in Pabna, for instance, encouraged similar rebellions in the neighbouring districts. The movement pertaining to the Bengal Tenancy Bill was also fairly widespread. But here also the organizational base was very weak. In the first case, the rebels of Pabna had only tenuous links with

rian relations in Bengal, 1859-1885" (unpublished Oxford D.Phil dissertation, 1968), Ch. 5.

their followers in other districts, such as transmission of inflammatory messages by the emissaries from Pabna. The basis of the second movement was identical hopes shared by a large section of the peasantry. With the growing disenchantment of the peasants over the Bill, the movement soon petered out.

A far more serious shortcoming was the absence of what may be called a philosophy behind the programme of action of the rebel peasants, which, by relating the peasants' grievances to some fundamental social and economic institutions, could provide the rebels with a broad perspective for their movement. The main concern of the peasants was the removal of some specific immediate grievances. The criterion of judging what particular set of conditions properly constituted a grievance was whether the existing law approved or disapproved of such conditions. For instance, the asking by *zamindars* of a larger quantum of rent irrespective of form or occasion, constituted a grievance where the law disapproved of it. The abruptness with which such demands were made by the *zamindars* made them all the more galling to the peasants. The acceptance by the peasants of this criterion, naturally imposed serious restraints on their movements, from the very beginning. This meant that they did not question those institutions the working of which added to their grievances. The removal of such grievances, therefore, deprived the movement of the basic impulse which could sustain it over a long period.

It was once thought that the participation of a section of the intelligentsia in the movement of the peasants, which was a particularly striking phenomenon during the agitation over the Bengal Tenancy Bill (1879-85), gave the movement a radical tone. Jatindra Mohun Tagore, Secretary, British Indian Association (an organization dominated by zamindars) explained the social roots of this alleged radicalism and its nature thus:

> They have neither status nor stake in society, and to attain the one or the other or both, they resort to various kinds of agitations, social, religious, reformatory and so on....They are for the most part East Bengal men, joined by some English-returned natives, who also hail from that part of the country. Many of them have seen something or read still more of the doings of the Irish agitators, and with a natural love of emulation and a highly ambitious

mind, they would fain try their chance in the socialist line to eke out, if possible, a living, or create a position for themselves by following in the footsteps of their European examplars.... They go to the ryots, pretend to be their friends, sow seeds of dissension between them and the zamindars, and thus set class against class....In their pretended zeal in the interests of the ryots they had, two years ago, nearly brought the country to a blaze by inciting agrarian insurrection....The Bengal Tenancy Bill... has proved a powerful weapon in their hands for setting class against class.[2]

Such a characterization of their plans of action was far from correct. It was not enough that some of them had radical faiths. In fact the peasant movement was not appreciably affected by such faiths, and they scarcely left any trace after the Tenancy Bill agitation had died out.

The nationalist movement led by the Congress had in its early phase an elaborate agrarian programme, but could not provide an appropriate "philosophy" for a broad-based peasant movement. The Congress agrarian programme was mostly confined to a critical analysis of the British land revenue administration in India. The British land revenue policy, a feature of which was believed to be a drive for the maximization of land revenue, was denounced by the Congress as one of the most vital causes of India's poverty, since the high revenue demand was thought to be the biggest single drain on the surplus generated in the agricultural sector, thus keeping the accumulation of capital at a frightfully low level and making the peasant economy increasingly vulnerable to occasional failures of crops. Arguing from this premise, the Congress concluded that a demand for the fixation of the land revenue would help to resolve the crisis in the nation's economy. Hence its plea for the extension of the permanent settlement of the Bengal type to other parts of India. The support for the Bengal model however did not necessarily imply a support for the particular zamindari system of Bengal, with which the permanent settlement was associated from its beginning.

[2]*Private Correspondence of Ripon with persons in India,* 1883, Vol. 1; Letter No. 335; Tagore wrote the letter to Bayley, Member of the Viceroy's Council, and it was enclosed in Bayley's letter to the Private Secretary to the Viceroy, 5 June 1883.

Curiously enough, the Congress accepted the zamindari system for granted, and tended to ignore the fact that most of the zamindars were mere parasites living off the labours of peasants, and that the numerous exactions on their part did constitute a factor in the impoverishment of the peasantry.

Some Congress leaders occasionally took part in the peasants' struggle, but the fact was that sometimes they were drawn into it in spite of themselves and this participation was not part of any commitment by the Congress as an organization to the struggle. We can take Gandhiji's defence of the interests of the indigo cultivators of Champaran (1917) as an illustration. The Congress had nothing to do with the movement. In fact, as Gandhiji wrote, it was practically unknown in those parts. His confessions are revealing:

I did not then know the name, much less the geographical position, of Champaran, and I had hardly any notion of indigo plantations. I had seen packets of indigo, but little dreamed that it was grown and manufactured in Champaran at great hardship to thousands of agriculturists.[3]

To Gandhiji, however, the indigo system appeared as an isolated instance of an unjust system, and not as a part of a wider institutional set-up. Moreover, he was cautious not to give the movement a political colour. His stand was justifiable once we assume the correctness of his understanding and characterization of the indigo system and of the aims of his movement, i.e. to reform the indigo system for the time being and not to destroy it.[4]

The first significant contacts of Jawaharlal Nehru with the peasantry too were quite fortuitous. "I was thrown," he tells us, "almost without any will of my own, into contact with the peasantry."[5] This is explicable once we keep in mind the particular aims of the

[3]M.K. Gandhi, *An Autobiography* (Ahmedabad, 1945), Part V, Ch. 12.

[4]"I had decided that nothing should be done in the name of the Congress... For the name of the Congress was the *bete noire* of the Government and their controllers—the planters.... Therefore we had decided not to mention the name of the Congress and not to acquaint the peasants with the organization called the Congress." (*Ibid*, Ch. 14).

[5]*Ibid.*, Ch. 8.

Congress at the time, and also the nature of the social groups whose interests the realization of such aims would have promoted. What Nehru wrote of the kind of politics he had been engaged in, till 1919-1920, largely applies to the politics of the dominant Congress leadership at the time:

> My politics had been those of my class, the bourgeoisie. Indeed all vocal politics then were those of the middle classes, and Moderate and Extremist alike represented them and, in different keys, sought their betterment. The Moderate represented especially the handful of the upper middle class who had on the whole prospered under British rule and wanted no sudden changes which might endanger their present position and interests. They had close relations with the British Government and the big landlord class. The Extremist represented also the lower ranks of the middle class. The industrial workers, their number swollen up by the war, were only locally organized in some places and had little influence. The peasantry were a blind, poverty-stricken, suffering mass, resigned to their miserable fate and sat upon and exploited by all who came in contact with them—the Government, landlords, money-lenders, petty officials, police, lawyers, priests.[6]

II

It was in the period under review that we find the gradual emergence of a strong peasant movement equipped with the philosophy of a kind which enabled it to transcend peculiarly local limits. Such a movement, however, cannot be traced from the beginning of this period. A great upsurge did occur among the peasantry in 1920-1921, primarily as a consequence of the Non-Cooperation movement. For the first time after the widespread agitation against the partition of Bengal (1905), the nationalist leadership sought to draw the masses into the nationalist movement. This by itself could not move the peasants much. The Congress leadership did not intend it either. But the Non-Cooperation movement created an atmosphere which was favourable to the growth of an

[6]Jawaharlal Nehru, *An Autobiography* (Calcutta, 1962), p. 48.

independent peasant movement. The scope of the Non-Coop-erators' programme tended to widen, and included at one time agitation against the payment of *choukidari* (village police) tax and land revenue. Examples of non-payment of land revenue to the Government by the peasants (where such a system of direct payment prevailed) undoubtedly encouraged similar evasions of payment of rent to *zamindars*. It is also probable that some local leaders having radical faiths and acting on their own judge-ment irrespective of Congress leadership had a hand in the peasant agitations, which gradually grew to an alarming extent.[7]

With the calling off of the Non-Cooperation movement, the main impulse behind the peasant agitations quickly disappeared. Even if the former movement had continued it is doubtful whether the Congress leadership could have for long ignored the implications of the growing peasant movement for the nationalist movement. Though the Congress wanted the peasants to participate in the nationalist movement the emphasis throughout was on how to strengthen it through such participations. If the peasants through an independent movement of their own threatened to be a divisive force in it then the Congress would have preferred doing without them. The resolution of the Congress Working Committee at Bardoli (12 February 1922) was bitterly critical not only of the occurrence of violence in the movement, but also of any indepen-dent peasant movement inevitably developing into a kind of "No Rent" movement:

[7]This was how some of the local journals reacted :—
Tippera Guide, Comilla, (24 January 1922): "The spirit of non-cooperation has spread into the lower stratum of society. The non-cooperation movement has assumed threatening proportions and the storm of unrest is blowing over the villages."
Herald, Dacca (9 February 1922) : "If the proportion of private owners of land be taken to be 10 per cent, it would be much more in Eastern Bengal, then the campaign of non-payment of taxes would at once mean a fight between this 10 per cent, on one side and the 90 per cent on the other. On the one side will be skill, resource and accumulated strength and on the other shall be num-bers to swamp the other side. There will be set in the country a regular civil war."
Atma Sakti, Calcutta (5 April 1922) : "A social revolution without political freedom will be injurious to a dependent country.... Who will deny that if the ire of the masses is once roused against social oppressions, etc., to which they have been subjected for centuries, it will consume the whole community like a volcanic eruption."

The Working Committee advises Congress workers and organizations to inform the peasants that withholding of rent payment to the zamindars is contrary to the Congress resolutions and injurious to the best interests of the country. The Working Committee assures the zamindars that the Congress movement is in no way intended to attack their legal rights, and that even where the ryots have grievances, the Committee desires that redress be sought by mutual consultation and arbitration.

As a result the peasant movement suffered a great set-back. However, peasants got opportunities to renew their activities when the Government brought a Bill in 1923 for amending the Bengal Tenancy Act of 1885. The changes that were contemplated were many, but the one that created quite a stir at the time related to the sharecroppers, *bargadars,* who constituted a considerable group. They had neither legal rights, nor in most cases any customary rights in the lands they cultivated. The zamindars or the richer peasants whose lands the *bargadars* cultivated could evict them without much ceremony. The Government contemplated conferring on them the status of "occupancy ryots," a group enjoying special legal protection in regard to the tenure of their holdings and the level of their rent. This daring move created much enthusiasm among the *bargadars.* They formed, for the first time, their own associations in various places. But their enthusiasm was not enough to create a strong movement for which they needed active co-operation of other social groups. This was mostly wanting. On the other hand the zamindars and the substantial peasants whose interests were threatened by the Bill opposed it strongly. Several newspapers and journals which used to uphold their point of view also joined the protest. So did the members of the Swaraj Party and, of course, the representatives of the zamindars in the Legislative Council. Moreover, some zamindars and richer peasants fearing that some revolutionary measures would soon be adopted, hastened to evict their *bargadars,* in a desperate attempt to save as much as possible before the worst came to the worst, even though this rash step resulted in an appreciable contraction of cultivation. This opposition persuaded the Government to leave *bargadars* and landowners to themselves.

III

The formation of the Workers' and Peasants' Party (1926-28), constituted a turning point in the history of the growth of the peasant movement, particularly in Bengal. Its origin and programme was thus described by the Defence Counsel at the Meerut Conspiracy Case:

> Its world outlook was Marxian, and it applied Marxian principles to its study of the contemporary political situation and the social and economic organization in India. The background of the formation of the party was the result of a growing feeling that the way the Congress had been leading the country's struggle for freedom was wrong. The Congress, the founders of the Party felt, misunderstood the class character of the groups hostile to this struggle, and this had resulted in weakening the struggle.

The *Principles and Policy* of the Party says:

> The chief exploiting interests were British imperialism, Indian capitalists, landlords and princes, and there were no chances of any serious divisions among the ruling classes, and they jointly exploited the large masses of workers and peasants.

The Congress was not sufficiently aware of this. The members of the Workers' and Peasants' Party felt indignant

> at the way the Congress had been used for their own purposes by the landlords and capitalists. The collapse of the Non-cooperation Movement and the experience of the Swarajists in the Assembly had convinced them that the programme based on the co-operation of the exploiting classes, who were themselves in part a creation of an alien rule, was not enough to achieve national liberation. They decided that the dynamic force of a mass movement should be the sole basis of national struggle.

The Programme of the Party was "complete national independence from British imperialism and a democratic organization of society involving the nationalization of key industries and appropriation of land without any compensation." For achieving this the Party "decided to establish contacts with all anti-imperialist organizations and work among all politically revolutionary social strata." To increase the momentum of the mass movement it was decided to establish mass organizations and organize mass demonstrations and mass non-payment of taxes and rent and general strike.

The Party preached these ideals in Bengal through two Bengali journals, *Langal* (Plough) and *Ganavani* (Voice of the People). Here was a plan of integrating an independent peasant movement with the general anti-imperialist struggle.

It is not known whether Marxian ideas influenced the leaders of the peasant movement before the October Revolution in Russia. There is no doubt that such ideas quickly spread in Bengal after the Revolution. The reports of the Intelligence Branch of the Political Department of the Government of Bengal suggest that by 1920 the circulation of "Bolshevik" literature was large enough to attract the attention of the Government. A number of leading journals of the time (like the *Samhati, Atma-sakti, Samkha, Bijli, Dhumketu* and *Dainik Basumati*) show how deeply the revolution had moved a sizeable section of the Bengali intelligentsia. The stir created by it soon reached even the rural masses. The ideas that attracted them most were in fact simplified versions of the Marxian concepts of social classes and class struggle. The educated members of society, with whom rural masses presumably came into contact, taught them that the zamindars were mostly responsible for their poverty and misery, and that the destruction of the zamindari system would bring them prosperity and happiness. What had happened in Russia was presented as a prototype of the things to come in Bengal after the elimination of the tyrannical zamindars. Lenin represented to them the ideal type of leader to lead them to such a goal. Rathindra Nath Tagore, son of the poet Rabindra Nath Tagore, visited their estates in East Bengal a few years after the first world war. At that time he met a number of peasants who were inspired by such faiths. Once when he was discussing with a group of peasants how best to improve agriculture, a fairly old peasant intervened and talked disparagingly of the nationalist leaders. According to him, they talked big but were completely ineffective when it came to concrete action. He concluded his discourse thus: "Were there such a man as Lenin in the country, everything would be put right."[8]   The poet Tagore himself saw when he visited some parts of Eastern Bengal in 1926, how "innumerable" local literary journals were propagating a cult of violence directed against zamindars and money-lenders.[9]

The influence of the Marxian ideas was thus gradually spreading. The formation of the Workers' and Peasants' Party was, however, a significant point in the process. Instead of various agencies scattered over the country, including a number of literary journals which had seldom any consistent social and political philosophy, an organized group (in addition to one or two more) now took upon itself the propagation of Marxian ideas and it formed a nucleus for the growth of independent peasant associations.

One finds here the vital role of ideas in building up the base of a peasant movement. It is, however, doubtful whether a "philosophy" alone could produce, let alone sustain it. Without the presence of objective political and economic conditions, the new ideas would have soon lost their force. Such conditions emerged mainly as a result of the economic depression of the thirties. Awadheswar Prasad Singh, Secretary to the Bihar Provincial Kisan Sabha, emphasized the point in 1938: "The Kisan movement as developed today is the direct outcome of the objective situation intensified by the agricultural crisis."[10]

Fluctuations in the prices of agricultural produces occurred in Bengal and Bihar.   Changes in the state of crops, either a shortfall in the production or a bumper harvest in the context of a more or less fixed market, reacted sharply on the prices.   Two other characteristics of a predominantly peasant economy, particularly of its monetized sector, also account for such variations—the tendency of the output of primary products to be inelastic and the fluctuating demand for such products.[11]

[8]Rathindra Nath Tagore, *Pitri Smriti* (Reminiscences of my Father).

[9]"Raiyater Katha" (About the Peasants) in *Collected Works*, (Centenary Edition), Vol. 13, pp. 345-6.

[10]*Amrita Bazar Patrika,* 26 April 1938, Report on the Second Session of the Gaya District Kisan Conference, held on 23-24 April 1938.

[11]Discussions on the point are innumerable.   Here is a good summary: "The output of primary products tends to be inelastic, which means that it does not change very much in response to changes in the price.   This is essentially a matter of time-periods.   The output of manufactured goods can often be

When depression set in, the prices slumped. In the period between 1929 and 1935 a fall by 60 per cent to 70 per cent was a
common phenomenon in many districts of Bengal and Bihar.
There was a steep fall in the prices of jute, which was the most
important cash crop of the peasants in many districts. The crash
came abruptly. Since the beginning of the 20th century, the jute
prices showed a steady rise, aggregating to about 150 per cent
in the period between 1900 and 1929. The peak year was 1925,
when the prices shot to Rs 16 per maund. In 1933 the harvest
prices fell as low as a little over Rs 3/-. It was remarkable that
for the first time since 1900 there came about an organized move
for restricting the jute cultivation.[12]

The extent of the fall in the prices was not however entirely
unprecedented. What was particularly striking was the duration
of the depression and its universality. The steep fall in the prices
was of course a disaster for the peasants, but their recovery from
its effects would have been easier if the disaster had not continued
beyond a single year. It lasted for about eight years. Moreover,
the depression affected not only one or two agricultural produces,
but all the produces at the same time. Previously this was scarcely
the case, so that the loss from one crop was at least partly made
up by the gains from another crop. Where, for instance, the conditions of soil and climate made the cultivation of jute possible,
a slump in the prices of rice resulting mostly from a bumper harvest
led the peasantry to increase the cultivation of jute. Similarly,
a fall in the prices of jute, so much so that its cultivation scarcely

---

increased quite quickly by putting in new plant and equipment, or simply by
working overtime; but it takes a long time to grow more rubber trees or sink a
new copper mine. Similarly, the output of manufactured goods can be reduced
by laying men off; but coffee trees or cotton plants will go on producing
regardless. Moreover, the demand for primary producing fluctuates much
more than the demand for manufactured goods, precisely because it is known
that a shortage will not result in much extra production, so that people will react
to any hint of a shortage by intensive stock-piling; and similarly, when the threat
of a shortage disappears, will live off their stocks and thus drastically reduce
their demand for what is currently being produced." Big variations in price
inevitably result from a combination of these two circumstances. (Michael
Stewart, *Keynes and After,* a Pelican Original, pp. 260-1).

[12]*Report of the Bengal Jute Enquiry Committee,* 1934; Vol. 1, Majority Report,
Para 13.

repaid the producers, led them to abandon it for the time being and to concentrate on rice. The well-known phenomenon of the interchangeability of rice and jute thus partly resulted from the movement of their relative prices.

The depression suddenly aggravated all the ills from which the peasants had long been suffering. Where their income was derived almost entirely from the sale of their crops, the consequences are not hard to realize. The burden of their normal unavoidable financial obligations suddenly increased, since they had to part with a far larger quantity of their produce than before to meet their old obligations. The upward movement of rent during the long spell of high prices of nearly two decades and a half, particularly since 1905, made the rent obligations heavy indeed. Rents were not automatically reduced when the depression had set in, at least not proportionately to the fall in the prices. Arrears of rent thus tended to accumulate, leading in several cases to eviction of the peasants. Where the commutation of produce rent into money rent had taken place on a considerable scale during the period of the high prices, the distress of the peasants was naturally far greater, since the system of produce rent imposed a much heavier burden on the peasants in terms of the quantity of produce they had to surrender to the zamindars. It is, however, wrong to suppose, as Dr Walter Hauser did,[13] that the kisan movement in Bihar was mostly confined to the regions where the system of produce rent prevailed. The intensity of the distress resulting from the depression, varied of course from region to region, but it was severe enough to produce deep discontent in the peasants which resulted in kisan movements. That was why in Bengal proper where the system of produce rent was confined to small regions the kisan movement was no less widespread or intense. This was partly because of the fact that rent formed a small part of the total financial obligations of the peasants. In fact, their debt obligations were also quite heavy, and indeed exceeded the rent obligations in several places. Even where the peasants had

---

[13]Walter Hauser, *The Bihar Provincial Kisan Sabha, 1929-1942*; *A Study of an Indian Peasant Movement* (unpublished Ph.D. Thesis, the University of Chicago, 1961). I have used a copy in microfilm kept in the Nehru Memorial Museum and Library, New Delhi.

not incurred fresh debts, the falling prices by themselves made the debt obligations still heavier.

The depression with all its consequences seemed to reinforce the Marxian class analysis. The poverty and misery of the peasantry which the depression had suddenly brought to the surface, were attributed to the particular class composition or society, which according to the Marxists was mainly determined by the fact that the law had invested in the class of *zamindars* property right in the land. Elimination of this poverty and building up the base of a new peasant economy therefore necessitated the destruction of the *zamindari* system. For this the peasants had to organize themselves and fight the system out. In view of the magnitude of the economic crisis produced by the depression, it seems surprising that it was only in 1936 that the abolition of the system was formally stated as one of the basic aims of the kisan movement.

This formed a strikingly new feature of the peasant movement. Even earlier, peasant agitations had occasionally led to a complete suspension of rent payment. This, however, did not result from any doubts on the part of the rebel peasants as to the propriety or legality of the institution of zamindari, but from a dead-lock created by the resolve of the peasant community not to pay rent exceeding a certain rate which the zamindars on their part had found unacceptable. The warring groups soon found a way out, and rent payment became normal. The aim of eliminating the zamindari system was indeed revolutionary. This inevitably meant that the struggle would not end with the mere removal of some particular grievances.

Independent peasant movements in several places gradually came to be influenced by ideas derived mainly from the Marxian philosophy. This transformation can be clearly traced in Bihar.[14]

It was just humanitarianism, a deep compassion for the wretched peasantry, that first led Swami Sahajanand and others to try to organize them around some specific demands. Being nationalists they had no doubt whatsoever, in the beginning, about the priority of the nationalist movement, and did not hesitate to subordinate the kisan agitation to it. However they gradually outgrew their belief that this subordination would eventually do real good to the peasants. This happened as a result of ideological influences.

[14]*Ibid.*

It is significant to note that in the long period between 1920, the year in which he took a leading part in the Non-Cooperation movement in Bihar, and 1927, when he first began to take a keen interest in the problems of the peasantry, Swami Sahajanand seemed to have been completely unaware of the existence of a distinctively peasant question. This was partly due to the fact that after the movement of the indigo peasants in Champaran a peasant movement worth its name was virtually non-existent in Bihar. With the abrupt withdrawal by Gandhiji of the Non-Cooperation movement, the Swamiji, like a number of Congress leaders of Bihar at the time, became actively associated with an organization of the prominent zamindars belonging to the Bhumiar Caste—Bhumiar Brahmin Sabha. He was asked by the Bhumiar zamindars to establish at Bihta in Patna district, an *ashram* mainly for the purpose of giving their children lessons in Sanskrit. The *ashram* came into existence in 1927.

It was in the zamindari estates around the *ashram* that he had his first contacts with the peasants. He understood some of the worst features of the zamindari system, including the system of forced labour, *begar,* and thus gradually realized the need for an independent organization of the peasants. In 1929 the Bihar Provincial Kisan Sabha was set up with the co-operation of the major Congress leaders. To begin with, he conceived of the kisan movement "in the spirit of a reformist....At that time I did not know what revolution was, nor did I understand its import....What we had in our mind was to do some good to peasants by exerting constitutional pressure and getting their grievances redressed."

Even this "reformist" movement could not be reconciled with the nationalist movement. When the Congress started the Civil Disobedience Movement, the Swamiji promptly suspended the kisan agitation since he feared an independent kisan agitation would tend to "weaken our struggle for freedom."

A large number of peasants did participate in the Congress movement, but the utter indifference of the Congress leadership to the grievances of the peasants shocked the Swamiji. Peasants in numerous places, as in Gaya under the leadership of Sri Jadunandan Sarma, a close associate of the Swamiji, sent numerous petitions to the Congress Agrarian Committee (1931), explaining such grievances. The Committee, however, had scarcely anything new to say.

The disillusionment with the Congress leadership alone was not enough to make a radical peasant leader of the Swamiji. He also needed a social philosophy, and his close association with the leaders of the Congress Socialist Party soon provided him with one. The Programme adopted by the Party in October 1934 particularly impressed him. It included, among other things, transfer of all power to the producing masses, elimination of zamindars and "all other classes of exploiters without compensation" and redistribution of land to the peasants. The Swamiji's radicalism can in fact be dated back to 1934 when he started thinking in terms of abolition of the zamindari system. Initially, however, he feared that this stand would alienate a considerable number of supporters from the Kisan Sabha, particularly the small landholders. Such doubts were soon overcome. The manifesto of the Bihar Provincial Kisan Sabha (11 July 1936) outlined some of the Sabha's "basic" demands. These included abolition of the zamindari system, the creation of a system of land tenure where peasants could own land and the provision of "gainful employment" to the landless.

Similar Kisan Sabhas were gradually formed in other parts of the country. Such sabhas, however did not for long remain isolated from their counterparts. The first session of the All-India Kisan Sabha with Swami Sahajanand as the President, was held on 11 April 1936. The "Manifesto of Demands of the Kisans of India" adopted by the All-India Kisan Sabha Committee (21 August 1936) formulated the "main object" and the "main task" of the Kisan movement. The "object" was—"complete freedom from economic exploitation and achievement of full economic and political power for peasants and workers and all other exploited classes." The "task" was—"organization of peasants to fight for their immediate political and economic demands in order to prepare them for emancipation from every form of exploitation," and this was to be done through "active participation in the national struggle for independence."

IV

The Kisan Sabha was not, however, the only organization of the peasants at the time. In Bengal the Muslim League sought to "wean away" the peasants from the influence of the Kisan Sabha. The League feared that increasing activities of the Kisan Sabhas among the Muslim peasants would endear the Congress to them and thus eventually result in weakening the League's hold over them. To prevent the Muslim peasants from attending the session of the All-India Kisan Sabha at Comilla (in Eastern Bengal, May 1938), the League members went to the extent of scattering pages from the Koran on the main road to the Conference, believing that the Muslim peasants would not be bold enough to trample on them.

The success of the League was only partial. Whatever success it had, was largely attributable to the particular composition of the Bengal peasantry. The majority of them were Muslims, while their zamindars were mostly Hindus. The League, professing to defend the interests of the Muslim community, succeeded to a certain extent in influencing the Muslim peasants by playing on their religious sentiments. It, however, did not set up any separate peasant organization.[15]

The Krishak Proja Party, another organization working among the peasants in Bengal, had a much wider influence on the peasantry, though it was mostly confined to the richer section of the Muslim peasantry. The proclaimed aims of the Party gave it the look of a radical peasant organization. The Party's programme advocated the abolition of zamindari as also the elimination of the host of intermediaries between the state and the actual peasant cultivators. It stood for a "permanent peasant proprietary system of land" where "all proprietors of land will be the actual cultivators," and would pay a fixed tax, not rent or revenue to the state."

The differences between the Krishak Proja Party and the Kisan Sabhas were, however, fundamental. The former conceived of the peasant movement primarily as an economic movement, unrelated to the struggle for the country's freedom. To the latter, the peasant movement formed a vital part of the freedom struggle, since the *zamindari* system, which the movement aimed to destroy, was propped up by British rule. Moreover, the Krishak Proja Party had serious reservations about the way the Kisan Sabhas had

[15]The Muslim League leaders, unlike the *wahabi* and *ferazee* leaders working among the peasantry in Bengal in the 19th century, were not in the least influenced by the social radicalism of Islam.

been leading the peasant movement, and strongly disapproved of
any class struggle of the Kisan Sabha style, which necessarily involved some violence at a certain stage.   This was how two leaders
of the Proja Party felt over the question.   Qazi Imam Husain
remarked :

> The distinction between the kisan movement in the United
> Provinces...and the Proja movement of Bengal is remarkable in
> the fact that the former one is a little aggressive, inclined towards
> socialism...while the latter is purely economic,   parliamentary
> in its demand and is averse to violence.[16]

The worsening situation in regard to rural indebtedness which
reduced several small owner-peasants to the status of agricultural
labourers provoked M. Azizul Haque, another Proja leader, who
remarked :

> The process has to be stopped if a universal agrarian unrest with
> its disastrous repercussions on the province as a whole has to
> be avoided.   The average Bengal agriculturist is much too
> conservative, spiritual and resigned to his fate to be easily amen-
> able to socialistic and communistic preachings.   But a province
> with a vast mass of landless labourers as one of the features of
> its rural economy has within it the seeds of real danger.   Dic-
> tatorship of the proletariat is a very comprehensive phrase and
> may be twisted and distorted to appeal to the sentiments of the
> aggrieved and suffering classes.   Release the cultivator from
> the bonds of indebtedness, help him to make agriculture pay and
> the country will be saved from some of the dangers of commu-
> nism.[17]

The Proja leaders, naturally, wanted the peasants to keep away
from mass movements.   The initiative of the peasants inevitably
languished under such circumstances, and often the leaders acted
on behalf of the peasants.   Through the Provincial Legislatures
they put pressure on the Government for the adoption of particular

[16]Qazi Imam Husain, "Nature of the Proja Movement in Bengal," in *Amrita
Bazar Patrika,* 31 March 1937.
[17]M. Azizul Huque, *The Man Behind the Plough*, pp. 151-2.

measures for redressing some of the grievances of the peasants. The peasants were mainly supposed to elect them to the legislature. The Proja movement was aptly described by Qazi Imam Husain as being "parliamentary in methods." Such a movement could do little harm to the radical kisan agitation.

V

The ultimate aim of the Kisan movement was, as we have noted earlier, "complete freedom from economic exploitation and achievement of full economic and political power for peasants and workers and all other exploited classes." The achievement of political power for peasants was part of the larger question of the country's political freedom. And until the political freedom was achieved the Kisan movement aimed mainly at the destruction of the zamindari system. The demand for the abolition of the zamindari system came from various other quarters also. The assumption that the abolition would have a big role to play in the economic regeneration of Bengal was so widespread that an enquiry into its feasibility formed one of the terms of reference of the newly set-up Bengal Land Revenue Commission (November 1938). The Kisan Sabhas did not, however, leave the question to the Commission. It launched a countrywide agitation to press its demands. The Commission in fact recommended the abolition of the zamindari system.

The immediate programme of the Kisan Sabhas had various aspects. The struggle for the reduction of rent and debts was by far the most important.

The Civil Disobedience movement had already created among the peasants a spirit of defiance against their zamindars. Some zamindars of the Tamluk sub-division of Midnapur, for instance, were threatened by their tenants that "they would not any longer receive the customary services of the labourers, barbers, *dhobis* (washerman) etc."[18] The Depression made reduction of rent an increasingly urgent question for the peasants. And with the increasing strength of the Kisan movement, the struggle for such reductions soon developed into a virtual "no rent" movement.

[18]Bengal Land Revenue Administration Report, 1930-1931, para 38.

By 1932, the spread of the movement was alarming enough to call for the adoption of preventive measures by the Government. In the worst-affected districts like Noakhali and Tippera, the Government promulgated Ordinance No 111 of 1932 under which any person who instigates directly or otherwise any person or class of persons not to pay rent was made liable to six months' imprisonment. Notices under Section 144 of the Criminal Procedure Code were issued by the Sub-divisional Officers prohibiting meetings organized by the Krishak Sabhas. A common slogan of the peasants in many parts of Bihar was "*Malguzari lo ge kaise, danda hamara zindabad*" (How could our rents be realized ? Long live our cudgels).

The militant peasants could not, however, be tamed. In fact, several developments between 1934 and 1939 tended to harden their attitude. The anti-money-lender legislation of the period was one such development. Initially it had a modest scope and aimed at curbing mostly the non-Bengali money-lenders, particularly the itinerant Pathans and Kabulis. More stringent measures were taken in 1936. By the Bengal Agricultural Debtors Act, the Government imposed ceilings on interest rates and set up arbitration Boards (called Debt Settlement Boards) empowered to write off a portion of agricultural debts. The existing debts were thus considerably reduced. The peasants however were reluctant to pay even the reduced debts. The result was a virtual moratorium on the payment of debts in many places.

The question of rent was outside the purview of the Act, but an idea increasingly gained ground among the peasants that the Act applied to payment of rent as well. This naturally strengthened the "no-rent" campaign. Complaints of the zamindars on this score became nearly universal,[19] and the Government admitted that they

---

[19]Bengal Land Revenue Commission (also called the Floud Commission) heard these complaints day after day. The Jessore Landholders' Association said: "The Bengal Agricultural Debtors Act has supplied additional impetus and strength to the agrarian agitation and no-rent campaign, and has caused an all-round suspension of rent.... It has engineered a class war and an all-round communist spirit" (Volume IV of the Commission's Report, p. 67). One of the popular slogans was : "Rent is payable when able, land belongs to those who plough." According to the Khulna Landholders' Association, "The ignorant mass has been over-encouraged to think that they can avoid all sorts of payment by taking resort to the law" (*ibid.*, p. 95). The Maldah Land-

were well-founded.[20]

The peasants were encouraged in this by the "electioneering speeches" in 1937. The new Act of 1935 greatly increased the size of the electorate, and during the first election held under the Act (1937) the candidates made big promises to the peasants with a view to getting their votes.   Townend, then Commissioner of the Burdwan Division observed:

> This tendency to refuse rents undoubtedly has its origin in the irresponsible electioneering speeches made by candidates of all parties who sought election to the legislature.... To get the cultivators' vote they spoke as if the interests of the cultivators alone would be considered in future. There was talk of the abolition of the Permanent Settlement, which was understood to mean the abolition of all tenures, and everything possible was done to arouse discontent and to inflate expectations.[21]

Such expectations further arose as a result of the country-wide agitation in 1937 and 1938 over the amendment of the Bengal Tenancy Act.   Some provisions of the Bill, debated in the provincial legislature in April 1937, were quite favourable to the peasants. The Bengal Provincial Kisan Sabha launched an agitation demanding the resignation of the Coalition ministry if it failed to pass the Bill. (The Act was passed in August 1938). An official report noted that partly as a result of this there occurred "a general change in the ideas of the tenants regarding their own rights in the land."[22]

The organization of the Kisan Sabha vastly improved at the same

---

holders' Association remarked: "By the passing of the Act an impression has been firmly rooted in the minds of the agriculturists that they have been released from all liabilities of payments of debts as well as rents" (*Ibid*, p. 111). Equally categorical was the observation of the Bengal Landholders' Association: "Tempers have been roused to such a pitch by incessant preaching of class hatred and zamindar-baiting in particular that cool reasoning can no longer be expected.... The impression is now common that all debts and even arrears of rent can be wiped out by executive order or legislation. (Vol. III, pp. 84 and 107).

[20]*Bengal Land Revenue Administration Report, 1938-1939*, para 39.

[21]*Report of the Floud Commission*, III, 423.

[22]*Bengal Land Revenue Administration Report, 1937-1938*, para 38.

time. This was due to the fact that a number of political workers
who relied till then on "terrorist methods" increasingly lost faith
in their efficacy and were attracted by the Marxian ideas relating
to class struggle and organization of industrial workers and agricultural labourers. The terrorist activities appreciably declined
by 1935. A police report of the year records :

A fresh wave of revolutionary activity is gathering momentum.
A large number of the terrorists are involved in this new movement, which is closely connected with communism and the
methods adopted by the Russian revolutionaries. Terrorists
have already realized that a revolution cannot be brought about
by terrorism alone. It does not produce the social and economic
chaos which is the necessary preliminary to a violent revolution.
Vigorous propaganda on these lines is going on in many quarters...among students, industrial workers and agricultural
labourers.[23]

This trend was not later reversed. Another police report of
1938 says:

Information in the possession of the Government shows beyond
a shadow of doubt that a large proportion of the ex-terrorists
and revolutionaries...are obsessed in varying degrees by theories
of communism....These doctrines are being assiduously propa-
gated among youths and students, labourers and peasants...
The influence of prominent communists is visible in practically
every organization.[24]

The release, by the end of 1938, of most of the persons detained
under Regulation III of 1818, the Bengal Criminal Law Amendment Act of 1930, and the Bengal Suppression of Terrorists Outrages
Act of 1932, resulted in bringing a new vigour to the kisan sabha
and similar other "mass" organizations.[25] The Mymensingh
Landholders' Association despairingly told the Land Revenue
Commission in 1939 that "the leadership of rural areas has fallen

[23]*Bengal Police Administration Report*, 1935, para 32.
[24]*Bengal Police Administration Report*, 1938, para 32.
[25]*Bengal Police Administration Report*, 1939, para 32.

into unworthy hands, and the result is going to be chaos, confusion and communism." By "unworthy hands" the Association meant "socialists, who are a class of educated landless people having no stake in the country."[26] The Bengal Land Revenue Commission had to admit that the growth of a "no-rent mentality among the raiyats had threatened the stability and security of the land system as a whole."[27]

A similar resistance was organized against money-lenders. In fact the no-rent movement and the anti-money-lender movement progressed side by side. In Noakhali, for instance, prior to the launching of a no-rent campaign, anonymous notices were reported to have been received by several money-lenders threatening them with execution if they failed to return the bonds.[28] A meeting in Noakhali of the representatives of the Joint Stock Banks and Loan Offices on January 4, 1932 "viewed with alarm the present situation arising out of the propaganda carried on by some agitators through-out the district instigating people for non-payment of all rents, debts and other dues."[29] A resolution passed at another meeting in the district held on the same day urged the money-lenders "to exempt debtors from all interests and to accept the principal only in 20 instalments in view of the present economic crisis."[30] A police report of 1934 attributed the increase in "dacoity" in Tippera and Noakhali "to the activities of the *krishak samities* which are secret organizations whose main object was to loot wealthy money-lenders and destroy their documents."[31]

When the Congress formed the ministry in Bihar (1937), the Kisan Sabha persuaded it to intervene on behalf of the peasants. The measures of the Congress, however, disappointed the kisan leaders. At the 1937 session of the All-India Kisan Sabha, it was resolved that, if by December 1937 the Congress had failed to adopt more effective measures, "the peasants should be entitled to declare a moratorium themselves and further to boycott any legal machinery set up for reducing or negotiating debts and take

[26]*Report* of the Land Revenue Commission, IV, pp. 286 and 314.
[27]*Report*, I, para 88.
[28]*Amrita Bazar Patrika*, 5 April 1932.
[29]*Ibid.*, 8 January 1932.
[30]*Ibid.*, 7 January 1932.
[31]*Bengal Police Administration Report*, 1934, para 31.

all the concerted measures they might deem fit to promote the object in view."[32]

The Kisan Sabhas also succeeded to some extent in organizing the sharecroppers (*bargadars*). The *bargadari* system was in many places part of the larger question of rural indebtedness. Small owner-peasants, unable to repay the accumulating debts, gradually lost their lands to the money-lenders. The latter, not considering it worthwhile to cultivate such lands themselves, let them out to the expropriated peasants. These peasants continued to cultivate them agreeing to surrender half the gross produce to their creditors.

The *bargadars* were not a docile group. There are several instances of combined resistance by them particularly in the 1920's. This resistance owed much to the hopes aroused in them by a move on the part of the Government for a better legal definition of their rights on land. Towards the end of 1924, the Muslim *bargadars* of the *Manikganj* subdivision of Dacca district collectively decided to "boycott the Sabha community," to which their creditors mostly belonged, "on the ground that members of the caste ill-treat their servants, charge interest at exorbitant rates and foreclose on their debtors' lands." Despite its apparent "religious tinge," the movement was "fundamentally economic—a case of peasant versus capitalists," as an official report put it.[33] The movement gradually spread to other parts of Dacca and to Mymensingh, and continued upto 1930.[34] In 1929, in some parts of Jessore the *bargadars* demanded two-thirds of the crop as their share. The zamindars disagreed with their demands with the result that cultivation was stopped. As a consequence the area under cultivation shrank considerably.[35]

The Depression further aggravated the plight of *bargadars*. The high level of rent, usually half the gross produce, was by itself enough to reduce them to dire poverty. Their distress increased in the context of a steep fall in the prices of agricultural produce. At the same time, the number of *bargadars* went on increasing, primarily because more owner-peasants lost their lands to money-lenders. The anti-money-lender measures of the Government, like reducing the

[32]*Amrita Bazar Patrika,* 18 November 1937.
[33]*Bengal Land Revenue Administration Report,* 1923-1924, para 2.
[34]*Ibid.,* 1925, para 35. *Ibid.,* 1927-1928, para 35. *Ibid.,* 1929-1930, para 38.
[35]*Ibid.,* 1928-1929, para 2 and 38.

debts of the peasants, gave them some relief. This was, however, temporary and before long the peasantry realized the adverse effects of these measures. Scared by such measures, the creditors refused to lend any money at all. Rural credit was nearly frozen as a result. But since the peasants in the grip of the depression could scarcely do without borrowing, they eventually agreed to borrow on more stringent conditions than before. Curiously enough, though the size of indebtedness actually diminished in the late 1930's, the number of distress sales of peasants' holdings largely increased. The Bengal Land Revenue Commission estimated the size of the *barga* cultivation in 1939 at more than 20 per cent of the total cultivation.

The influence of the Kisan Sabhas among the sharecroppers was mainly visible in some districts in northern and eastern Bengal. In northern Bengal, the main centre of their activities was the district of Dinajpur where their primary concern was the problem of the *adhiyars,* the local name for sharecroppers. The *adhi* system was quite extensive, and about 25 per cent of the cultivation in the south and west of the district was done by the *adhiyars.*[36] They were indebted to the landowners, *jotedars,* as they had a precarious tenure in the lands they cultivated. Indeed, such was their "precarious position" that "instances have been found where the threat of withholding *adhi* settlement has been used to force surrender in social quarrels."[37]

The *adhiyars* had tamely accepted their fate without a protest till the Kisan Sabhas appeared on the scene. The Kisan Sabhas found it very difficult to break this inertia. But once roused from difference they seldom relapsed into it thereafter. The struggle of the *adhiyars* developed mainly over two demands. The first related to the question of the place where the crops would be stored before division. Previously the place used to be the *khamar* (own place) of the *jotedars.* This gave the *jotedars* opportunity for intrigues, and it often happened that the *adhyar's* share dwindled to insignificance, because they claimed much of it on one pretext or another. The *adhiyars* now demanded that the place for storing the crop should be of their choice. The second demand related to the rates of interest charged on the grain-loans made by the *jotedars.* The *adhiyars* could scarcely do without such loans, since their stock of grain used to be insufficient. The rate of interest used to be about

[36]F.O. Bell, *Dinajpur Survey and Settlement Report,* 1934-1940, para 20.
[37]*Ibid.*

50 per cent. They now refused to pay more than 25 per cent. If the grain lent was exclusively seed-grain, they were reluctant to pay any interest.

The struggle began in 1939 and gradually intensified. Even severe police repression on the Kisan leaders could not suppress it. The *jotedars* eventually came to a compromise, mainly as a result of the intervention of the Magistrate. The settlement of the main points of dispute was now left to a Board (panchayat) composed of members chosen by both *adhiyars* and *jotedars*.

In eastern Bengal, the main area of the Kisan Sabha activities among the sharecroppers was the pargana Susang, in the district of Mymensingh, inhabited largely by tribes, including the Hajangs and Garos. The Kisan movement, beginning in 1938, was aimed against the most widely prevailing system of rent payment— the *tanka* system. Under it a fixed portion of the produce had to be paid as rent, whatever the produce. The movement partly succeeded. The *tanka* system was not formally abolished, but the Hajangs were given the option of paying their rent in kind or cash. This was no small gain, in view of the tendency of the agricultural prices to rise since 1939.

In 1939 the Kisan Sabha sought to organize a larger movement in northern Bengal. It demanded an increase in the share of the *bargadar* from one-half to two-thirds. The movement did not catch on. However, it was the beginning of the *te-bhaga* movement, which started in 1946.

The Kisan Sabha was aware that such reforms were only partial solutions of the problem of *bargadars*. To the Sabha the real solution was the abolition of the *barga* tenure altogether and the eventual conversion of *bargadars* into occupancy ryots, defined and protected by law. While struggling for the reforms the Sabha did never lose sight of this ultimate goal. It is quite likely that the arguments of the Bengal Land Revenue Commission (1940), in favour of abolition of the *barga* system were influenced by the constant preachings of the Kisan Sabha.

In Bihar the Kisan Sabhas had another grim battle to fight to stop evictions of peasants by *zamindars* from the so-called *bakhast* land. These lands were the zamindars' "own" lands, distinguishable from the lands cultivated and owned by the peasants. The origin of the *bakhast* land can be traced to the dispossession by zamindars of the owner-peasants on grounds of non-payment of rent. The formal dispossession, however, rarely resulted in the change of cultivators. Evictions on a considerable scale began in 1937. The zamindars were provoked largely by the agitation at the time over the amendment of the Tenancy Bill. They feared that the amended Act would confer on the cultivators the status of occupancy ryots, which in fact was precisely one of the demands of the Kisan Movement.

The Kisan Movement was aimed both at restoring to the owner-peasants the lands they had lost and preventing the evictions from the *bakhast* lands. The measures of the Congress ministry in regard to the first question disappointed the kisan leaders. These measures provided for the restoration of all lands, in respect of which the rent was enhanced or commuted into cash in the years between 1911 and 1937, and also of the lands sold in the years between 1929 and 1937. They, however, did not apply in cases where the zamindar was exempted from the payment of agricultural income-tax and where the land had already been settled with other tenants "in good faith." Thus only a small portion of the *bakhast* land was affected.

Far more difficult was the problem arising out of the evictions from the *bakhast* land. The Kisan Sabhas organized *satyagrahas* by the evicted peasants—thereby preventing others from cultivating the land. This resulted often in violent clashes. Such clashes were most numerous in Barhayiatal in Monghyr district, a place mostly inhabited by the low-caste *Dhanuks*. The Kisan Sabha had a strong hold there, having led in 1936 a fight against *begari* (unpaid labour). The All-India Kisan Sabha observed the "Bihar Kisan Day" on 18 October 1937 as a mark of protest against the severe police repression on the *satyagrahis*.[38]

Another problem which the Bihar Kisan Sabha had to face was that of the sugarcane growers. The peasants cultivated sugarcane with or without advances from the sugar mills. With decreasing demand for sugar, the demand of the sugar mills for sugarcane suddenly fell. Earlier in similar circumstances the sugarcane growers could partly make up for the loss by pressing the sugarcane themselves and making molasses, *gur*. Now that the market for *gur* also shrank, the producers had no other alternative but to accept whatever

[38]*Amrita Bazar Patrika,* 16 November 1937. "Agrarian trouble in Barhayiatal" A statement by Karyanand Sarma, Secretary, Monghyr District Kisan Sabha, 15 November 1937.

prices the sugar mills had offered. The Kisan Sabha organized a movement for securing higher prices. In 1933, it asked the producer not to enter into contracts with the mills except through the newly set-up Provincial Sugarcane Sabha. The Kisan Sabha contended that in face of combined opposition by the sugarcane growers the mill-owners would eventually prefer paying higher prices to shutting their mills for want of sugarcane. Similar agitations on a much larger scale took place in 1935 in the Dinajpur subdivision. The Sugar Factories Control Act passed by the Congress ministry fixed a minimum price for sugarcane. In fact this did not help the producers. The Kisan Sabha soon found that "the minimum has invariably become the maximum, as millers have never thought it fit to pay even a pie more than the minimum price fixed by the Government." The Kisan Sabha's success was only partial in respect of this problem.

In the context of the falling prices of agricultural produce, the rates fixed on the basis of the pre-depression prices for the use of the canal water in the Sone canal area in Sahabad and in the Damodar Canal area in Burdwan bacame extremely iniquitous for the peasants using water for canals. A significant aspect of the Kisan Sabha acti-vities was a fight for a reduction in the water-rates. The peasants won a complete victory in the Damodar canal area.

VI

The peasantry in Bengal and Bihar was not at all a homogeneous group. This again posed problems for the Kisan Sabha. The strategy of the Kisan movement in its early phase does not seem to have been influenced very much by the heterogeneous nature of the pea-santry. The earliest constitutional document of the Bihar Kisan Sabha (1929), defined a peasant as anyone whose primary source of livelihood was agriculture. The more elaborate constitution of the Sabha (1936) said essentially the same thing.[39] The Sabha ignored the different aspects of production in agriculture. In fact agriculture provided means of livelihood to different groups in different ways.

It was in the introduction to the Hindi edition of the *Manifesto of the Bihar Kisan Sabha* (1936), that Swami Sahajanand for the first

[39]Hauser, n. 13, Ch. 1.

time considered an agricultural labourer as a peasant. He said: "A peasant is known as a *Grihasta,* a person who earns his livelihood by cultivation and agriculture, be he a petty landlord, ryot or labourer working on wages for ploughing fields."

A separate organization of agricultural labourers was not however considered necessary: "The Kisan Sabha does not desire that by creating a separate organization of agricultural labourers any strife should be let loose between them and landlords and ryots, nor should the latter oppress agricultural labourers."[40] At the 1937 session of the Bihar Provincial Kisan Sabha at Niyamatpur in Gaya district (15 July 1937), Sahajanand said: "The interests of the agricultural labourers and the Kisan are the same."[41]

The ideas of the Kisan leaders gradually changed, presumably because of a better understanding on their part of the then existing agrarian structure. At the first session of the Mymensingh District Krishak Samiti (24 February 1938) the President Muzaffar Ahmed classified the peasants into four groups: (*a*) those who tilled other men's lands; (*b*) those who tilled their own lands and also other men's lands, because their own holdings were not large enough for their subsistence; (*c*) those who had lands just enough for them, and (*d*) those who had enough land and got it cultivated by hired labour. Ahmed felt that the last group should not join the Kisan movement, and that its strength should come from the first three groups.[42] The Secretary of the Bihar Provincial Kisan Sabha, Awadheshwar Prasad Singh, also thought alike, though he thought that the Depression had tended to blur the distinction between a large number of owner-peasants and agricultural labourers.[43]

Gradually the emphasis further changed, and the Bihar Kisan Sabha under the leadership of Swami Sahajanand tended more and more to rely on the "lowest strata of the peasantry" as the backbone of the Kisan movement. He said in 1944:

It is they, the semi-proletarians or the agricultural labourers who have very little land, or no land at all, and the petty cultivators who anyhow squeeze a most meagre living out of the land they

[40]*Ibid.*
[41]*Amrita Bazar Patrika,* 18 July 1937.
[42]*Amrita Bazar Patrika,* 27 February 1938.
[43]*Amrita Bazar Patrika,* 26 April 1938.

cultivate... who are the kisans of our thinking...and who make and must constitute the Kisan Sabha ultimately.[44]

It seems, however, that the Kisan Sabha's success was only partial in bringing the "lowest strata of the peasantry" into the Kisan movement as a permanent force. An enquiry made in 1939 by the Bengal Provincial Kisan Sabha into the nature of the composition of the membership of the Sabha in the Kishoreganj subdivision of Dacca showed that "the majority were raiyats, and a smaller number were under-raiyats and *bargadars*."[45] Swami Sahajanand admitted that even as late as 1944 it was "really the middle and big cultivators ... (who were) for the most part with the Kisan Sabha." He even suspected that the "middle and big cultivators" were "using the Kisan Sabha for their own benefit and gain."[46]

VII

The thirties in which the Kisan movement came into existence and became a powerful force in rural Bengal and Bihar was also the period of great advances in the nation's struggle for freedom led by the Congress. The Kisan Sabha had therefore to define its relations with the Congress. For the sake of convenience the present study of these relations is confined to Bihar. Apart from other reasons, the evaluation by the Kisan Sabha of the performance of the Congress ministry in Bihar, particularly in regard to the peasant question, was a decisive factor that influenced the attitude of the Sabha to the Congress.

The relations were at first quite cordial. This was partly due to the nature of the Kisan leadership. Most of the Kisan leaders in the early phase of the Kisan Movement were also actively connected with the Congress. They believed that by drawing the peasants into the freedom struggle they were only strengthening the Congress organization. They were naturally averse from doing anything which would result in weakening the Congress. Indeed, where the Kisan Move-

---

[44]Hauser, n. 13, Ch. 1.
[45]Oral Evidence of the Bengal Provincial Kisan Sabha before the Floud Commission, 22 March 1939. *Report of the Floud Commission,* Vol. IV, p. 62.
[46]Hauser, n. 13, Ch. 1.

ment was thought to be a divisive force in the nationalist movement, the Kisan leaders promptly called it off.[47]

At the same time, the Kisan leaders had no doubt about the need for an independent organization of the peasants. This was not because of any assumption that by its very structure and composition the Congress would necessarily be hostile to the peasants, but because of a feeling that the Congress was too preoccupied with political questions to take interest in a distinctively peasant question. "The Congress included in its fold various interests," but such diverse interests did not at first appear irreconcilable to the Kisan leaders. On the contrary, they believed that the Congress could be made a real Kisan organization. In fact they justified an independent Kisan organization precisely on the ground that the pressure put on the Congress by it through a broadbased Kisan Movement could prevent the domination of the Congress by vested interests hostile to the Kisan.

This optimism gradually disappeared. During the Civil Disobedience movement, the Kisan leaders did much to draw the peasants into it and went to the extent of calling off an independent movement of the Kisans out of a fear that the former might suffer, only eventually to find the Congress utterly indifferent to the woes of the Kisans. The Kisan leaders gradually started doubting the earnestness of the Congress in this regard. Such doubts developed into a positive mistrust after the Congress Ministry had begun to function (August 1937).

The Bihar Kisan Sabha had serious reservations about the acceptance of office by the Congress. The Bihar Provincial Kisan Council at a meeting on 24 February 1937, with Swami Sahajanand in the chair opposed it on the ground that "the Government of India Act was brought with a view to entrenching the vested interests in power and making the imperialist grip stronger."[48]

However, when the Congress finally decided to form the government, the Kisan Sabha did not in any way seek to undermine it. On the contrary, the Sabha decided to make use of it, as far as possible for promoting the peasants' cause. It tried to convince the government of the urgency of the peasant question by organizing big pea-

[47]Swami Sahajanand, for instance, did it once during the Civil Disobedience movement.

[48]*Amrita Bazar Patrika*, 27 February 1937.

sant rallies. The Kisan leaders, for instance, asked the peasants throughout Bihar to muster strength before the Legislative Assembly on 23 August 1937, the opening day of the Assembly. The Kisan leaders thus exhorted the peasants on the occasion:

> Constant agitation should be made...so that you can be free from rural indebtedness, imposition of numerous taxes, and oppressions of many a person. It is you, tillers of the soil, who have chosen your representatives in the Assembly, and it is you who shall draw their attention to your needs and wants.... Your fight has reached a critical stage, and it is time for you to keep alert...Simply saying that the Congress is now the Government will not take you anywhere.[49]

The peasants responded warmly. Twenty thousand peasants gathered near the Assembly shouting the slogans: "Give us water, we are thirsty; give us bread, we are hungry; remit all our agricultural loans; down with zamindars and save us from oppression."[50] The Kisan demonstration was unprecedented in the history of Bihar.

The Kisan leaders evidently expected much of the new government, and sought to persuade the Congress to make a firm commitment to the defence of the peasants' interests. The Bihar Provincial Kisan Council, at a meeting held on 4 November, 1937 said: "There are numerous interests which are opposed to the interests of the Kisans, but the responsibility of the Congress is towards the exploited and the downtrodden rather than towards the privileged and vested interests."[51]

The performance of the Congress Ministry disappointed the Kisan leaders although some of its measures undoubtedly helped the peasantry.[52] Rent was reduced by about 25 per cent, on an average. Peasants' holdings were made transferable without the prior consent of zamindars, and the *salami* that was previously payable to them at the time of such transfers was greatly reduced. Sales by zamindars of the entire holdings of peasants on grounds of non-payment of

[49]*Ibid.,* 20 August 1937.

[50]*Ibid.,* 24 August 1937.

[51]*Ibid.,* 6 November 1937.

[52]For details see Rajendra Prasad, *Autobiography* (Hindi), New Delhi, 1955, pp. 454-9.

due rent were made illegal. Zamindars could sell only a part of the holdings, which was enough for the realization of the arrears of rent. The Ministry persuaded the zamindars to agree not only to a reduction of the cash rent, but also of the share of the crop.

The Kisan leaders however expected much more. The problem of rural indebtedness remained as chronic as before. The Congress ministry did very little towards solving the *bakhast* land question. A meeting of the All India Kisan Committee in Calcutta on 27 October 1937, expressed "strong dissatisfaction with the piecemeal, superficial and perfunctory manner in which the Congress ministries have dealt with only some of the problems affecting the Kisans."[53] The kisan leaders in fact wanted the Congress to establish a kind of *Kisan raj. "Kisan raj kaem ho"* (a kisan regime would soon be coming) was one of the popular slogans with the Kisan demonstrators.[54] This involved confiscation of the zamindar estates and the distribution of the lands thus acquired among the landless.

The Congress ministry found the Kisan slogans much too radical for their taste, and made no bones about it. The Prime Minister Srikrishna Sinha once observed, "If lands are taken without compensation, volcanic eruption will be sure to follow."[55] The Kisan leaders sought to explain the failure of the Congress ministry in terms of class interests. "All the fights of the Congress," said Swami Sahajanand at a Kisan rally at Siwan on 26 November 1938, "had been fought by the masses, whilst the capitalists and landlords sided with the imperialist forces. Zamindars and capitalists seeing that they had no hope from the imperialists, were now joining the Congress and monopolizing it."[56] According to the Kisan leaders the failure of the Congress ministry was due to the structural weakness of the Congress movement. Pandit Jadunandan Sarma observed:

Unfortunately politics have so far dominated the Congress.... The masses have so far been kept in a mere state of emotional exaltation, and the Congress has always tried to reconcile the irreconcilable interests in its attempts to keep intact its national character.... The masses who staked their all have not been al-

[53] *Amrita Bazar Patrika,* 30 October 1937.
[54] *Ibid.,* 12 January 1938.
[55] *Ibid.,* 30 January 1938.
[56] *Ibid.,* 29 November 1938.

lowed to ventilate their genuine grievances against their exploitation by Indian feudalism and rising capitalism. It is time for the
leaders to realize that the exploiters and the exploited cannot
be benefited at one and the same time. It is high time for them
to realize the absurdities of the position that there cannot be
compromise between landlords and tenants.[57]

Swami Sahajanand stressed the point at the Comilla session of
the All-India Kisan Conference (May 1938):

It is dangerous to agree that the Congress is a Kisan organization.
... I do not want that the Congress should be a Kisan organization in name only. I want it, if ever, to be so in its ideology.... I
want that the Congress should reflect the class interests of the
Kisans and cease to be dominated by those who fatten on the
exploitation of the Kisans.[58]

The Congress could not for long afford to ignore such criticisms.
The criticism that the interests of the Kisans were not safe in their
hands and aspersions at their moral integrity[59] incensed the Congress
leaders. The Congress also reproved the Kisan Movement for its
being prone to violence. Gandhiji went to the extent of saying that
such a movement "would be something like fascism." Reforming
the land system, the Congress believed, did not at all necessitate
violence.[60]
   In December 1937, the Congress took the decision forbidding
Congressmen from participating in the Kisan Sabha activities.
The Saran District Congress Committee on 7 December 1937, asked
Swami Sahajanand to suspend his proposed tour in Saran district,

[57]*Amrita Bazar Patrika*, 23 January 1938.
[58]*Ibid.*, 15 May 1938.
[59]Congressmen with *khaddar* and their Gandhi caps were compared to *Sadhus*
who with their *tilaks* and other marks cheated the people." Rajendra Prasad's
statement on 11 January 1938, *Amrita Bazar Patrika*, 12 January 1938.
[60]Gandhian notion of eventual change of heart of the property-owners greatly
influenced them. He said : "I want them (zamindars and ruling chiefs) to
outgrow their greed and sense of possession, and to come down in spite of their
wealth to the level of those who earn their bread by labour." *Economic and
Industrial Life*, I, 119. In the *Harijan* of 23 April 1938, he remarked that if the
zamindars did not change, "they will die a natural death."

since it feared "his presence might lead to unrest among the Kisans and tenants."[61] The Congress members were asked "not to attend, or organize or help in organizing Kisan Sabha meetings to be addressed by Swami Sahajanand." Other district committees soon followed suit. The Bihar Provincial Congress Committee formally approved of the ban of 14 December 1937. In justification of their action they said that the propaganda of the Sabha "has been responsible for producing a poisonous atmosphere.... Attacks are being made on the principle of Ahimsa which is the cherished creed of the Congress. An atmosphere is developing in certain parts of the province which, it is apprehended, is likely to do much harm to the country and put obstacles in the way of the country's march toward freedom."[62] Prominent Congress leaders toured different parts of the province and sought to explain the Congress stand to the Kisans. In his two-day tour in Saran in April 1938, Vallabhbhai Patel asked them not to be misled by

> what is inspired by western ideas and also by the Red Flag, which is the symbol of violence and against the culture and tradition of India.... Comrade Lenin was not born in this country and we do not want a Lenin here. We want Gandhi and Ramachandra. Those who preach class hatred are enemies of the country.[63]

Misunderstanding between the Congress and the Kisan Sabha thus tended to increase. At the Gaya session of the All India Kisan Conference (9-10 April, 1939) radical Kisan leaders like Swami Sahajanand wanted a complete breach with the Congress. Moderate opinions, however, ultimately prevailed, and the formal breach did not occur.

VIII

During the period under review, unlike the earlier period, the Kisan Movement was sure of its ground from the point of definition of aims and also of organization. The Kisan leaders sought to build

[61]*Amrita Bazar Patrika,* 9 December 1937.
[62]*Amrita Bazar Patrika,* 16 December 1937.
[63]*Ibid.,* 10 April 1938.

an appropriate organization, though it remained, admittedly, an imperfect one.[64]

However, the elements of weakness in the Kisan Movement should not be overlooked. In view of the Depression and the aggravation by it of the manifold evils of the agrarian society, the movement would have been stronger. Barrington Moore found the Indian peasants far less rebellious than the Chinese peasants, and attributed the phenomenon partly to the particular character of the nationalist leadership in India. "The character of nationalist leaders imparted to their movement a quietist twist that helped to damp down what revolutionary tendencies there were among the peasants."[65] The point is debatable. The disapproval by the Congress of the particular form of the Kisan agitation in Bengal and Bihar has been noted. The Congress occasionally succeeded in drawing the peasantry into the nationalist movement, but it did not lead any appropriate peasant organization. It had failed not only to keep up their enthusiasm, but also alienated them when "violence" on the part of the peasants, as the Congress understood the word at the time, sometimes led it to call off the nationalist movement. Indeed, the Kisan Movement developed in spite of the adverse reactions of the Congress leadership. Such reactions, therefore, could not be a real source of weakness of the Kisan Movement.

Moore was aware of "the huge size and appalling misery of India's rural proletariat,"[66] but he pointed out that tension of

[64]The presence of these two features also distinguished the Kisan movement from the radical millenarian peasant movements in several parts of the world, of which much has been written. The essence of the millenarianism was "the hope of a complete and radical change in the world which will be reflected in the millennium, a world shorn of all its present deficiencies." (E.J. Hobsbawm, *Primitive Rebels,* Ch. 4). This hope gave the movement a tremendous force. However, they shared "a fundamental vagueness about the actual way in which the new society will be brought about," and a notable thing about them was their indifference to the question of organization. "Its (the movement's) followers are not makers of revolution. They expect it to make itself, by divine revelation, by an announcement from on high, by a miracle—they expect it to happen somehow. The part of the people before the change is to gather together...to undertake certain virtual measures against the moment of decision and change, or to purify themselves, shedding the dross of the bad world of the present so as to be able to enter the new world in shining purity" (*Ibid.*).

[65]Barrington Moore, *Social Origins of Dictatorship and Democracy,* p. 378.
[66]*Ibid.,* p. 455.

the kind that one would, under the circumstances, assume to have built up in the rural society, was largely nonexistent. According to him apart from the fact that "many" of the agricultural labourers were "tied to the prevailing system through possession of a tiny plot of land,"[67] the caste system provided a niche for landless labourers and tied them into the division of labour within the village, while its sanctions depended for their operation less directly on the existence of property."[68] Moreover, "the system of caste did enforce hierarchical submission. Make a man feel humble by a thousand daily acts and he will behave in a humble way. The traditional etiquette of caste was no mere excrescence; it had definite political consequences."[69]

A "very high correlation between caste ranking and superior and inferior rights to land"[70] was undoubtedly a significant feature of the land system in Bengal and Bihar. But how did the caste system, involving as it did a system of sanctions, correct the imbalance in the rural society resulting from the reduction of a sizeable sanction of owner-peasants to the status of agricultural labourers? Could it just sanction away such a reality ? The caste system could not surely provide employment for the dislocated group. The relative infrequency of rebellions by the agricultural labourers? need not be related to the "submissiveness" enforced by the caste system. They hesitated to rebel, partly because they were not sure of the results of such rebellions.

For the sources of weakness in the Kisan Movement we must therefore look elsewhere. The Kisan Sabha had a formal organizational structure, but, as Hauser puts it, "It is more accurately characterized as a movement than an organization as such. Its primary instruments were numerous meetings, the rallies and annual sessions."[71] The number of formal members seems impressive (250,000 in Bihar in 1938 and 50,000 in Bengal in 1939), but the organization largely depended on a small group of dedicated

[67]*Ibid.*

[68]*Ibid.*, p. 213.

[69]*Ibid.*, p. 383.

[70]Gunnar Myrdal, *Asian Drama* (London, 1968), Vol. II, p. 1059. For some evidence on the point see Benoy Chaudhuri, "Agrarian economy and agrarian relations in Bengal 1859-1885," in *History of Bengal, 1757-1905* (published by the University of Calcutta), pp. 315-16 and 321-2.

[71]Hauser, n. 13, p. 87.

workers. It, therefore, sometimes failed to cope with the task of organizing large movements.

Another source of weakness can be attributed to the particular agrarian relations in Bengal and Bihar. The Depression created for the peasantry an extremely difficult situation, but the class relations did not admit of any adjustment, though whether the Indian caste system made the process any easier, as Gunnar Myrdal thinks,[72] is an open question. The zamindars were not a particularly rapacious tribe enforcng their rent demands regardless of whatever had happened to the peasantry. The steep fall in the prices made the old level of rent grossly iniquitous to the peasants, but, in fact, many of them just defaulted without necessarily provoking "legal actions" on the part of the zamindars. Rent arrears and also arrears of debt tended to accumulate. Zamindars had the legal power to evict them and money-lenders to force the payment in various ways. But many of them did not go as far as they could. The forbearance of the zamindars was not entirely a matter of kindness for the afflicted peasantry. They realized that as long as the Depression continued, changing peasants for the cultivation of their lands would not be of much use. Moreover, where the majority of the peasant community defaulted, other legal steps short of eviction were seldom more effective, particularly because the legal process was tardy as well as costly.

The elements of weakness in the Kisan movement also partly resulted from the particular composition of the peasant community itself. It is wrong to describe a village in Bengal and Bihar as one "composed entirely of mass of poor tenants united in opposition to the absentee landlords and their agents." The peasant community was not a homogeneous group. It was a complex structure composed of elements which were sometimes naturally hostile. The Kisan Sabha, therefore, found it difficult to organize all the groups in a united movement. For instance, where *bargadars* were employed by richer peasants, as was often the case, the Kisan Sabha, fighting with the former, risked alienating the latter, which had backed them once in their fight against zamindars. In Bihar,

[72]Myrdal, n. 70, p. 1061. He writes : "A social environment in which high status is accorded to abstinence from physical work encourages adjustments by the more privileged strata to relieve at least the direct distress of the dispossessed."

Swami Sahajanand was shocked to find how big occupancy ryots had largely succeeded in turning the Kisan Sabha into an instrument for promoting their own interests. This was the reason for the increasing emphasis afterwards on the need to bring the agricultural labourers and "the lowest strata of the peasantry" into the Kisan Movement.

Where *bargadars* or agricultural labourers were involved, the Kisan Sabha sometimes failed to attract them largely because of their fear that by opposing their employers they risked losing their tiny plots of land, which were their only means of subsistence. Such fears, as we have seen earlier, were not baseless. This was the reason why the settlement officers carrying on survey and settlement work often failed to persuade a sizeable section of the *bargadars* to declare their status, so that this could be included in the settlement records. Such was the hold of their employers over them that many *bargadars* altogether denied that they had at all cultivated lands on a crop-sharing basis.

<h2 style="text-align:center">IX</h2>

The Kisan Movement began to decline towards the end of the period under review particularly in Bihar. Hauser attributed it partly to the tactical mistake of the Kisan Sabha leadership dominated by the personality of Swami Sahajanand and partly to a series of developments which tended to reduce the misery of the peasants.

The Kisan Sabha was a strong movement of agitation. It was not organized structurally because of the impatient and articulate leadership which Swami Sahajanand provided. He was a Swami who sought change, a charismatic revolutionary. So long as he maintained that attitude within the framework of the nationalism which sustained all political activity in India during this period, the movement was effective. When he was attracted to ideological politics of the anti-national Left, he and the movement he had created found no support among the peasants of Bihar.[73]

[73]Hauser, n. 13, p. 156.

According to Hauser, the new legislative measures reducing the rents in the south Bihar districts between 1937 and 1940, and the improved price situation of the war period, were responsible for diminishing the distress of the peasants.

Hauser's view in regard to the responsibility of Sahajanand for the decline of the Kisan Movement seems to be of doubtful validity. The main strength of the movement lay not in its appeal to nationalist sentiments, but in its particular stand on the basic grievances of the peasantry. It may, however, be true that the Swamiji's increasing inclination towards the "Left" in the country's politics alienated a number of persons actively connected with the leadership of the Kisan Movement. The rank and file of the peasants do not seem to have been much affected by the alleged political bias of the Swamiji.

The tendency of the prices to rise since the end of 1938, particularly since the beginning of the second world war, undoubtedly helped the peasantry in making a recovery from the effects of the long Depression. So did the measures reducing the rent burdens. Needless to say, these were temporary reliefs. The basic maladjustment in the peasant economy and agrarian society persisted. In fact, certain developments made this still worse, particularly the drying up of rural credit as a result of the legislative measures designed for reducing rural debts. We have seen how more peasants lost their land as a result. The famine of 1943 left the peasant economy in ruins. The background for a wider Kisan agitation was thus formed. It began soon after the end of the war and became stronger year after year.

IMPACT OF SOCIALISM ON MARATHI LITERATURE DURING THE INTER-WAR YEARS

PRABHAKAR PADHYE

THE FOUNDING CONFERENCE of the Progressive Writers' Association was held in Bombay in 1936, under the presidentship of Raosaheb Patwardhan. As is well known, PWA is an association of Marxists and Fellow-travellers. Of course, Raosaheb was no Marxist; nor was he, unlike his brother Achyutrao, even a proclaimed socialist. However this fact did not conceal the true nature of the Conference. It unfurled the flag of Marxism and socialism in the world of Indian literature, at one of the leading centres of Marathi writing. And yet the doctrines of the Progressivists, particularly Marxism, had a remarkably feeble impact on Marathi literature during the period we are considering (1919-1939), and the years immediately following.

Why this should be so need not be a mystery to those who are acquainted with the generally sceptical attitude of the Marathi intellectuals. This natural scepticism was amply fed by the appearance in 1935 of a book called *Sahitya ani Samaj-jeevan* (Literature and Society) by Laljee Pendse, a well known communist. The book was a flaming proclamation of the Marxist faith in the world of Marathi literature. Now Marxism is a viable socio-economic doctrine, however tenuous its philosophical credentials may be. Its view of man and society has a large socio-psychological basis. Man may be born as an individual, but he is brought up in and grows up in society. His very perceptions, which are the foundations of his living, are his negotiations with the environment. He lives by assimilating a part of nature and in the process adjusts himself to it. It is true that he looks at the world through the window of his consciousness, but his consciousness has no meaning unless it comes into contact with the environment. Marx talked glowingly of this consciousness. In a famous passage in *Capital*, he compared man with the bee and the bird and the spider which build their combs, nests and webs with astonishing accuracy, but lack man's vision who builds and manufactures with a previously conceived image. Marx was conscious of these mental powers of man, and yet he was not willing to forget the socio-economic foundations of this consciousness. Marx maintained that man's life was a constantly changing relationship with nature. It was a relationship between two systems of energy and could not, in the nature of things, be anything but dynamic. It was expressed in the prevailing mode of production symbolized by the productive forces. The mode of production therefore tends to change and with it the relations of production which are created by it. The fabric of human life was therefore an innately social fabric. But human life also connoted the life of the mind and Marx insisted that man's mental life was only a reflection of his social life. What he called the superstructure of society, by which he meant man's cultural edifice, was built on the foundations of the mode and the relations of production. Man's mind, he indicated, was rooted deeply in the socio-economic foundations of society. When a cynic said that culture was rooted in the deep dung of cash he was merely venting his ire on a deep truth of life.

Literature and art are alluring products of the human mind. By definition therefore they should be rooted in the socio-economic conditions of society, and should bear socio-economic interpretations. But precisely at this point a number of questions arise. Do the socio-economic roots of art and literature make the artist a conscious, or even an unconscious, agent of socio-economic changes ?

Is man's mind a blind tool of social reality or has it an element of autonomy ? If it has, where do we seek the roots of this autonomy ? Again is the mode of production the only power behind the social dynamic ? And then is the mind of man so closely bound to the relations of production ? Does it not reflect other aspects of social reality and do these not have a measure of autonomy ?

These questions have plagued the Marxian doctrine ever since it was born. Marx first stated his doctrine of Historical Materialism in his Introduction to the *Critique of Political Economy*. "The mode of production," he said, "*conditions* the social, political and spiritual life process" and in the very next sentence added: "It is not the consciousness of men which *determines* their consciousness." He interchanged the words *condition* and *determine* as if they meant the same thing. (This is not some trick of translation. The original German words he used are *bedingt* and *bestimmt*). Obviously there is some confusion here between necessary cause and sufficient cause. The spiritual processes of life might take place within its socio-economic framework, but does it mean that the latter is a sufficient cause of them ? This confusion between limiting condition and determining cause has plagued Marxist theory throughout its history. There is another confusion in the doctrine that ought to be mentioned. By relations of production Marx meant only ownership relations, but there are other relations like professional relations, geo-spatial relations and so on. These make not only the superstructure but also the socio-economic foundation much more complex than is allowed in the Marxian theory. That is why in spite of the tremendous insights of Marxist sociology, the doctrine has always remained a little unsatisfactory.

This is particularly so in the case of art and literature. To explain the socio-economic origin of a work of art is not to explain the appeal of its beauty. The genetic or even the conditioning factor may not adequately tell what makes it beautiful. The laws of beauty (whatever they are) remain separate. When, therefore, Trotsky said that art had its own laws he was putting his finger unerringly on a profound truth. But even Trotsky was too much of a Marxist to see the problem in all its complexity. Why then speak of the small fry ? Laljee Pendse's book proved that he was singularly incapable of taking a measure of the problem. He wrote with the assurance that in Marxism he had spotted the secret of art and literature. With this assurance he went on to explain the class basis of Russian, French and Persian literatures, not to mention the Indian literatures which he took in one sweeping stride. This would have perhaps amused the Maharashtrian reader, had it not been for the chapter reviewing the 800 years of Marathi writing. It is unnecessary to trace the course of Pendse's embattled reasoning. I will only produce his remarks about two of the celebrated architects of Marathi literature—one ancient and one modern. Writing about Jnaneswar he says:

> Jnaneswar has sung the import of the Bhagwadgita. Five hundred years earlier Shankaracharya also had given an interpretation of the Geeta. Both of them seem to have erected a conspiracy of non-action against Shrikrishna, the author of the Geeta. Shankaracharya considered that in the Geeta 'knowledge' was supreme and he dislodged "action." Jnanoba gave pre-eminence to *bhakti* and contrived the neglect of 'action.' This playing fast with the meaning of Geeta helped the upper classes in making the hard-working labouring peasantry neglect its duty (p. 77).

About Ram Ganesh Gadkari, Pendse pontificates as follows:

> There is no difference of opinion about the fact that Gadkari was a great artist of classical genius. But his intoxicated art-enamoured imagination looks lifeless though alluring. His artistic efflorescence has become disenchanting like the decoration of a corpse. It is difficult to find another example of such glaring discrepancy between spiritedness and a writer as one finds in Gadkari (p. 103).

This interpretation of Jananeswar and this judgement of Gadkari could not but strike as utterly outrageous to any discerning student of Marathi literature. Pendse's book abounds in such judgements. It was one of the crudest operations that Marathi literary criticism had experienced. Not being very familiar with the dialectics of Marxism the Marathi reader concluded that the doctrine was too outrageous to be taken seriously. He did not find it necessary to spend time over the challenge that Marxism in fact presented to the world of letters.

This challenge is considerable in spite of the fact that Marxism as a doctrine is bound to be ill at ease in the world of literature. Whereas art and literature are the products of intrinsic perception, Marxism is par excellence a doctrine of instrumentalism. Marxism is as much grounded in praxis as in gnosis. Marx himself complained that philosophers till then had specialized in interpreting the world. He warned that the time had now come to dissolve philosophy and the way to do it was to ground your theory in praxis. Marxism therefore was not primarily a way of thinking; it was a way of living. A Marxist man of letters was not merely a writer; he was a practitioner. Stalin accurately called him the engineer of the soul. His was not primarily the life of the mind; it was the life of action. For him thought was action and was to be judged by the tests of action. Marxist literature therefore represented some kind of a built-in contradiction. As literature it had to be the product of intrinsic perception; as a feat of engineering it had to fix its gaze on the instrumental qualities of experience. The relations between intrinsic perception and instrumental perception is not an easy one. Even in purely contemplative literature the pulls of both entangle each other. In literature that avowedly glorifies the life of action, intrinsic perception tends to be smothered by instrumental perception. But one must remember that action has certain perceptual qualities which can be intrinsically explored and savoured, and transformed into art and literature. Not merely this. Marxism invokes a grand future for mankind. It dreams of the future when there is no exploitation of man by man. To an idealistic mind to which man is the measure of all things, Marxism represents a flaming ideal. As George Steiner said, "Communism, even where it has gone venomous, is a mythology of the human future, a vision of human possibility rich in a moral demand" (*Language and Silence,* p. 356). Myth has always an irresistible appeal to the poet and the artist. The myth of the future is always alluring in its infinite possibilities.

But the situation in India, in the twenties and the thirties, was a little more complicated. Gandhi was already dominating the minds of the people. If Marx represented one mythology of the future, Gandhiji represented another. The golden horizon of the Gandhian myth could be scanned, if only dimly, here and now. It was not a myth that was to be realized by a series of dialectical contradictions where today's repression was the promise of tomorrow's liberation, where today's inhumanity was supposed to lay the basis for the triumph of tomorrow's humanism. Gandhism sought to realize the virtues of humanism here and now. Gandhi's truth and non-violence represented some kind of a perennial ethical code, and his programme sought to embrace and affirm the little virtues of life that religion and culture had always preached.

Gandhism in practice was therefore a kind of realization of the future
in the present. This, in Maharashtra, gripped the mind of Sane
Guruji who produced tale after tale of simple virtues, sacrifice
and suffering. His stories and novels written in straight, simple
but emotional prose were little literary capsules of love, of truth,
of service, sacrifice, suffering, sympathy and renunication of ease.
For him Indian culture epitomized these simple virtues which
lived in the form of various symbols through our myths and epics.

The very simplicity and sentimentality of this approach gripped
the minds of the unsophisticated young. For Sane Guruji, socialism was another name for this simple kind of humanism. The
struggle against the British which Gandhiji, in a way, had remarkably simplified, provided a background against which Sane Guruji
constructed, almost non-stop, a series of simple fable-like tales.
But when independence came after a series of agonizing experiences
of war and partition, when the new postwar world began to manifest many complicated features which were indifferent to his treas-
ured codes of life, living was too much for Sane Guruji and he
chose to quit, and it appeared as if an epoch of writing had come
to an end.

No other mind in Maharashtra was gripped by Gandhian humanism in the way Sane Guruji's was. Prema Kantak wrote a
couple of Gandhian novels but they were largely ignored.
Gandhism produced a couple of remarkable theoreticians who were
also remarkable stylists. I need not say here much about Vinoba
Bhave who became some kind of a metaphysician of Gandhism.
But, like Marxism, his metaphysic was grounded more in praxis
than in gnosis, and it was not an accident that he later became the
architect of a soul-stirring movement. I want to talk here of another theoretician who was not merely a Gandhian but a conscious
socialist. I refer to Acharya Jawadekar. He tried to assimilate
Marxist philosophy to the classical Indian idealism and claimed
that the *moksha* ideal was to be realized here on earth. He produced
the philosophy of *Satyagrahi Samajwad*, which was socialism
based on the doctrines of truth and non-violence. He even toyed
with the idea of a new aesthetic, with his concept of *Kranti-rasa*
(revolutionary emotion), which was however largely ignored by
critics in Maharashtra.

This marriage of Marxism and Gandhism did one important

thing. It emphasized the humanism that was common to the ideals of both. And this humanism was relevant to the problems that were peculiar to India. Indian society was not cut out to suit the prescriptions of Marxism. Along with oppressed classes there were in India oppressed castes and they often tended to cut across class divisions. The situation in India was much more complex than suited the book of Karl Marx. In India several eras and ages were telescoped into one and it presented a complex which defied analytical powers and prescriptive remedies. But humanism enabled the creative writer, if not a critical thinker, to get over the difficulty. He could fuse the conflicting ideologies of Gandhism and Marxism into a pantheistic theory of simple humanism. Khandekar has done this more effectively than most others. The hero of his famous novel *Kraunch-vadh* says:

> While returning from Ramgad my mind was gravitating more towards socialism than Gandhism. But after having roamed over the whole country and after having stayed in different villages for months on I have come to feel that although Gandhism and socialism appeared outwardly antagonistic, at heart they embraced each other. Socialism looks at the world through the eyes of a father, whereas Gandhism looks at it through the gaze of a mother. Socialism wants to create a new world, but no new world could be created without a new man, and even if it were so created it would not exist for long. Gandhism wants to create a new man.

Khandekar's typical way of looking at things (which he has consecrated into a typical style) could be seen in his observation that socialism looks at things through a father's eyes whereas Gandhism looks at things through a mother's eyes. At heart he is a glorified Sane Guruji. The simple little virtues of daily life appeared to him to be the essence of humanity, and it was not an accident that in his first novel he tried to show that a school-teacher served society better than a lawyer. Like Sane Guruji's, therefore, his writings had a great appeal to the adolescent mind. But there was one difference—and a great one. Khandekar was a self-conscious artist. He was extremely conscious of literary modes and implications. He tried to turn his sentimental humanitarianism into

cultivated humanism. It is difficult to say if he succeeded. Almost
always he did not. But his basic humanistic persuasions enabled
him to transcend theoretical schemes and embrace the confusing
problems of Indian society. His *Don Dhruva* (The Two Poles,
1934) is an example. He succeeded in constructing a plot where
the elemental inhumanity of capitalism and the elemental cruelties
of the caste-ridden society appeared to comingle. Khandekar's
great forte is his plot construction. His widely dispersed characters somehow manage to come together in a well-knit pattern.
He tries to adorn the pattern with a lot of literary flourish. But
it cannot conceal the basic simplicity of his vision.

Class and caste were not the only things that confused the political picture of the time. There was another confusion which was
romantic and therefore ensnaring. This was a confusion between
communism and terrorism. In the early decades of the 20th
century, Maharashtra had produced a number of notable terrorists
whose careers were sagas of courage and sacrifice and the Maharashtrian mind was easily enchanted by tales of terrorism. Equally
fascinating was the new wave of communism that had already
started engulfing the working classes of Bombay. The new communist leaders had launched and led a number of textile workers'
strikes that had culminated in the Meerut conspiracy case. Terrorism and communism easily mingled in the imagination of
Maharashtra. This fascination was given a literary form in
Madkholkar's *Muktatma* (The Liberated Soul, 1933). Dange
complimented Madkholkar by saying that in this novel he had
faithfully portrayed the early phases of the communist movement in
Bombay. If this is correct, the movement as it emerges from the
pages of *Muktatma* was confusion worse confounded. The hero
of *Muktatma* was a romantic petit-bourgeois whose mental make-
up hardly matched the demands of the movement he was in. His
communism scarcely went beyond disturbing a few meetings and
lecturing to some odd political groups. His liaison with the
revolutionary Veerandra came to grief through his singular ineptness. Madkholkar's political heroes revel in discussions. There
is a fair measure of them in *Muktatma*, but they do not deal princi-
pally with the problems of revolution—either terrorist or communist. The fact is Madkholkar never really sorted these problems
out. The same kind of confusion between terrorism and commu-

nism appears in his later political novels like *Kanta* (1939), and
Mukhavate (Maska, 1940), and it comes to the same sorry end
because of the ineptness of the revolutionaries. Madkholkar's
romanticism persisted in toying with the subject of terrorism and
communism. But he had hardly the discipline of an artist or even
of a thinker to give them a credible form. Madkholkar's political
passion was anti-Gandhism. He was a romantic and not a huma
nist. His political novels lack the saving grace of Khandekaria
humanism.

Muktatma is said to be the first political novel of Maharashtra
But Mama Varerkar claims the distinction for his novel *Dhavta
Dhota* (The Running Shuttle, 1931) and he seems to be right. This
novel deals with a textile strike in Bombay and the picture of the
working class that Varerkar draws is credible and meaningful
Unlike Madkholkar he does not indulge in big theories or flam
boyant politics. He presents the story of a single textile strike in
Bombay. But he is able to portray the strike situation with
remarkable realism. He pictures the men and women of working
class in flesh and blood—flesh that is shrinking through poverty
and blood that is boiling with wrath. But Varerkar also has hi
own romanticism. One of the leaders of the strike is no other
than the son of the mill-owner, who has been living incognito as
a common worker. In the dramatic version of this novel, *Sonyache
Kalas* (The Golden Spire, 1934), Varerkar makes his hero hand
over his mill to the workers ! All the realism that Varerkar was able
to invest his story with was woefully marred by this unreal solution

But apparently such solutions tempt even the otherwise discern
ing minds of much better thinkers than Mama Varerkar. D
Ketkar was an eminent sociologist and a man of massive intellect
His *Brahman-Kanya* (The Daughter of a Brahmin, 1931), was a
brilliant study of an outcaste marriage with all its psycho-social
complications. But even in such a sophisticated study Dr Ketka
could not resist the temptation of introducing a labour-leader who
conceives the scheme of co-operative ownership for workers of a
textile mill in Bombay. Fortunately the solution is not worked
out in the body of the novel and remains purely on the conceptual
level. Even so the working class atmosphere in the novel (what
ever little we have of it) does smell of the smoke and dirt that dis
figure the working class areas of Bombay. The sociologist-turned

novelist Ketkar has shown greater powers of depiction than the novelist-turned-politician Madkholkar.

But none of these writers was a conscious theoretician of art. Their socialism (whatever there was of it) was of an incipient variety. But the thirties saw a writer who was a conscious socialist, of a characteristically individualistic type. That was P. Y. Deshpande who today has travelled so far as to be a *bhashyakar* of J. Krishnamurthy. Deshpande was not a mere onlooker. He was a participant. But more than anything else he was a passionate thinker. He reacted vehemently to the crudities of Laljee Pendse. Starting with Trotsky's dictum that "a work of art should be judged by its own laws.... The Marxian methods are not the same as the artistic" he warned that it was impossible to explain the beauty of *Abhijnam Shakuntal* or *Meghdoot* by their class character. He insisted that the artistic impulse was to be sought in the individual's mental furnace. There was no such thing as class art. All art was basically human. Art always projected the humanistic freedom of the individual. Deshpande postulated that every new work of art was a new synthesis of the conflict between Man and Nature, or rather between the individual and his environs. Every new synthesis of this conflict opened up a new horizon of human progress.

He worked out his individualistic faith in his novel *Vishal Jeevan* (Life Expansive, 1942). This novel opens with one particular economic problem of an individual. This leads to a struggle with the government. This struggle quickly becomes social, because it highlights the difficulties of the entire peasantry. That makes the hero a Marxist revolutionary. He goes to Bombay to participate in the workers' struggle. But instead of identifying himself with the class struggle of the workers he gets involved with a rich man's daughter who however had identified herself entirely with the Communist Party. Deshpande's analysis of the artistic impulse had a great deal of truth in it, but his novel did not prove an apt illustration of his theory. But he was involved. He did not shout slogans on the sidelines.

One writer who dramatically unfurled the red flag in literature by writing a poem in tribute to the red flag and who had berated those who wrote songs of cheap love, only gave the impression of being a dilettante. That was Anant Kanekar. He gave proof

of his brilliance in a number of essays, *Pikalin Panen* (Withered
Leaves, 1935) which had in them some Shavian influence. In
these essays he created a character called *Ganukaka* who was an
amiable petit bourgeois with his share of respectable hypocrisy.
Kanekar used this character to expose some of the petit bourgeois
cant of the Maharashtrian middle class, in literary pieces full of
intelligent gossip. These essays had a scintillating quality that put
some life into a literary form that had never shone consistently in
the firmament of Marathi letters. Kanekar soon ceased to be a
Marxist, and, although he never threw away his socialism he became thoroughly disillusioned with the Marxist variety of it.

A writer truly significant for socialist thinking was Professor
Vaman Malhar Joshi. Joshi was not a socialist; rather he was a
rationalist with a strong streak of Vedantic idealism in him. But
in his two novels, *Sushilecha Dev* (Sushila's God), and *Indu Kale
ani Sarala Bhole,* he turns his attention to certain social problems
and reveals himself as a thinker with impeccable insights.. In
Sushilecha Dev, for instance, he brings up the question of the
abolition of private property and that of public management of
things. In a little debate on this question, Sushila's friend Bal-
vantrao, neatly points out the *cul de sac* of this endeavour. He
asks : These public enterprises would need managers and assistant
managers; but who is going to manage the manager ?" In 1930,
when James Burnham's *The Managerial Revolution* had not yet been
written and Galbraith's *The New Industrial State* was decades off,
Wamanrao raised a question which has had no answer yet.

In the other novel, he posed yet another social riddle. He is
concerned to show there that men should not be one-track beings,
some concerned exclusively with art, others with learning, still
others with social service, and so on. In our society men are
forced into a single-track, with the result that they become warped
and wasted. But they have urges and impulses which refuse to die,
and raise their hoods like cobras and continue to haunt men's
inner being. He pleads for a society where an all-sided development of people would be possible.

One would immediately discern here a shrewd mixture of Marx
and Freud, or rather a Freud socialized. It is not only individuals
that suffer from suppressed desires; societies also suffer likewise
and become lop-sided, with disastrous results for its members.

This Joshi said in 1935, when the idea of applying Freud to the problems raised by Marx was not quite the fashion. Vaman Joshi was indeed a pioneer in this line of thinking. One can imagine how important was all this for the development of socialistic thinking in Maharashtra.

One writer who never courted fanfare but who stood forth as a genuine poet of revolution or even red revolution was Kusumagraj (V. V. Shirwadkar). It could be said that he became a genuine revolutionary poet because he was never ideologically initiated. His poems clearly show that his imagination was never burdened with theoretical lumber. But his poems breathe fire against the injustices of society—both of the class and of the caste. His is a fiery humanism which is untarnished either by pity or by prose. His was a fire-eating realism that looked unblinkingly into the facts of oppression of every kind—political, social, economic. He was not concerned with political or party labels. He went to the heart of the matter and shone forth in his poetry with fiery brilliance of passion and metaphor.

He did not have to enter with fanfare, because he was directly in the tradition of modern Marathi poetry whose founder Keshavsut had the same vision and the same passion. If Keshavsut could be called the poet of the philosophy of the French Revolution, Kusumagraj could be called the poet of the philosophy of the Russian Revolution; but the gifted imagination of these two poets blossomed forth because both were supremely unconscious of their respective philosophies. Rather they had dissolved their philosophies, if ever they had formulated them consciously, in the crucible of perennial humanism. This enabled them to fuse their imagination and revolutionary passion into a fine alchemy of art. This is more so in the case of Shirwadkar. He has never succumbed to the temptation of slogan-shouting. Even in the case of the poem—

Cry hail to the revolution, to the revolution
And bare your breasts to the blows of the sabre

he introduces into the resolve of the hunger-striking Dum Dum prisoners, the dramatic element embodied in an address to the motherland.

They assure Mother India that

> At every step we spread burning embers on our path
> And run defiantly on them.

They ask her not to worry because

> In the womb of night dwells the dawn of morrow.

This dramatic element has been strengthened by powerful symbolization. "Earth's Love-song" is a good example of this. The earth's lover is, of course, the sun. The sun is Kusumagraj's supreme symbol of revolution. The sun means light, fire and the red colour of revolution. Rightly does Kusumagraj call his poem "*Sacrificial Wood*" in which the divine fire inheres. This is how he invests his symbol with the import of freedom. In one of his poems he invokes the sun and asks it to fill the expanse with flaming light; he says:

> Let the red flag flutter in the East
> Let the shackled bird fly in the sky.

But it is not merely the love of fire, the love of revolution that impels Kusumagraj. The strength of his poetry lies in his brilliant imagination. In his poem *Ahi-Nakul* (The Cobra and the Mongoose) he calls the red lips of a mongoose the flags of blood, suggesting the red flags of revolution. But this does not allow his passion for revolution to cloud his imagination. In this poem the play of imagination is simply fascinating. He compares the cobra successively to the erupting fire of a volcano, to the blade of a sabre, to the lightening streaks of a silken sari, to the running trail of a fire, to the flash of Yama's dagger, and to a singer's flourish of *Malhar raga*. It is this powerful imagery that invests Shirwadkar's revolutionary poetry with brilliance and beauty. But there is one more factor which is of even greater importance. That is the depth of understanding revealing flashes of wisdom. Note how the fight between the cobra and the mongoose ends:

The battle was over; blood had spattered around

Grass blades were delightfully bathing in blood
The snake was lying like so much tousled wool
And insects were swarming around to eat the pieces.

Shirwadkar knows that warriors win the war and cunning politicians enjoy the fruits thereof.   He has another beautiful poem called
Murtibhanjak (Idol-Breaker). An idealist leaves the world,
retires to the mountains, carves a magnificent temple out of a rock,
instals an idol therein and starts worshipping it; but the idol does
not respond.   He is terribly disappointed.   In a fit of rage he breaks
the idol, scatters the pieces around and sits at the temple-door
looking searchingly into the sky.   Some tourists come along and
are fascinated by the sculpture, but when they see the broken idol,
their fascination turns into anger.   They see the man at the ent-
rance, conclude that he is the breaker of the idol and shower curses
on him.
   It is the understanding along with the poetic brilliance of his
imagination that saves Shirwadkar's poems from being slogan-
shouting compositions and saves him from being a breast-beating
propagandist.   He remains the best socialist poet of the period.
   But as indicated above, this period in Maharashtra was not
favourable for the appearance of avowedly Marxist poetry.   It
did appear later in the compositions of Saratchandra Muktibodh.
But it had to wait several years, before it could do so.   In between,
Anil (A. R. Deshpande) had a stint of Marxism, but this exotic
affair was bound to prove short-lived.

IMPACT OF SOCIALIST IDEOLOGY
ON TELUGU LITERATURE
BETWEEN THE WARS

D. ANJANEYULU

THE YEARS BETWEEN the two World Wars were undoubtedly a period
of intense creative activity in Telugu Literature. It was during the
twenties and thirties of this century that what could roughly be
described as the Romantic Movement in Telugu Poetry swept the
whole Andhra country like the west wind of Shelley. It is possible
that the "new poetry," as it was so called in those days, representing
a revolt against the classical tradition, was largely pioneered by
Gurazada Appa Rao who died in 1915, and Royaprolu Subha
Rao, who wrote some of his earliest poems a few years before the
First World War. But the Romantic Movement, as such, was
spearheaded by D. V. Krishna Sastri (Devulapalli Venkata-
krishna Sastri, to give him his full name), still happily with us.
He was, perhaps, the most significant of a group of highly talented
poets, including Basavaraju Appa Rao, Nanduri Subba Rao,
Nayani Subba Rao, Vedula Satyanarayana, among others, who
are hardly equalled, in some respects, by those before or after them.
All these poets, mostly men of good academic education, had
certainly heard and read of the Russian Revolution of 1917 and the
experiment in Socialism (or Communism, as we understand it),
but one looks in vain for socialist ideology or any specific political
ideas in their poetry. They were broadly humanist, inspired as
they were by the poets of the Romantic Revival in England, who,
in turn, were influenced by the ideas of the French Revolution.
Wordsworth's identification with Nature, Keats's quest for Beauty
and Truth and Shelley's thirst for Liberty had all found their
expression in the work of their distant successors in Telugu. But
the liberty they had sung about was wider than political liberty

and the quality they had dreamed of was unrelated to economic equality.

Possibly, the earliest public notice taken of the October Revolution of 1917 and subsequent happenings in Russia, was by Dr B. Pattabhi Sitaramayya, who was later to become the historian of the Congress and later still Congress President. In an article on "Soviettulu" (or "The Soviets") contributed to the Ugadi special number of the *Andhra Patrika* for the year 1920-21, he tried to examine the ideas thrown up by the Revolution with consideration and sympathy, to the extent it was possible for a man of his social position, and political and intellectual background. He gave voice to his doubts if a political state thrown up in this upsurge and sustained by its ideas of Marxism would succeed in implementing its ideals or last for any considerable length of time. He, however, invoked the parallel of the French Revolution, whose basic ideas had fired the imagination of Europe and the world, though the Revolution itself could be termed a failure in a narrow sense. An editorial of the *Andhra Patrika* special number commenting on this subject, unequivocally advocated the methods of peace, in harmony with the Indian, or Hindu, tradition, quoting the well-known saying : "Those who take up the sword shall perish by the sword."

One of the earliest references to socialist ideas in general and to the Bolshevik experiment in particular could be found in the novel, *Maalapalli* (literally "Harijan Hamlet"), first published in 1922, and banned for some time by the British Government of the day. It was written by the later Unnava Lakshminarayana, a contemporary of Dr Pattabhi, and a Congress leader like him, closely influenced by the philosophy of Truth and non-violence as propounded by Mahatma Gandhi. The scene of the story of this novel was laid in the countryside of Guntur District (south of the River Krishna) in coastal Andhra, also known as the Northern Circars. The theme could roughly be described as the relation between the caste Hindus and the Harijans and of the landlords and tenants of the village and the use of methods inspired by the philosophy of the Mahatma and the teachings of the Bhagavad-Gita. We do not find here any suggestion of the class war usually encouraged by some of the modern writers' treating of these themes. The author believed, with Gandhi, in the efficacy of "turning the other cheek," commended by the Sermon on the Mount in effecting the desired change to heart in the wrongdoer. He could countenance the suffering of the just and the poignant tragedy that might sometimes overtake the lives of those who least deserve it. But not the policy or retaliation—meeting violence with violence—to an equal or even a greater degree. This is particularly significant when we remember that the author had his share of admiration for the Irish Rebellion—and the peasants' revolt—with which he was familiar as a law student in Dublin before the First World War.

That he was fairly well acquainted with the ideology of socialism, as understood by the leaders of the Bolshevik Revolution in Russia, would be evident in a long passage (in the book) from an address to a gathering of Harijans by one of the characters, named Venkata Reddi, who works in co-operation with Sanga Das, who can be considered the hero of the novel (which also bears the alternate title of "Sanga Vijayam" or the "Triumph of Sanga Das"). The points mentioned in the address are briefly summarized for the benefit of those not acquainted with this novel in the original.

A government of the Soviets has been established in Russia. Their movement is called "Bolshevism," which literally means the ideology of the majority party, according to which the government of the land is to be run. The Soviet Government have taken over all the wealth, including the palaces and factories of the millionaires. There could be no individual rights for the rich or the poor in a country where everything belongs to the State. He is only allowed to consume who is able to produce, with the exception of the old, sick and disabled. The lazy will have to starve. This is a great experiment. Similar was the spirit of the sermons of Jesus Christ. Our hermits of old possibly used to live on the same lines, as far as I could imagine it. This was also the general pattern of our rural life in the days gone by. It is difficult to say how long this new system of government would last. But its builders are working with great enthusiasm. It is their conviction that every man has a right to share in the enjoyment of the world's material wealth. Everyone must work and earn his share. It is not fair that a chosen few should roll in wealth and luxury, while others starve and go naked in their struggle for existence. No one could doubt the inherent justice of these principles, but some have doubts of their own about their capacity for being put into practice. The poor were happy when the farms and factories of Russia's rich were taken over on their behalf by the Soviets, but not so happy when the surplus income on them was sought to be appropriated by the State. The Bolshevik theory is contrary to all the concepts of equality currently accepted by us. The Bolshevik ideas are eating like white ants into all the old structures of social organization.

"It looks as though only the British political system will be able to withstand the impact of the Bolshevik Revolution. In our country, the caste system and the pattern of occupational distribution that goes with it have long been under fire. But few are ready to give up the old system with its own advantages, while many are eager to benefit from the new. But they do not seem to realize that new benefits bring new problems in their wake. We should not adopt the means of Revolution. It is best for us to wait and watch, after the British example. Will the landlords oblige if they are asked to distribute their land among the landless ? Nor is it fair on our part to ask them. When we think of the ultimate goal, they would have to agree, in the long run, to sharing a part of the harvest with the landless labour and permit them to occupy, on request, the more fertile parts of the *poramboke* fallow land on the outskirts of the village and forest lands. It is the responsibility of the rich to promote the cause of our education.... It is not too much for us to demand that labour should have its due share in the administration of the country. Ours is a holy cause, with no room for hatred in the movement. No movement will succeed, if it is filled with the feeling of hatred."

It is not difficult to see that while the author is not unaware of the new-found gospel (of Bolshevik socialism) according to Lenin and goes to the extent of conceding its basic compulsion, he is not able to give it his whole hearted approval. His enthusiasm is reserved rather for the Gandhian concept of all property being held in trust by the rich, for the poor, and the need for a change of heart to persuade the former to do their duty by the latter. But there is another side too to this problem. Appa Das, the younger brother of the hero Sanga Das (with whose approach to life the author obviously identifies himself), equally moved by lofty impulses, is not half so patient as the latter in the methods he chooses for

achieving his objective of improving the lot of his brethren of the
Harijan community. He leaves the village for an unknown des-
tination and rumour has it that he is moving about the countryside
incognito as the leader of a gang of robbers. But they are robbers
with a difference, robbing the rich to feed the poor and he is their
Robin Hood.

Snatches of a ballad attributed to him and sung by an itinerant
party give us an inkling of his social and economic philosophy.
The thought content may not be profound or well-organized, by
contemporary standards, but its direction is unmistakable:

Time was when men were equals all
No grades of high and low to fall
Nor prince or pauper to call,
When no one felt it hard to toil.

As humans fell, by and by, from their noble State,
Greed and graft came to be our fate;
Who was then to check the rulers of the State,
In their crafty game—the World's wealth
                                                 to appropriate.

Isn't it high time
We knew the price of labour prime?
Workers of the world unite
We have nothing to lose but our chains tight!

There is strength of unity in numbers,
We need no one's favours;
Strike work when the employer is perverse,
Stick on and on, till victory is yours!

Some of the uncommitted onlookers among the passengers in the
train who listen to these words admit the substratum of truth underlying them. They are harsh and unpalatable like many other rugged
truths, adds another. The unreliability of modern rulers and the
strangle-hold of moneyed classes over society are freely commented
upon. The futility of empty homilies is exposed and the need to
face the hard realities of life is emphasized. As the conversation

proceeds, the unstated case for theft of property and the implied character of property as theft are discussed threadbare, apparently in jest, but really in earnest.

There is a natural time-lag in sensibility among writers, no less than among peoples in general, in their response to the thought-currents set out by the economic or political movements of the world originating abroad. In addition to the barrier of distance created by geographical factors, there are the other barriers of language and social tradition, which involve a process of translation at the different levels for being successfully got over. The categorical imperatives of Marx on capitalism containing within it the seeds of its own destruction, to be followed by a socialist revolution, leading ultimately to a classless society, took some considerable time to get across to the different regions of India. The impact of the ideas leading to the Russian Revolution and the ideas thrown up by it in turn was not widely noticeable among the writers in Andhra in the early Twenties. Nor could we say that the Fabian concept of socialism by persuasion (through the machinery of legislation) and in gradual stages, evolved by the Webbs, Shaw and Graham Wallas, had made any impression until well after the thirties. Other varieties of socialism like the Christian socialism of William Morris and the other Romantics of nineteenth century England were possibly not powerful enough to cross the limited national borders. (It is quite a different matter that Gandhi was deeply influenced by Ruskin's *Unto This Last* and Tolstoy's *Whither Are We Going.* This had to do more with the evolution of Gandhi's own personal philosophy comparable to socialism of the Marxian or any other accepted variety).

It was in the early thirties that the rumblings of socialist thought began to be heard in Telugu literature, indirectly though. If there was one book, more than any other, which had a powerful influence on the youthful writers of the day to the extent of effecting a marked change in their outlook on society, it was Maxim Gorky's *Mother.* The vividness and poignancy with which Gorky represented the struggles and sorrows of the poor in general, and of the working class in paticular, gripped the imagination of the readers and writers alike. K. Linga Raju, a Congress leader of Rajahmundry, translated the work (under the title *Amma*) in 1932, while he was in jail, though it had had to wait for two years to find publication.

After its first publication in 1934, it has seen several editions. It is also known to be the first translation of this novel in any Indian language (though one has to keep oneself open to correction in making a claim in this behalf). A whole generation of writers, from its earliest translator in Telugu to the latest, had exposed themselves to its invigorating influence. As a result of this, stark realism came to be widely accepted in Telugu fiction and the heroism implicit in the sufferings of the common people, including the peasants and the workers, gained increasing recognition. A few years later, Premchand's *Godan* (first published in Hindi in 1936), found its way into Telugu and the translation, as well as the original, has won a wide circle of admiring readers. Some novels were also written in Telugu on the model of *Mother* and *Godan,* though they do not claim a high place as literature. The novels of Dr. Mulk Raj Anand, particularly *Coolie* (1933), *Untouchable* (1935), and *Two Leaves and a Bud* (1937) were read with keen interest and were translated in Telugu. But the Telugu versions cannot truly be said to have made the grade.

The years 1930–1931 were notable not only for Gandhi's Salt Satyagraha and the no-tax campaign, but the founding of the Congress Socialist Party as a ginger group within the parent organization. Professor N.G. Ranga (leader and till recently president of the Swatantra Party), who started as a Kisan leader, used to serve as one of the focal points of leftist opinion within and outside the Congress in Andhra. Periodicals like *Vauhini, Chitragupta* and *Prajabandhu* (both of which were edited by the late Mrs S.G. Acharya), starting publication a few years later, used to provide the forum for discussion of socialist ideas, strengthening the leftist forces and encouraging the younger elements in the national organization. It is worth mentioning at this stage that Leftism in Telugu periodical journalism at the time was apt to be rather a vague and inchoate affair, with no well-defined ideas about economic revolution or social organization. It was broadly assumed that their editors had reserved their enthusiasm for the younger national leaders like Jawaharlal Nehru, Subhas Bose, M.N. Roy and Jayaprakash Narayan rather than for the old guard led by Sardar Patel, Bhulabhai Desai, Rajaji, and Dr Pattabhi, the no-changers who swore by the dictates of the Mahatma.

A number of publications during this time, inspired by the freedom fighters of the world, were launched as a contribution to the national struggle, with little regard for the economic side of these ventures. The late Gadde Lingaiah, a writer in his own right, and an able translator (who is better known as the founder of the publishing venture, Adarsa Grantha Mandali), started the Red Flag Publications, under whose imprint were brought out *The Lives of Terrorists (Viplava Veerulu),* promptly banned by the British government. Some years later, round about 1937 or so, a series of patriotic publications with a socialist slant, under the title *Navya Sahitya Maala* was started at Anantapur under the joint editorship of Vidwan Viswam (now Editor in charge of the *Andhra Prabha Illustrated Weekly*) and T. Nagi Reddi (presently leader of an extremist group of Andhra Communists). The establishment of socialism was assumed by the sponsors to be the goal of the struggle for freedom. Biographies of Lenin and Stalin, among others, were brought out in this project. Viswam wrote a long poem entitled *Paapam,* in which an intellectual active in the national movement describes his own life and inner struggle. He also wrote another poem called *Naa Hrudayam* ("My Heart") during the period, which was published in the well-known literary and cultural periodical, *Bharati.*

In the field of poetry, a new epoch can be said to have started with a single poem of Sri Sri (the famous initials standing for Srirangam Srinivasa Rao) called *Maha Prasthaanam,* written probably in 1932 but published in 1934. The first few lines of the poem, meant to be rendered as a marching song, read as follows, in the author's own translation (with the caption *Forward March*):

The waves are rolling
The bells are tolling
The voice of another world is calling
Another another another world
Is rolling tolling calling on
Forward march
Oh onward forge
Ahead ahead let's always surge.

What that "another world" really was or might look like is left to the reader's imagination, which is vigorously stimulated by the martial tempo of these resounding numbers. The author is not clear enough about its positive content or its vital details, but he could not possibly be more definite about his impatience with the old outmoded world around him, rotten to the core with "hoax and humbug," with "senility and orthodoxy." Though he had never been actively connected in his personal life with the freedom struggle or with any political party, the sympathies of young Sri Sri (then in his early twenties) were undoubtedly with the terrorists. He was deeply moved by the death sentences on Bhagat Singh and his two colleagues (Rajguru and Sukhdev) and gave vent to his feelings in the now famous song, which reads in the original *Maro Prapancham, Maro Prapancham, Maro Prapancham Pilichindee* (literally meaning "another world, another world, another world is calling"). He is known to have been influenced in composing this song by the rhythm and words of another song by a brother-poet (the late Sishtla Umamaheshwar), beginning "Maaro,Maaro ...etc." (Hindi expression, referring to the lathi charge). It is a measure of the time-lag in political sensibility, typical of the contemporary establishment, that this poem was promptly returned to the author by the editor of a respectable literary periodical, not unfriendly to patriotic versification. They had, possibly, reasons of their own to grow nervous at these blood-and-thunder lines:

> Our blood is floods
> Shall drench all roads
> We leap the deep and sweep all shores
> Reshaping geography amain
> Remaking history again
> Nor deserts nor forests nor hills nor rivers
> Our forward march shall halt or reverse
> East and West and North and South
> Eagles and lions and hounds of youth
> Attack the turrets of humbug and hoax
> The conservative the orthodox
> Shall go to the wall shall come to the dock
> Rotten marrowed
> Senile time harrowed
> Haggard laggards shall die on the spot...

The poet wants the people to go ahead "shot by shot," though he knows not where. He urges "Freedom's Zealots," proud heirs of "tomorrow's thought" to surge forward:

Their drizzling blood dazzling red hot
With shouts of "Om
Hari Om, Hari Om"
Storm the Bastille Reaction's home
And surge forward
Converge skyward
Lo another world a grander world
The banner of liberty has unfurled

His appeal is specially to the youth, for he is inspired by a faith in the future. He is not one of those whose golden age is always in the past. The clarion call rings on and on:

Youthful blood ignites the future
Youth awake is on the march
Towers of new life for us to catch
Is this oil boiling? Oh no,
This is a lake of blood aglow
Like Niagara like Nynza
Like resistless waterfalls
Bounce forward
Advance onward
Announce the birth of another world
Hear ye not the ringing singing
Drumbeatings of another world?

Proceeding further, the poet gives us a glimpse of what he hopes the marchers to see. He cannot help being vague here too, but he is perhaps less vague than at the beginning:

See before us rise the glorious
Mankind's hope lit spire of fire...
Hail the morn
And sound the horn
A newer truer world shall be born

then sing in chorus
Lo before us there is another world
Yonder, yonder
Lo the splendour
And the wonder
Of its faery fiery crown
And the red flag of its dawn
Like the ritual flame of time.

The mention of the red flag would leave the reader in no doubt as to what he is talking about. It was an unmistakable reference to the flag of Soviet Russia (with the emblem of hammer and sickle in white against a red background). He was obviously in complete sympathy with the new ideal of a classless society, sought to be achieved by the Soviet Union. In this, he was one with many of the progressive leaders in India and elsewhere (including Nehru and Laski) who had, for long, looked upon Soviet Russia as the promised land for the subject peoples of the world. The impression nursed by many was that Russia was a kind of earthly paradise, where social and economic inequalities had been destroyed, unemployment, poverty and hunger abolished, heralding an era of equality and justice, peace, progress and plenty. This was perhaps in keeping with the spirit of the age and the impression, true enough in its broadest outline and not easy of verification by a distant observer, was shared by most of the intellectuals who prided themselves on being more forward-looking than their parents and predecessors. The naivety of their belief had not yet been exposed to the latter-day revelations and disillusionments about the dictatorship of the proletariat in practice.

There were few modern writers coming of age in the thirties who had not been inspired, in some way, by the socialist movement, of which each had a personal vision of his own. Books on Soviet Russia had a strange attraction for readers, though the information that could then trickle down to the world outside, across the many barriers was by no means complete, or even correct in some vital matters of detail. The frequent and often thoughtless bans imposed on such books by an obtuse bureaucracy served considerably to enhance their attraction. Among the popular books of the day in Telugu was *Neti Rashyaa* (Russia Today) by

V.R. Narla, a journalist and writer of promise then, and now a respected leader of the profession. It was topical and informative and was a fair measure of the general interest in the subject in Andhra. It soon went out of print and became out of date equally soon, which was only in the nature of things.

Among the other Telugu writers who had attained intellectual maturity and political identification in the thirties were T. Gopichand, and G.V. Krishna Rao, Mahidhara Ramamohana Rao, and Maddukuri Chandrasekhara Rao. They were all conscious of the growing power of socialist ideology. The first two understood socialism through the eyes of M.N. Roy and the last two did so, accepting the Soviet view, like so many of their political co-workers. Gopichand was basically a student of philosophy, with an admiration for Bertrand Russell and company, interested primarily in the workings of the human mind. He wrote simple and readable essays on Marxism and other systems of thought in the Telugu Weekly *Prajamitra* (now defunct), for the benefit of the intelligent layman depending on Telugu as his only medium of information. Krishna Rao, a student of aesthetics and poetry, as well as a creative writer, was just then forming his ideas on socialism and allied subjects. In a novel published in the late forties (or may be early fifties), entitled, *Keelubommalu* (Puppets), he used the state of affairs obtaining in some of the Andhra villages, including the pro-Communist and anti-Communist factions to illustrate how the leaders at the back of the trouble, having the levers of economic power and political advantage in their hands, were exploiting the common man for their own personal ends. Ramamohana Rao, substantially a self-educated man with a Sanskrit background, wrote articles and stories in *Prajabandhu, Vauhini* and *Prajamitra,* totally accepting the Marxian interpretation of history and social organization in his understanding of the contemporary situation in Andhra, with particular reference to the villages in the Godavari delta. His major works in fiction were yet unwritten at this time, but his close observation through the ideological microscope had given him the necessary personal insights. Adivi Bapiraju, in his novel, *Narayana Rao,* and even more in *Konangi,* both of which have some political references reflecting the contemporary situation, had made no secret of his impatience with the then powerful feudal set-up and a desire for replacing it with something more desirable in common interest. But his idealism was by and large non-political, looking back to the art of Ajanta and Ellora, Hampi and Lepakshi, and looking forward to the renaissance of Andhra culture, under the inspiration of a golden age of its distant past.

There were a few short story writers like "Cha So" (Chaganti Somayajulu) and Ana Sarma (Ayyala Nrusimha Sarma) who had revealed a social consciousness not too common in their day. So did Kosaraju Seshaiah, who wrote a few novels, including one or two on the plight of the landless agricultural workers. The late Veluri Sivarama Sastri, a scholar and creative writer of an older generation well steeped in the Indian cultural tradition, had to his credit a few stories that reflect an awareness of the economic factors responsible for the social situation in the dismal thirties. (One of them entitled *Depression Chembu* is particularly notable). Kodavatiganti Kutumba Rao, one of the novelists and short story writers of major importance with a progressive outlook, had started writing in the thirties, but his most representative work really comes after the outbreak of the Second World War.

Apart from the economic interpretation of social and political phenomena, the impact of socialist ideology had quite a few other significant repercussions on the Telugu writers in the choice of theme and its treatment, in the use of language and style, in the evolution of technique and workmanship. For one thing, poetry, in particular which had for long, been stifled in the heavy coat-of-mail of an outmoded and Sanskritized poetic diction, and merci-lessly stretched on the procrustean bed of metre and rhyme, began to break away from all its rusty shackles. The Romanticists of an earlier generation had already raised the banner of revolt against the classical tradition with all its rigours and rigidities. As a result of which, there was a notable relaxation of the rules of poetics, including prosody *(Chhandas)* and aesthetics *(Alankara Sastra)*, which were until then held sacrosanct by the poets and pandits alike. But the new spirit of a total revolt, a lot more far-reaching in its consequences, was symbolized by a number of youthful poets (like Narayana Babu, Sishtla Umamaheshwar and Pattabhi) led by Sri Sri, who sang:

Old walls are cracking

Old songs are croaking
Old ways are breaking
Why are you not waking?

He repudiated the time-honoured assumption that there were a
few "approved" subjects fit for poetic treatment and many others
beneath its notice. A writer like G.K. Chesterton, tradition-bound
in some respects and unconventional in others, could write a
short moving poem on *The Donkey* (the poor long-eared thing
that had its hour of glory mounted by Jesus Christ) but such a
thing was unheard of in the poetic tradition of Telugu. It was
left to Sri Sri to come out with a new manifesto, as it were, that
sought to widen the areas of poetic experience.   He put it as spicily
as he could:

Tweeny weeny pups
Eeny meeny ships
Sheeny shiny soaps
All world silent or noisy
Is material for poesy.

Nothing that was part of the gamut of man's daily life, was outside
the range of his poetic vision:

Cottage lamps
Postage stamps
Dreams and 'dromes and shrimps and gamps
Rule the realms of Art for sure
All Art is grand, all Art is pure.
A slice of bread
A piece of wood
A rotten plantain that's no good
Each shares with you
Joy shares with you.

Once the scales had fallen from the poet's eyes, he could see beauty,
where he had not learned to recognize it before. Not unlike Wordsworth, who could contemplate on a tiny blade of grass or a waving
ear of corn, but the approach is very different.

There is beauty, there is grace
Here and there and everywhere
Inspired be
By sea, by tree
Everything see and anything say.
The world is a labyrinth strangely arranged
And poesy a deep thirst ever unquenched.

The new poetic movement of Sri Sri, socialist in its ideological framework, was inspired, on the linguistic side, by Gidugu Venkata Ramamurti's campaign for adopting spoken Telugu as a medium for literary expression. Most of the writers who responded to Rama-murti's call began the experiment in prose—starting with novels and short stories. Sri Sri was, perhaps, the first to try the experiment in verse—and with phenomenal success, in due course. He used the words of common parlance with an uncommon power. He was able to exploit their hitherto untapped potentialities. To change the metaphor again, he breathed life into words of common clay. Not for him the petrified usage of poetic diction. He hoped to tear up the old straight-jacket into which the poor versifier was obliged to squeeze himself. He could not have been more deadly earnest than when he wrote these lines, apparently in jest:

Chhando bando bastu lannee
Chhat! Phat phat mani Trenchi
Dammit! Emitraa idante
Pray! It's poetry Andaam.

A marriage between prose and verse was also another thing he wanted to achieve. To read it in his own words,

Ardhaanni adhwaannapu Adavilo vadali
Gadyaanni Padyaaniki Pelli Chedaam.

Discarding the Sanskritized word-compounds (which, however, he could use to good effect, when he so desired), and the traditional metrical patterns, he went back to some of the folk metres and rediscovered the untold wealth of their instant suggestion and intimate association in the minds and hearts of the common men and women. He also went forward to the experimentalists of Europe including the *avant garde* school of French poets. In fact, the models for his inspiration were far flung—from Gurazada and Gidugu at home, to Walt Whitman in America, from Browning and Swinburne in England to Francois Villon and Baudelaire, Valery and Sartre in France, to Dali in Spain and Mayakovsky in Russia. By the frequent use of English expressions right in the midst of the body of Telugu verse (which began to be adopted even more widely by a younger poet, Arudra) he freed the language of poetry from all its old-fashioned inhibitions. Internationalism in political ideology was well matched by an unrestricted cosmopolitanism in poetic technique.

One of the notable consequences of this movement is a growing rejection of the aesthetic theory of Art for Art's sake (reminiscent of Oscar Wilde and Aubrey Beardsley) which, however, had never been able to strike any deep roots in Indian literature. The old Indian ideal of universal good *(Vishwasreyah Kaavyam)* was restated in terms of a new social commitment, identified as the greatest good of the greatest number. Literature was brought back closer to the people and the poet was forced to come down from the ivory tower in the clouds, of his own making, not only to the clubs and coffee houses but to the fields and factories as well. Not that there has been no blatant political propaganda and readymade slogan-mongering in the process of democratization and under the pretext of relating literature to the daily life of the common people. But the social consciousness and the awareness of contemporary problems was a distinct gain. There was, in fact, more of this in Telugu literature during the years after 1939 than before it. But the beginnings were made here and the harbinger of the age echoed the desire of all poets, when he sang:

> This is my one desire
> That when I begin to sing
> The race of man take up that song
> And like a gong's
> Its tintinabulations
> Be carried to the farthest limits of the earth
> And the utmost reaches of the sky.

REFERENCES

Sri Sri (Srirangam Srinivasa Rao), *Maha Prasthaanam* (collection of poems).

Sri Sri (Srirangam Srinivasa Rao), *Three Cheers for Man* (English renderings of selected poems).

Sri Sri (Srirangam Srinivasa Rao), *Khadga Srushti* (poems).

Anisetti and others (Compiled by), *Sri Sri Yugam* (anthology of poems).

Reddi, K.V. Ramana, (Compiled by), *Adugujaada Gurajadadi* (anthology of poems).

Arudra, *Twamevaaham* (poems).

Progressive Writers, *Nayagaraa* (anthology of poems).

Rao, Maddukuri Chandrasekhara, *Andhra Sahitya Punarvikasam,* Visalandhra Publishing House.

Unnava Lakshminarayana, *Malapalli* (novel).

Rao, Mahidhara Ramamohana, *Radha Chakraalu* and *Kollayi gattitenemi* (both novels).

Sitapati, Dr G.V. *History of Telugu Literature,* Sahitya Akademi.

Reddi, Dr C. Narayana, *Adhunika Andhra Kavitwamu.*

Andhra Darsini, Visalandhra Publishing House, Vijayawada.

Telugu Encyclopeadia (Vol.III on Andhra Culture), Telugu Bhasha Samiti, Madras.

Back numbers of *Bharati* (literary monthly periodical in Telugu, Madras).

Back numbers of *Sravanti* (literary monthly, Hyderabad).

Back numbers of *Adhyudaya* (Telugu periodical, organ of the Andhra Progressive Writers' Association, Vijayawada).

Yetukuri Balaramamurti, *Andhrula Samkshipta Charitra,* Visalandhra Publishing House.

Reddi, K.V. Ramana, *Kavikokila* (a literary biography of Duvvuri Rami Reddi).

Reddi, K.V. Ramana, *Mahodayam* (Life and work of Gurazada).

A SELECT BIBLIOGRAPHY

List of Abbreviations

AICCL   All India Congress Committee Library, New Delhi.
DUL   Delhi University Library, Delhi.
GSS   Gandhi Smarak Sangrahalaya, New Delhi.
ICWAL   Indian Council of World Affairs Library, New Delhi.
NL   National Library, Calcutta.
NMML   Nehru Memorial Museum & Library, New Delhi.

1. ABID ALI
     The Indian communists exposed. 3d ed., New Delhi, I.N.T.U.C., 1965. vi, 44 p.

                                       NMML

2. ADHIKARI, G.
     Communist Party and India's path to national regeneration and socialism: a review and comment on E.M.S. Namboodiripad's revisionism and dogmatism in the Communist Party of India. New Delhi, C.P.I., 1964, 205 p.
     "Roots of our left-sectarian and reformist errors in the pre-independence period, 1922-1947," pp. 51-86.

                                         NMML

3. ——, ed.
     From peace front to people's war. 2d enl. ed. Bombay, People's Pub. House, 1944. 444 p. (Marx-Engels-Lenin-Stalin series, no. 25)

                                       NMML

4. AHUJA, B.N., comp. & ed.
     "J.P." : India's revolutionary number one. Lahore, Varma Pub. Co., 1947. viii, 220 p.

                                       ICWAL

5. ALL INDIA FORWARD BLOC
     Programme of post-war revolution: draft manifesto of the Forward Bloc, the vanguard of Indian revolution. Bombay, National Youth Publications, 1946, 65 p.
     "Rise and growth of left movement": pp. 10-16.

                                       NMM

6. ALL INDIA TRADE UNION CONGRESS
    Reports, 1920-21, 1923-29, 1931-33, 1935-36 and 1938.

7. AVASTHI, RAM KUMAR
    Social and political ideas of M. N. Roy.
    Thesis—Agra Univ. 1960.

8. BALABUSHEVICH, V.V., AND DYAKOV, A.M., *eds.*
    A contemporary history of India. New Delhi, People's Pub. House,
    1964. viii, 585 p.
    First published in Russian under the auspices of the Institute of
    Oriental Studies, Academy of Sciences of USSR, Moscow, in 1959.
    "The anti-imperialist movement, 1920-22": pp. 57-95.
    "Birth of the communist movement": pp. 140-62.
    "Simon Commission and new tide of struggles": pp. 163-72.
    "Rise of the working class movement and boycott of the Simon
    Commission": pp. 192-226.
    "Mass civil disobedience and popular uprisings"; pp. 227-50.
    "India in 1931-1933": pp. 251-73.
    "Federal scheme and new features of struggles": pp. 291-311.
    "Introduction of provincial autonomy": pp. 312-33.
    "Struggle for a United National Front": pp. 334-47.

                                                                                    NMML

9. BALARAM, N.E.
    A short history of the Communist Party of India; with an introduction
    by C. Achyutha Menon. Trivandrum, Prabhath Book House, 1967.
    ii, 72, xii p.

                                                                                    ICWAL

10. BANDOPADHYAYA, JAYANTANUJA
    Indian nationalism versus international communism: role of ideology
    in international politics. Calcutta, K. L. Mukhopadhyay, 1966,
    ix, 368 p. bibl.

                                                                                    NMML

11. BASAK, V.
    Some urgent problems of the labour movement in India. London,
    Works Library Publishers [1933], 43 p.

12. BASU, CHANCHAL KUMAR
    A survey of ideologies in Indian politics. Calcutta, Calcutta Pub.
    Concern, 1940.

                                                                                    NL

13. BEAUCHAMP, JOAN
    British imperialism in India. Prepared for the Labour Research

Department. London, Martin Lawrence, 1934. 224 p. bibl.
"The trade unions and the rising tide of militancy": pp. 135-59.

NMML

14. BENIPURI, RAMAVRIKSH
Jayaprakash. Patna, Sahityalaya, 1947. 240 p.
Hindi.

GSS

15. BESANT, ANNIE
Socialism in India [a lecture]. Madras, 1920. 22 p. (National Home
Rule League pamphlet, no. 15)

16. BHAGOLIWAL, T.N.
Economics of labour and social welfare: an authoritative account
of labour problems in India and other countries of industrial importance. Agra, Sahitya Bhawan, 1966. vii, 470 p.
"Trade union movement in India": pp. 92-112.

NMML

17. BHARGAVA, G.S.
Leaders of the left; with an introduction by M. Venkatarangaiya.
Bombay, Meherally Book Club, 1951. vii, 73 p.

NMML

18. ———
A study of the communist movement in Andhra; with a foreword by
Asoka Mehta. Delhi, Siddharta Publications, 1955. 48 p.

NL

19. BIHAR SOCIALIST PARTY
Bihar Socialist Party aur Bihar ka kisan andolan. Patna [n.d.]
Hindi.

20. BOSE, SUBHAS CHANDRA
The Indian struggle 1920-1942; comp. by the Netaji Research Bureau.
Bombay, Asia Pub. House, 1964. xii, 476 p.

NMML

21. BRADLEY, BEN. F.
Trade-unionism in India. London, Modern Books [1932] 63 p.

NL

22. BRECHER, MICHAEL
Nehru: a politica biography. London, Oxford Univ. Press, 1959.
xi, 682 p. bibl.
"Hero of the left," p. 212-29.

NMML

23. Brij Narain
     Charkha, Marxism, Indian socialism. Lahore, Rama Krishna, 1941.
     195 p.

                                                                    NMML

24. ———
     Indian socialism. Lahore, Atma Ram, 1937. xxiii, 158 p.

                                                                    NMML

25. ———
     Marxism is dead. Lahore, Rama Krishna, 1939. 265 p.

                                                                    NMML

26. ———
     Supplement to Marxism is dead. Lahore, Rama Krishna, 1939.
     30 p.

                                                                    NMML

27. Chaddha, Tilak Raj
     A study of the communist movement in the Punjab. Ghaziabad,
     Jyoti Prakashan [1954] 50 p.

28. Chakrabarti, A.N.
     An analytical review of democratic socialism: Faizpur to Jaipur
     ['36-63]. Calcutta, Thacker, Spink [n.d.] 28 p.

                                                                    ICWAL

29. Coatman, J.
     Years of destiny: India 1926-32; with a foreword by Lord Irwin of
     Kirby. London, Jonathan Cape, 1932. 384 p.
     "Parties and personalities in India": pp. 86-114.

                                                                    NMML

30. Communist International. 6th congress, 1928 Programme. Bombay,
     People's Pub. House, 1948.   viii, 72 p.
     Comments on the present C.P.I. and shows the difference between
     C.P.I. and the Communist International.

                                                                    ICWAL

31. Communist papers: documents selected from those obtained on the
     arrest of the communist leaders on the 14th and 21st October, 1925.
     London, H.M.S.O., 1926. 132 p.

32. Communist Party of India
     Draft platform of action of the C.P. of India. [n.p., 1933?] 5 p.

                                                                      NL

33. ———
      A manifesto to the All India National Congress. London, Dorrit
      Press [1926] 15 p.

                                                                    NL

34. The communist reply. Bombay, Workers' Literature [n.d.] 60 p.
      Abridged ed. of joint statement of 18 communists accused in Meerut
      Case.

35. Communists challenge imperialism from the dock; introduction by
      Muzaffar Ahmad. Calcutta, National Book Agency, 1967. xiv,
      316 p.

                                                                  NMML

36. Congress Socialist. Bombay, All India Congress Socialist Party, 1936.
      2v.
      Microfilm.

                                                                 ICWAL

37. CONGRESS SOCIALIST PARTY
      The C.S.P., the Reds and Roy. Bombay [1937?] 16 p.
      Statement of C.S.P. executive of 9 August 1937 in reply to attacks on
      party by communists and Royists.

38. ———
      Communist plot against the C.S.P. Bombay (1938?) 12 p.

39. ———
      Reports, 1934, 1936 and 1938.

40. ———
      Socialist disunity and the Communist International. Bombay, 1942.
      12 p.

41. CRANE, ROBERT I.
      The Indian National Congress and the Indian agrarian problem,
      1919-1939: an historical study.
      Thesis—Ph.D.—Yale Univ. 1951.
      Microfilm

                                                                  NMML

42. CROUCH, HAROLD
      Trade unions and politics in India. Bombay, Manaktalas, 1966.
      x, 315 p. bibl.

                                                                  NMML

43. Dandavate, M.R.
          Evolution of socialist policies and perspective: 1934-1964. Bombay,
          Lokamitra Publications, 1964. 19 p.
                                                                NMML

44. ————
          Gandhiji's impact on socialist thinking. Bombay, Praja Socialist
          Party, 1957. 13 p.
                                                                NMML

45. ————
          Three decades of Indian communism.   Bombay, Praja Socialist
          Publication [n.d.] 33 p.
                                                                NMML

46. Dange, S.A.
          Gandhi vs. Lenin. Bombay, Liberty Literature Co. [1921]. iii, 64 p.
                                                                GSS

47. ————
          Hell found.   Calcutta, Vanguard Literature Co. [1928] ix, 123 p.
                                                                ICWAL

48. ————
          On the Indian trade union movement: reports to a convention of
          Communist Party members working in the trade union movement,
          Calcutta, May 20-22, 1952. Bombay, Communist Party Publication,
          1952. 62 p.
          "Trade unions, political parties and unity": pp. 28-37.
                                                                NMML

49. Das, Rajani Kanta
          The labour movement in India. Berlin, Walter De Gruyter, 1923.
          x, 122 p.
                                                                GSS

50. Democratic Research Service, comp.
          Indian Communist Party documents 1930-1956; with an introduction
          by V. B. Karnik. Bombay, 1957. xx, 345 p.
                                                                NMML

51. Desai, A.R.
          Social background of Indian nationalism. 4th ed. Bombay, Popular
          Prakashan, 1966. xix, 461 p.   bibl.
          "Rise of new social classes in India": pp. 174-220.
          "Rise of political movements as the expression of Indian nationalism":
          pp. 307-380.

"Problem of nationalities and minorities": pp. 381-431.
"Epilogue": pp. 432-441.

NMML

52. DEVANANDAN, P.D. AND THOMAS, M.M., *eds.*
Communism and the social revolution in India: a Christian interpretation. Calcutta, Y.M.C.A. Pub. House, 1953. iii, 88 p.
"History of the Communist Party of India": pp. 25-44.

NMML

53. DHANAPALA, D.B.
Eminent Indians. Bombay, Nalanda Publications [n.d.] 180 p.
"Jawaharlal Nehru": pp. 20-35.
"Jai Prakash Narain": pp. 144-51.

NMML

54. DRUHE, DAVID N.
Soviet Russia and Indian communism 1919-1947: with an epilogue covering the situation today. New York, Bookman Associates, 1959. 429 p. bibl.

AICCL

55. DUFFETT, W.E., AND OTHERS
India today: the background of Indian nationalism. New York, John Day Co., 1942. 173 p. bibl.

ICWAL

56. DUTT, R. PALME
India today. Bombay, People's Pub. House, 1947. 532 p.

NMML

57. ———
Modern India. London, Communist Party of Great Britain, 1927. 174 p.

ICWAL

58. EDATATA NARAYANAN
Praja socialism; monopoly's pawn. Bombay, People's Pub. House, 1952. 74 p.
"The Socialist Party": pp. 11-22.

NMML

59. FISCHER, LOUIS
Gandhi and Stalin: two signs at the world's crossroads. Delhi, Rajkamal Publications, 1947. 147 p.

NMML

60. ——, *ed.*
   The essential Gandhi: an anthology. London, Allen & Unwin,
   1963. 369 p.
   "Gandhi on socialism and communism": pp. 303-07.

                                                           NMML

61. GADRE, KAMALA
   Indian way to socialism; foreword by V.K.R.V. Rao, New Delhi,
   Vir Pub. House, 1966. 136 p. bibl.

                                                           NMML

62. GAHRANA, G.K.
   On Indian socialism. Agra, Agra Univ., 1965. 52 p. (Agra Univ.
   extension lectures)

                                                           ICWAL

63. GANDHI, M.K.
   Communism and communists; comp. by R. K. Prabhu. Ahmedabad,
   Navajivan Pub. House, 1959. 24 p.

                                                           NMML

64. ——
   My socialism; comp. by R. K. Prabhu. Ahmedabad, Navajivan Pub.
   House, 1959. 56 p.

                                                           NMML

65. ——
   Socialism of my conception; ed. by Anand T. Hingorani. Bombay,
   Bharatiya Vidya Bhavan, 1957. xii, 315 p. (Gandhi series, 2)

                                                           NMML

66. ——
   Towards non-violent socialism; ed. by Bharatan Kumarappa.
   Ahmedabad, Navajivan Pub. House, 1951. xi, 165 p.

                                                           NMML

67. ——AND JOSHI, P.C.
   Correspondence. Bombay, People's Pub. House, 1945. vi, 63 p.
                                                           NMML

68. GHOSH, GOPAL
   Indian trade union movement. Calcutta, T.U. Publications, 1961.
   1pt., 93 p.
   "The development of trade union movement": pp. 65-82.
   "The birth of the A.I.T.U.C.": pp. 83-93

                                                           NMML

69. Ghosh, P.
    Personnel administration in India.   New Delhi, Sudha Publications,
    1969. xiv, 440 p.
    "Trade unionism in India": pp. 304-39.

                                                                    NMML

70. Ghosh, Shibdas
    A critique of communist movement in India. Calcutta, Socialist
    Unity Centre [1940]

71. Glading, Percy
    The Meerut Conspiracy Case.   London, Communist Party of Great
    Britain [1933?] 19 p.
    Includes result of trial with sentences.

72. Goyal, O.P.
    Contemporary Indian political thought.   Allahabad, Kitab Mahal,
    1965. ii, 104 p. bibl.
    "Political thought of M.N. Roy": pp. 1-14.
    "Political thought of Jawaharlal Nehru": pp. 15-37.
    "Indian socialist movement and thought": pp. 38-57.
    "Indian communist movement and thought": pp. 76-90.

                                                                    NMML

73. Gregg, Richard B.
    Which way lies hope ? : an examination of capitalism, communism,
    socialism and Gandhiji's programme.   Ahmedabad, Navajivan Pub.
    House, 1952. viii, 219 p.

                                                                    NMML

74. Griffiths, Percival
    The changing face of communism.   London, Bodley Head, 1961.
    223 p.
    "Communism in India": pp. 135-54.

                                                                    AICCL

75. Grover, D.C.
    M.N. Roy's political philosophy with special reference to India.
    Thesis—Ph.D.—Kurukshetra Univ. 1967.

76. Gupta, R.C.
    Socialism, democracy and India.   Agra, Ram Prasad, 1965. 203 p.
    "Political parties in India": pp. 129-53.
    "Socialist movement in India": pp. 154-68.

                                                                    NMML

77. Gurha, Lakshmi
    The growth of socialism in India.
    Thesis—Allahabad Univ. 1954.

78. HAITHCEX, JOHN P.
     Nationalism, communism and twentieth century Jacobinism : Royist
     tactics in India, 1927-1940.
     Thesis—California Univ. 1965.
     Microfilm
                                                                    NMML

79. HARI KISHORE SINGH
     A history of the Praja Socialist Party, 1934-59. Lucknow, Narendra
     Prakashan, 1959. 239 p.
     "The background" : pp. 1-25.
     "The Congress Socialist Party and the Indian National Congress
     1934-42" : pp. 26-51.
     "The Congress Socialist Party and the Communist Party 1934-42" :
     pp. 52-78.
                                                                    NMML

80. ———
     The rise and secession of the Congress Socialist Party of India, 1934-
     1948. In Raghavan Iyer, ed., South Asian Affairs. London, Chatto
     & Windus, 1960. pp. 116-40. (St Antony's papers, no. 8; South
     Asian Affairs, no. 1)
                                                                    NMML

81. HAUSER, WALTER
     The Bihar Provincial Kisan Sabha, 1929-1942 : a study of an Indian
     peasant movement.
     Thesis—Ph.D.—Chicago Univ. 1961.
     Microfilm.
                                                                    NMML

82. Hindi, A.K.
     M.N. Roy, the man who looked ahead. Ahmedabad, Modern Pub.
     House [1938] 242 p.

83. Hutchinson, Lester
     Conspiracy at Meerut; preface by Harold J. Laski. London, Allen &
     Unwin, 1935. 190 p.
                                                                    NMML

84. ———
     Meerut trial, 1929-37. Manchester, Manchester Meerut   Defence
     Committee [n.d.] 71 p.
     Statement given in defence at trial.

85. Ilyas Ahmad
     Trends in socialistic thought and movement: being a lecture on the

origin, growth and development of socialism down to our own times
with special reference to the onslaught of that movement in India.
Allahabad, Indian Press, 1937. x, 221 p.

86. India. *High Court (Allahabad)*
        Criminal appeal no. 122 of 1933. Allahabad, 1933.
        Appeal judgment in Meerut Communist Conspiracy Case.
        Typescript.

87. ———
        East India [conspiracy] copy of the judgment of the High Court of
        Judicature at Allahabad in the Revolutionary Conspiracy Case.
        London, H.M.S.O., 1924. 16 p.

88. ———
        King—Emperor vs. Nalini Bhushan Das Gupta, Muhammad Shaukat
        Usmani, Muzaffar Ahmad, and Shripat Amrit Dange in the High
        Court of Judicature at Allahabad, Criminal side: appeal no. 588 of
        1924, Cawnpore District. Allahabad, Government Press [1924?]

89. India. *Home Deptt.*
        Communism in India, 1924-27; comp. by the Intelligence Bureau,
        Home Deptt., Govt. of India Calcutta, Govt. of India, 1927. xix,
        415 p.

90. Indian National Congress
        Report of the General Secretary, March 1938—Feb. 1939. [Allahabad,
        A.I.C.C., 1939] 72 p.

                                                                NMML

91. ———. 49th *session, Lucknow,* 1936
        Report, Allahabad, A.I.C.C. [1936] vii, 115, viii, v, iv, 8, viii p.
                                                                NMML

92. ———. 51st *session, Haripura (Dt. Surat, Gujarat)* 1938 Report. Haripura,
        A.I.C.C. [1938] 232 p.

                                                                NMML

93. Jayprakash Narayan
        Democratic socialism: our ideal and our method. Bombay, Socialist
        Party [n.d.] 20 p.

                                                                ICWAL

94. ———
        Gandhiji's leadership and the Congress Socialist Party. Bombay, All
        India Congress Socialist Party (1940?) 12 p. (Congress Socialist tracts,
        no. 1)

                                                                ICWAL

95.   ————
       My picture of socialism. New Delhi, Delhi Congress Socialist Party
       [n. d.] 14 p.
                                                                    ICWAL

96.   ————
       Socialism, sarvodaya and democracy: selected works; ed. by Bimla
       Prasad. Bombay, Asia Pub. House, 1964. xliii, 287 p.
                                                                    NMML

97.   ————
       Socialism versus the A.I.V.I.A. Bombay, Congress Socialist Publication,
       1935. 34 p. (Indian Socialist Research Institute tract, no. 6)

98.   ————
       Socialist unity and the Congress Socialist Party. Bombay, Congress
       Socialist Party [1941] 46 p.
                                                                    ICWAL

99.   ————
       Towards a new society.   New Delhi, Congress for Cultural Freedom,
       1958.   170 p.
       "Letter to PSP associates" : pp. 1-48.
                                                                    NMML

100.   ————
       Towards struggle: selected manifestoes, speeches and writings; ed.
       by Yusuf Meherally.   Bombay, Padma Publications, 1946. 244 p.
                                                                    NMML

101.   ————
       Vichardhara; ed. by Ramavriksh Benipuri. Patna, Pustak Jagat,
       1948.   iv, 326 p.
       Hindi.
                                                                    NMML

102.   ————
       Why socialism ?   Benares, All India Congress Socialist Party, 1936.
       iii, 160 p.
                                                                    NMML

103.   Joshi, N.M.
       Trade union movement in India.   Bombay, 1927.

104.   Joshi, P.C.
       Congress and communists. 2d ed.   Bombay, People's Pub. House,
       1944.   26 p.

Reprinted from People's War, no. 22-26 Nov., 1944.
"Indian nationalism and communism": pp. 4-6.

ICWAL

105. KARNIK, V.B.
Indian trade unions: a survey. 2d ed. Bombay, Manaktalas, 1966.
ix, 343 p.
"Emergence of communists": pp. 48-60.
"The split and its aftermath": pp. 61-74.
"From disunity to unity": pp. 75-90.

106. KAUSHIK, P.D.
The Congress ideology and programme 1920-47: ideological founda-
tions of Indian nationalism during the Gandhian era. Bombay,
Allied Publishers, 1964. ix, 405 p.

NMML

107. KAYE, SIR CECIL
Communism in India. Delhi, Govt. of India Press, 1926. 154 p.
Covers period 1920-1924.

108. KENNEDY, MALCOLM D.
A short history of communism in Asia. London, Weidenfeld and
Nicolson, 1957. ix, 556 p. bibl.
"Ferment in India and Malaya": pp. 54-65.

DUL

109. KRISHNAMURTI, Y.G.
Jawaharlal Nehru: the man and his ideas; prefaces by Bhulabhai J.
Desai and Mrs. Rameshuri Nehru. Bombay, Popular Book Depot,
1942. xxxvii, 174 p. bibl.

NMML

110. LAJPAT RAI
Writings and speeches; ed. by Vijaya Chandra Joshi. Delhi, Univer-
sity Publishers, 1966. 2v.
Contents.—v. 1. 1888-1919.—v. 2. 1920-1928.

NMML

111. LAKHANPAL, P.L.
History of the Congress Socialist Party; with a foreword by Prem
Bhasin. Lahore, National Publishers [1946] viii, 158, iii p.

ICWAL

112. LAKSHMAN, P.P.
Congress and labour movement in India. Allahabad, A.I.C.C.
[1947] 174 p. (Congress Economic & Political Studies series, no. 3)

ICWAL

113. LIMAYE, MADHU
     Communist Party: facts and fiction. Hyderabad, Chetana Praka-
     shan, 1951. 101 p.

                                                                    GSS

114. ─────
     Evolution of socialist policy. Hyderabad, Chetana Prakashan, 1952.
     33 p. (Chetana pamphlet, 2)

                                                                   NMML

115. LOHIA, RAMMANOHAR
     Marx, Gandhi and socialism. Hyderabad, Navahind Publications,
     1963. xxxxvii, 550 p.

                                                                   NMML

116. MAEWALL, ANUPURNA
     Influence of International Labour Organization on labour movement
     in India.
     Thesis—Ph.D.—Agra Univ. 1963.

117. MALAVIYA, H.D.
     Socialist ideology of Congress: a study in its evolution; foreword by
     K. Kamaraj. New Delhi, Socialist Congressman Publication, 1966.
     ix, 75, lxxiv p.
     "Nehru's teachings: the basis and the background": pp. 1-10.
     "The groping": pp. 10-25.

                                                                   NMML

118. MARTIN, MARGARET HEATH
     The Indian National Congress and the labour unions.
     Thesis—M.A.—Pennsylvania Univ. 1950.

119. MASANI, M.R.
     The Communist Party of India: a short history; with an introduc-
     tion by Guy Wint. London, Derek Verschoyle, 1954. 302 p.
                                                                   NMML

120. ─────
     Communist plot against the Congress Socialist Party: for members
     of the C.S.P. Bombay, Comet Press [1938]. 12 p.

121. ─────
     Socialism reconsidered. 2d ed. Bombay, Padma Publications,
     1944. 70 p.

                                                                   NMML

122. MASHRUWALA, K.G.
     Gandhi and Marx; introduction by Vinoba Bhave. Ahmedabad,

Navajivan Pub. House, 1951.   vii, 112 p.

                                                                NMML

123. MATHUR, A.S., AND MATHUR, J.S.
      Trade union movement in India.   Allahabad, Chaitanya Pub. House,
      1957.   xvi, 303 p.

                                                                NMML

124. MATHUR, J.S.
      Indian working-class movement.   Allahabad, the author, 1964.
      xvi, 424 p.

                                                                NMML

125. MEERUT. *District Court*
      Meerut Communist Conspiracy Case: magistrate's order of committal
      to trial (Meerut, Saraswati Press, 1929?) 287 p.

126. ─────────
      Proceedings of the Meerut Conspiracy Case, in the court of R. Milner
      White...on 19th July, 1929.   Meerut, Saraswati Press (1929) llv.

127. MEERUT. *Sessions Court*
      Judgment delivered by R. L. Yorke [on the 16th January 1933
      in the Meerut Communist Conspiracy Case: King Emperor versus
      P. Spratt and others.   Simla, Govt. of India Press, 1932-33. 2v.

128. Meerut Conspiracy Case, March 1929—July 1933.   London, Meerut
      Prisoners release Committee [1933?] vi, 21 p.

                                                                ICWAL

129. The Meerut trial: facts of the Case.   London, National Meerut Prisoners
      Defence Committee, 1929.   15 p.

130. MEHTA, ASOKA
      Socialism and Gandhism.   Bombay, Congress Socialist Publication,
      1935.   23 p. (Socialist Research Institute tract, no. 4).

131. MISHRA, RAMNANDAN
      Socialism, Gandhism and Masani. 3d ed.   Chapra, Socialist Party,
      1947. 48 p.

                                                                NMML

132. MOHAN DAS, S.R.
      Communist activity in India, 1925-1950.   2d ed. [Bombay] Demo-
      cratic Research Service, 1951. 16 p.

                                                                NMML

133. MUKERJEE, HIREN
Gandhiji: a study. 2d rev. ed. New Delhi, People's Pub. House,
1960. vii, 225 p.

NMML

134. ⸺
The gentle colossus: a study of Jawaharlal Nehru. Calcutta, Mani-
sha Granthalaya, 1964. vi, 239 p.
"Towards socialism": pp. 158-178.

NMML

135. MUKHTAR AHMAD
Trade unionism and labour disputes in India. London, Longmans,
1935.

136. MUZAFFAR AHMAD
The Communist Party of India and its formation abroad; tr. from
Bengali by Hirendranath Mukerjee. Calcutta, National Book
Agency, 1962. 177 p.

ICWAL

137. ⸺
Communist Party of India: years of formation 1921-1933. Calcutta,
National Book Agency, 1959. 42 p.

ICWAL

138. ⸺
Myself and the Communist Party of India 1920-1929. Calcutta,
National Book Agency, 1970. xiv, 527 iii p.

NMML

139. NAG CHOWDHURY, NEMAI
Subhas Chandra and socialism. Calcutta, Bookland, 1965. 49 p.

NMML

140. NAMBOODIRIPAD, E.M.S.
Economics and politics of India's socialist pattern. New Delhi,
People's Pub. House, 1966. ix, 419 p.
"The new left and Nehru": pp. 48-60.
"Right-left conflict": pp. 61-76.

NMML

141. ⸺
The Mahatma and the ism. New Delhi, People's Pub. House, 1958.
130 p.

NMML

142. ⸺
A short history of the peasant movement in Kerala. Bombay, 1943.

143. NARENDRA DEVA
     The Indian struggle: next phase. Bombay, All India Congress
     Socialist Party [1940?] 16 p. (Socialist tracts, no. 2)
                                                              ICWAL

144. ————
     The peasant problem. Benares, Kashi Vidyapith [n.d.]

145. ————
     Rastriyata aur samajvad. Benares, Gyanmandal, 1949.
     Hindi.
                                                              GSS

146. ————
     Samajvad aur rastriya kranti; ed. by Yusuf Meherally. Agra, S.
     Agarwal (1946) ii, xiii, 265 p.
     Hindi.
                                                              GSS

147. ————
     Socialism and the national revolution; ed. by Yusuf Meherally.
     Bombay, Padma Publications, 1946. xvi, 208 p.
                                                              NMML

148. ————AND OTHERS
     Socialist hi kyon ? Lucknow, the author, 1947. 39 p.
     Hindi.
                                                              NMML

149. NATARAJAN, S.
     Indian parties and politics. London, Oxford Univ. Press, 1947.
     32 p. (Oxford pamphlets on Indian affairs, no. 41)
     "Leftist leanings": pp. 10-13.
                                                              NMML

150. NATIONAL JOINT COUNCIL
     Meerut release the prisoners: a statement upon the Meerut trial and
     sentences issued by the National Joint Council representing the Trade
     Union Congress, the Labour Party and the Parliamentary Labour
     Party, London [1933] 7 p.

151. NEHRU, JAWAHARLAL
     An autobiography: with musings on recent events in India. London,
     John Lane the Bodley Head, 1936. xiv, 618 p.
                                                              NMML

152. ————
     A bunch of old letters: written mostly to Jawaharlal Nehru and

some written by him.   Bombay, Asia Pub. House, 1958. xvii, 511 p.
NMML

153. ————

The discovery of India.   Calcutta, Signet Press, 1946.   xii, 514 p.
NMML

154. ————

Eighteen months in India 1936-37: being further essays and writings.
Allahabad, Kitabistan, 1938.   viii, 319 p.
NMML

155. ————

The first sixty years: presenting in his own words the development
of the political thought of Jawaharlal Nehru and the background
against which it evolved; ed. by Dorothy Norman.   Bombay, Asia
Pub. House, 1965. 2v.
NMML

156. ————

Glimpses of world history: being further letters to his daughter,
written in prison, and containing a rambling account of history for
young people.   Allahabad, Kitabistan, 1934-35.   2v. (1569 p.)
NMML

157. ————

Important speeches; ed. by Jagat S. Bright.   Lahore, Indian Printing
Works [1945-1951] 2v.
Contents.—v. 1. 1922-1945.
NMML

158. ————

India and the world: essays. London, Allen & Unwin, 1936. 262 p.
NMML

159. ————

Life and speeches; ed. by R. Dwivedi.   Allahabad, National Pub.
House [1929] lxxiv, 192 p.
NMML

160. ————

On socialism: selected speeches and writings.   New Delhi, Perspective Publications, 1964.   120 p.
NMML

161. ————

Recent essays and writings: on the future of India, communalism and other subjects. Allahabad, Kitabistan, 1934. 148 p.

NMML

162. ————
Report submitted to the All India Congress Committee, Haripura, February 1938. Allahabad, A.I.C.C., 1938. 12 p.

NMML

163. ————
Selected writings, 1916-1950: dealing with the shape of things to come in India and the world; ed. by J. S. Bright. New Delhi, Indian Printing Works [1950?] vi, 353 p.

NMML

164. ————
Soviet Russia: some random sketches and impressions. Allahabad, Ram Mohan Lal, 1928. x, 149 p.

NMML

165. ————
The unity of India: collected writings 1937-1940; foreword by V. K. Krishna Menon. (London) L. Drummond, 1941. 432 p.

NMML

166. ————
Where are we ? Allahabad, Kitabistan, 1939, 84 p.

NMML

167. NEVETT, A.
India going red ? Poona, Indian Institute of Social Order, 1954. viii, 318 p.
"How communism works in India": pp. 154-206.

NMML

168. ORGWALD
Tactical and organizational questions of the communist parties of India and Indo-China: in questions and answers. (n.p.) Pan-Pacific Worker (1933) 93 p.
"Conversations with Indian comrades": pp. 7-65.

ICWAL

169. OVERSTREET, GENE D.
Soviet and Indian communist policy in India 1935-1952.
Thesis—Columbia Univ. 1960.

170. ————AND WINDMILLER, MARSHALL
Communism in India. Bombay, Perennial Press, 1960. xiv, 603 p. bibl.

NMML

171. PANT, DEVIDATTA
     Socialism: its embryonic development in India. (Lahore, 1920)
     152 p.

172. PANT, S.C.
     Indian labour problems. Allahabad, Chaitanya Pub. House, 1965.
     xi, 515 p.
     "Trade union movement in India": pp. 69-108.

                                                                    NMML

173. PARAMESWARAN, C.
     Glimpses of the Indian ferment in communist crucible. New Delhi,
     New World Order Publications, 1952, iii, 34 p.
     "Advent and growth of socialism": pp. 11-14.

                                                                    NMML

174. PATTABHI RAMAN, N.
     Political involvement of India's trade unions: a case study of the
     anatomy of the political labour movement in Asia. Bombay, Asia
     Pub. House, 1967. x, 203 p.

                                                                    NMML

175. PATTABHI SITARAMAYYA, B.
     The history of the Indian National Congress; with an introduction
     by Rajendra Prasad. Bombay, Padma Publications, 1946-1947 2v.
     v. 1 first published by the Working Committee of the Congress in
     1935.

                                                                    NMML

176. ————
     Socialism and Gandhism. Rajahmundry, Hindustan Pub. Co., 1938.
     viii, ii, 244 p. (World Today series)

                                                                    NMML

177. PRAKASH CHANDRA
     The political philosophy of M. N. Roy.
     Thesis—Lucknow Univ. 1957.

178. PUNEKAR, S.D.
     Trade unionism in India. Bombay, New Book Co., 1948. 407 p.

179. RAJKUMAR, N.G.
     Nehru's ideas on nationalism, democracy and socialism.
     Thesis—Ph.D.—Osmania Univ. 1966.

180. RAJKUMAR, N.V.
     Indian political parties; foreword by Shankarrao Deo. New Delhi,
     A.I.C.C., (1948) 139 p.

                                                                    NMML

181. RAMANUJAM, G.
         From the Babul tree: story of Indian abour. New Delhi, I.N.T.U.C.,
         1967. xv, 252 p.

                                                                    NMML

182. RAMSWARUP
         Gandhism and communism: principles and technique. New Delhi,
         Jyoti Prakashan, 1955. 57 p.

                                                                    NMML

183. RANADIVE, B.T.
         Lenin and the Indian national movement. In Gupta, Anand, *ed.,*
         India and Lenin. New Delhi, New Literature, 1960. pp. 10-19.

                                                                    NMML

184. RANGA, N.G.
         Kisans and communists. Bombay, Pratibha Publications (n.d.)
         127 p. (Pratibha Publication, no. 6)

                                                                      NL

185. ———————
         The modern Indian peasant: a collection of addresses, speeches and
         writings. Madras, Kisan Publications, 1936. xxxii, 116, 70, 116 p.

                                                                    NMML

186. ———————
         Outlines of national revolutionary path. Bombay, Hind Kitabs,
         1945. 132 p.
         "The growth of socialist content of the Indian National Congress:
         in practice": pp. 26-34.

                                                                    NMML

187. ———————
         Peasants and Congress. Madras, All India Kisan Publications [1939]
         88, 64 p.
         Running title: Kisan handbook.

188. ———————
         Revolutionary peasants (a survey of the various revolutions that
         peasants have staged against capitalism all over the world). New
         Delhi, Amrit Book Co., 1949. 234 p.
         "Congress kisans and the Andhra movement" : pp. 60-101.

                                                                    NMML

189. ———————AND SAHAJANAND SARASWATI
         History of the kisan movement. Madras, All India Kisan publica-
         tions [1939]

190. ROSE, SAUL
        Socialism in Southern Asia. London, Oxford Univ. Press, 1959.
        278 p.
        "India": pp 14-53.
                                                                        NMML

191. ROTHERMUND, DIETMAR
        Nehru and early Indian socialism. In Mukherjee, S.N., *ed.,* The
        movement for national freedom in India. London, Oxford Univ.
        Press, 1968. pp. 38-111. (St. Antony's papers, no. 18; South Asian
        affairs, no. 2).
                                                                        NMML

192. ROY, M.N.
        The aftermath of non-cooperation. London, Communist Party of
        Great Britain, 1926. 136 p.
        Cover subtitle: Indian nationalist and labour politics.

193. ————
        The alternative. Bombay, Vora, 1940. 83 p. (Independent series,
        no. 6)
                                                                        ICWAL

194. ————
        Cawnpur Conspiracy Case: an open letter to the Rt. Hon. J. R.
        MacDonald. London, Indian Defence Committee, 1924. 11 p.

195. ————
        The Communist International. Bombay, Radical Democratic Party,
        1943. 73 p.
                                                                        NMML

196. ————
        Congress at cross-roads by a Congressman. Bombay, Independence
        of India League, 1934, 18 p. (Independence of India League pamphlet,
        no. 1).

197. ————
        Fragments of a prisoner's diary. 2d rev. ed. Calcutta, Renaissance
        Publishers, 1943-1957 (v. 1, 1957; v. 2, 1950; v. 3, 1943) 3v.
        Contents—v. 1. Crime and karma, cats and women—v. 2. India's
        message—v. 3. Letters from jail.
                                                                        NMML

198. ————
        Freedom or fascism? (Bombay?) Radical Democratic Party, 1942.
        110 p.

199. ———
>The future of Indian politics. London, R. Bishop (1926?) 118 p.
>
>> NMML

200. ———
>The future of socialism. Calcutta, Renaissance Publishers (1943?). 18 p. (Students' Club tract, no. 1).
>Talk to the Calcutta Students' Club, November 1943.

201. ———
>Gandhi vs. Roy: containing Roy's letter to Gandhiji, the latter's reply and the former's rejoinder. Bombay, V.B. Karnik, 1939, 18 p. (Independent India series, no. 5).

202. ———
>Gandhism, nationalism, socialism. Calcutta, Dharitri Ganguly, 1940. ii, 130 p.
>
>> NL

203. ———
>"I accuse": from the suppressed statement of Manabendra Nath Roy on trial for treason before Sessions Court, Cawnpore, India; with an introduction by Aswani Kumar Sharma. New York, Roy Defence Committee of India, 1932. 30 p.

204. ———
>India in transition: with the collaboration of Abani Mukherji. Geneva, Librarie J.B. Target, 1922. 241 p.
>
>> NL

205. ———
>India's problem and its solution. (Madras, 1923?) 55 p.

206. ———
>Jawaharlal Nehru. Delhi, Radical Democratic Party, 1945. 61 p.
>
>> NMML

207. ———
>Letters...to the Congress Socialist Party, written in 1934. Bombay, Renaissance Publishers, 1937. 78 p.

208. ———
>Memoirs. Bombay, Allied Publishers, 1964. xiii, 627 p. bibl.
>
>> NMML

209. ———
>My crime. Bombay, Ramesh D. Nadkarni (1937?).

210.   ————
        On stepping out of jail. Bombay, V.B. Karnik (1936?) 15 p.

211.   ————
        Our differences. Calcutta, Sarswati Library (1938) vi, 184 p.
                                                                    ICWAL

212.   ————
        Our problems; with the collaboration of V.B. Karnik. Calcutta,
        Barendra Library (1938) vi, ii, 274, xxviii p.
                                                                    ICWAL

213.   ————
        Our task in India. (n. p.) Bengal Committee of the Revolutionary
        Party of the Indian Working Class (1932?) 124 p.

214.   ————
        Political letters. Zurich, Vanguard Bookshop, 1924. 52 p.

215.   ————
        Presidential address at All India Sugar Mill Workers' Conference,
        Gorakhpur, held on 30 April and 1 May, 1938. Gorakhpur (1938?)
        17 p.

216.   ————
        Presidential address at the first All-India Conference of League of
        Radical Congressmen, Poona, 27 and 28 June 1939. Bombay (1939?)
        14 p.

217.   ————
        Problems of the Indian revolution. Bombay, Rajaram Pandey, 1941.
        27 p. (Scientific Politics, v. 10).

218.   ————
        Royism explained; ed. by D. Goonawardhana and D. Dasgupta.
        Calcutta, Saraswati Library, 1938. 65 p.

219.   ————
        What do we want? Geneva, Librarie J.B. Target, 1922, 43 p.
        and Roy, Evelyn

220.   One year of non-cooperation: from Ahmedabad to Gaya. Calcutta,
        Communist Party of India, 1923. 184 p.
                                                                    GSS

221.   RUSCH, THOMAS A.
        Role of the Congress Socialist Party in the Indian National

Congress, 1931-1942.
Thesis—Ph.D.—Chicago Univ. 1955.
Microfilm.

NMML

222. SAHAJANAND SARASWATI
Kisan Sabha ke sansmaran. Allahabad, Naya Literature, 1947.
Hindi.

223. ————
Mera jeevan sangharsh. Bihta, Patna, Sri Sitaram Ashram, 1952.
Hindi.

224. SAKLATVALA, S., AND GANDHI, M.K.
Is India different? (The class struggle in India: correspondence on the
Indian labour movement and modern conditions) London, Communist
Party of Great Britain, 1927. 35 p.

GSS

225. SAMPURNANAND
Indian socialism. Bombay, Asia Pub. House, 1961. x, 126 p.

NMML

226. ————
Memories and reflections. Bombay, Asia Pub. House, 1962. vii, 188 p.
"The Congress Socialist Party": pp. 72-86.

NMML

227. ————AND OTHERS
Samyavad ka bigul. Benares, 1940.
Hindi.

228. SAMRA, CHATTAR SINGH
India and Anglo-Soviet relations, 1917-1947. Bombay, Asia Pub.
House, 1959. xi, 186 p. bibl.

NMML

229. ————
India in communist perspective.
Thesis—Calfornia Univ. 1954.

230. SARDESAI, S.G.
India and the Russian revolution. New Delhi, C.P.I., 1967. 106 p.

NMML

231. ————
Why communists? Bombay, Popular Prakashan [1967] 91 p.
"Historical background": pp. 6-13.

NMML

232. SARIN, L.N.
     Studies of Indian leaders; with a foreword by Frank Moraes. Delhi,
     Atma Ram, 1963. ii, 128 p.
     "Aruna Asaf Ali": pp. 5-9.
     "Jawaharlal Nehru": pp. 37-42.
     "Jai Prakash Narain": pp. 43-8.
     "Narendra Dev ": pp. 74-80.
     "Ram Manohar Lohia": pp. 98-101.

                                                                    NMML

233. SARKAR, BIBEK BRATA
     The socialist movement in India from 1919 to 1947.
     Thesis—Ph. D.—Delhi Univ. 1964.

                                                                    DUL

234. SATINDRA SINGH
     Mahatma in the Marxist mirror. Delhi, Siddhartha Publications, 1962.
     35 p.

                                                                    NMML

235. SCALAPINO, ROBERT A. *(ed.)*
     The communist revolution in Asia: tactics, goals and achievements.
     Englewood Cliffs, N.J., Prentice-Hall, 1965. 405 p.
     "Revisionism and dogmatism in the Communist Party of India":
     pp. 309-342.

                                                                    NMML

236. SETH, HIRA LAL
     The red fugitive: Shri Jaiprakash Narain; prologue by M.K. Gandhi.
     Lahore, Dewan's Publications (n. d.) 66 p.

                                                                    NMML

237. SHAH, C.G.
     Marxism, Gandhism, Stalinism. Bombay, Popular Prakashan, 1963.
     xxx, 360 p.

                                                                    NMML

238. SHAKUNTALA NEHALCHAND
     Economic case for socialism in India.
     Thesis—Ph. D.—Bombay Univ. 1950.

239. SHARMA, B.S.
     The political philosophy of M.N. Roy. Delhi, National Pub. House,
     1965. 147 p.

                                                                    NMML

240. SHARMA, G.K.
     Labour movement in India: its past and present. Delhi, University

Publishers, 1963. ii, iii, 250 p. bibl.

NMML

241. SHUKLA, H.N.P.
The organization and working of trade unions in Uttar Pradesh.
Thesis—Ph. D.—Agra Univ. 1960.

242. SINHA, B.P.
Samajvad: niti tatha riti. Lucknow, Narendra Deva, 1947. 147 p.
Hindi.

NMML

243. SINHA, L.P.
The left-wing in India. 1919-1947. Muzaffarpur, New Publishers,
1965. xiv, 623 p. bibl.

NMML

244. SINHA, V.B.
The red rebel in India: a study of communist strategy and tactics;
foreword by Morarji Desai. New Delhi, Associated Pub. House, 1968.
vi, 262 p. bibl.
"Communist tactics till independence, 1947": pp. 8-41.

NMML

245. SPRATT, PHILIP
Blowing up India: reminiscences and reflections of a former comintern
emissary. Calcutta, Prachi Prakashan, 1955. 117 p.

NMML

246. ———
Communism and India. New Delhi, Janta Press, 1952 ii, 51 p. (Eastern
Economist pamphlets, 16).

ICWAL

247. ———
Gandhism: an analysis. Madras, Huxley Press, 1939. xii, 516 p.

NMML

248. TAGORE, SAUMYENDRANATH
The bourgeois democratic revolution and India. Calcutta, 1939. 48 p.

249. ———
Congress socialism. 2d ed. Calcutta, Ganavani Pub. House, 1946.
43 p.

ICWAL

250. ———
Gandhism and the labour: peasant problem. Gauhati, Radical Institute,
1940. 26 p.

251. ———
Historical development of the communist movement in India. Calcutta, Red Front Press, 1944.

252. TANDON, P.D.
Leaders of modern India. Bombay, Vora, 1955. 159 p.
"Jawaharlal Nehru": pp. 24-38.
"Jayaprakash Narain": pp. 66-73.
"Narendra Deva": pp. 106-13.

NMML

253. United States. *Office of Strategic Services. Research and Analysis Branch*
Communist Party of India. Washington, 1945. 73 p.

254. USMANI, SHAUKAT
Peshawar to Moscow: leaves from an Indian muhajireen's diary; with an introduction by P. Spratt. Benares, Swarajya Pub. House, 1927. v, 173 p.

NMML

255. VASUDEVA RAO, CHALASANI
Bharatha Communist Party nirmana charithrea; translation of excerpts from the Telugu original by Krishna Kumaran, with the assistance of Marshall Windmiller. [Berkeley, 1955]

256. WINDMILLER, MARSHALL
The left wing in India.
Thesis—M.A.—Calfornia Univ. 1954.

257. WINT, GUY
Communism in India. In Footman, David *(ed.)*, International communism. London, Chatto & Windus, 1960. pp. 105-127. (St. Antony's papers, no. 9).

DUL

258. WOOLACOTT, J.E.
India on trial: a study of present conditions. London, Macmillan, 1929. xv, 257 p.
"The red menace": pp. 222-33.

NMML

259. Workers' and Peasants' Party of Bengal. *3rd conference, Bhatpara,* 1928
A call to action, being the resolutions, theses and reports presented to the third annual conference. Calcutta, Sri Press, 1928. 58 p.

260. YAJNIK, INDULAL K.
Life of Ranchoddas Bhavan Lotvala; with an introduction by Anthony

Elenjimttam Bombay, Atmaram Dixit, 1952, xiv, 87 p.

NMML

261. Yusuf Meherally
      Leaders of India. 6th ed. Bombay, Padma Publications, 1946. 2v. (Current Topics series, no. 2).
      "Subhas Bose": v. 1, pp. 36-44.
      "Jaya Prakash": v. 1, pp. 64-73.
      "Subhas Bose": v. 2, pp. 21-6.
      "Kamala Devi": v. 2, pp. 27-36.
      "Aruna Asaf Ali": v. 2, pp. 37-46.
      "Achyut Patwardhan": v. 2, pp. 47-57.

NMML

262. ─────
      The price of liberty. Bombay, National Information & Publications, 1948. 261 p.
      "Pandit Jawaharlal Nehru": pp. 157-63.
      "Subhas Chandra Bose": pp. 164-81.
      "Ram Manohar Lohia": pp. 182-90.
      "Asoka Mehta": pp. 214-9.
      "Ram Nandan Misra": pp. 220-8.
      "Jayaprakash Narain": pp. 229-34.

NMML

263. Zafar Imam
      The effects of the Russian revolution on India, 1917-1920. In Mukherjee, S.N. (ed.), The movement for national freedom in India. London, Oxford Univ. Press, 1968. p. 74-97. (St. Antony's papers, no. 18; South Asian affairs, no. 2).

NMML

INDEX

Abhyudaya, Hindu nationalist weekly, 51

Act of 1935, 11, 15, 105, 111-12, 210

Advance Guard, journal, 33

Advocate, Government daily, 54

Afgan War, 50, 142

Afghanistan, 28-9; diplomatic mission at Tashkent, 29; relations with Soviet Russia, 52; turmoil in, 149

Afghanistan government, 29; reluctant to allow infiltration, 5; agrarian agitations in 1928, 180; disturbances in the Deccan, 2; reforms, 15

Agricultural producer in Bihar and Bengal, fluctuations in prices of, 200-2

Ahmedabad congress session, 7, 33; *see* Indian National Congress

Albareed, Khilafat urdu weekly, 53

All India Kisan Sabha, first session of, 205, 212; at Calcutta, 222; at Comilla, 206, 233; at Gaya, 224 Manifesto of, 205

All-Indian Socialist Youth Congress, 62

All-Indian Trade Union Congress, 3, 8, 55, 77, 84, 92, 103, 110; affiliation to the RILU, 87-8; efforts to affiliate with the international Federation of Trade Unions at Amsterdam, 88; foundation of, 142, programme of, 47; Nagpur session of, 99-100; Nehru's Presidential address at Nagpur, 138; resolution congratulating the Soviet Union on the tenth anniversary of the Bolshevik Revolution, 59

Allied war aims, 44-5

Amar Sakti 34

Amrit Bazar Patrika, 34

Amritsar Congress session, 51; *see* Indian National Congress

Amritsar massacre, *see* Jallianwala Bagh Tragedy

Andrews, C.F., 109, 112

Anglo-American bloc, 162

Anglo-Saxon bloc, 152

Anglo-Soviet relations, *see* Soviet Russia, foreign relations with Great Britain

Anglo-Soviet trade union co-operation, 90

Asian federation, 149-50; concept of, 147

Assembly Bomb case, 177, 188

Atshi Chakkar, leaflets, 168

Attlee, Clement, 97, 106-7, 110-11, 120; *The Labour Party in Perspective,* 112; Minority Report submitted by, 111

Autocracy, Tsarist, fall of, 3; British, 3

Barga system, abolition of, 215

Bengal Agricultural Debtors Act, 209

Bengal Criminal Law Amendment Act of 1930, 211

Bengal Land Revenue Commission, 208, 211-12, 214-15

Bengal Ordinance, promulgation of, 83

Bengal Suppress of Terrorists Outrages Act of 1932, 211

Bengal Tenancy Act, amendment of, 210; passed, 210

Berlin, Indian Independence Commitee in, 21; M.N. Roy in, 33-5